Trinity of the South

TRINITY OF THE SOUTH

POTENTIAL *of*

INDIA-BRAZIL-SOUTH AFRICA

(IBSA) PARTNERSHIP

RIS
Research and Information System
for Developing Countries

ACADEMIC FOUNDATION
NEW DELHI

www.academicfoundation.com

First published in 2008
by

ACADEMIC FOUNDATION
4772-73 / 23 Bharat Ram Road, (23 Ansari Road),
Darya Ganj, New Delhi - 110 002 (India).
Phones : 23245001 / 02 / 03 / 04.
Fax : +91-11-23245005.
E-mail : academic@vsnl.com
www. academicfoundation.com

in association with :

Research and Information System
for Developing Countries (RIS), New Delhi
www.ris.org.in

Cataloging in Publication Data--DK
Courtesy: D.K. Agencies (P) Ltd. <docinfo@dkagencies.com>

Trinity of the South: potential of India-Brazil-South Africa partnership / [prepared by Research and Information System for the Developing Countries (RIS)].
p. cm. Includes bibliographical references (p.)
ISBN 13: 9788171886791
ISBN 10: 8171886795

1. India--Foreign economic relations--Brazil. 2. Brazil --Foreign economic relations--India. 3. India--Foreign economic relations--South Africa. 4. South Africa—Foreign economic relations--India. 5. Brazil--Foreign economic relations--South Africa. 6. South Africa--Foreign economic relations--Brazil. I. Research and Information System for Developing Countries (RIS).

DDC 337.540 81 22

Typeset by Italics India, New Delhi.
Printed and bound in India.

Contents

List of Tables, Figures, Boxes and Appendices

TABLES

FIGURES

BOXES

APPENDICES

Preface

The formation of the India-Brazil-South Africa (IBSA) Dialogue Forum is a major landmark in the history of South-South Cooperation. The three partners represent leading economies in their respective continents and bring together an array of complementary strengths and capabilities that could be exploited for mutual benefit. The cooperation between India, Brazil and South Africa also has the potential of having important spillovers for the partners of each of these countries in their respective sub-regional groupings, namely, SAARC in the case of India, MERCOSUR in the case of Brazil, and SACU in the case of South Africa. Therefore, IBSA partnership could make a major contribution to the economic development of three sub-regions across Asia, Africa and Latin America.

This Report makes an exploratory attempt to examine the potential of IBSA economic partnership in the areas of trade in goods, services, investments, technology cooperation and other areas of economic cooperation. The Report finds an enormous potential of economic cooperation between the three countries given the extensive complementarities and synergistic capabilities that can make cooperation in a number of sectors highly fruitful. It makes a number of recommendations for exploiting this potential of the IBSA economic partnership.

This Report is a result of a Study conducted at RIS at the request of Ministry of Commerce and Industry. The Study is based on the analysis of secondary data at RIS, information gathered from various sources, including business chambers like, FICCI, CII, the Missions of Brazil and South Africa in New Delhi, India Missions in Brazil and South Africa and discussions with representatives of enterprises having business links with the concerned countries, among other experts. RIS organised a National Consultation on IBSA Economic Cooperation with stakeholders from trade, industry, academia and government on 18 September 2004 in New Delhi. Early versions of the Study have also been presented at the Discussion Meetings organised by the Department of Commerce of the Ministry of Commerce and Industry on 10 November 2004 and also on 6 October 2005 Chaired by Mr. G.K. Pillai, presently Secretary, Ministry of Commerce and Industry, and benefited from valuable discussions, inputs and feedback of senior officials of the Department. RIS also submitted Interim Reports and earlier versions of the Study to the Ministry in November 2004, March 2005, and in September 2005. We have benefited from detailed discussions with and support of Mr. R. Gopalan, Joint Secretary (TPD) and Mr. Sanjay Kumar, Director (TPD), Ministry of Commerce and Industry, among other officials.

The Report has been prepared by a research team led by the undersigned and comprising Dr. K.J. Joseph, formerly Visiting Senior Fellow; Dr. S.K. Mohanty, Fellow; and Dr. Prabir De, Fellow. Inputs were also provided by RIS faculty members including Dr. Mirza Allim Baig, formerly Research Associate of RIS.

New Delhi
September, 2007

Nagesh Kumar
Director-General
RIS

Executive Summary

The coming together of India, Brazil and South Africa in a trilateral commission to strengthen the economic partnership is to be seen as a major development in the area of South-South Cooperation. Besides shared political and economic history and development experiences, there are significant synergies between these countries as they have developed substantial capabilities in different sectors over the years. But these synergies are yet to be fully utilised for their collective benefit and development of the South in general. IBSA countries can reinforce the economic strength of each other by synergising their complementarities in areas of industry, services, trade and technology which in turn could create a market of 1.2 billion people, 2 trillion dollars of GDP and foreign trade of nearly 550 billion dollars. IBSA partnership is also of immense strategic value for multilateral negotiations and shaping their respective roles in the global governance.

IBSA COMPREHENSIVE ECONOMIC PARTNERSHIP ARRANGEMENT

IBSA constitutes a large and expanding economic space wherein their total trade is close to US$ 550 billion currently. The share of intra-IBSA trade in their total trade has been approximately 2.6 per cent (about US$ 7 billion) in 2005. The New Delhi Action Plan has put an ambitious goal for doubling the mutual trade by 2007. To exploit the synergies and potential of cooperation for mutual benefit, IBSA countries can explore an **IBSA Comprehensive Economic Partnership Arrangement** covering the following aspects among others:

1. An India-MERCOSUR-SACU FTA

At the Ministerial Meeting of IBSA in New Delhi in March 2005, it was decided to work towards evolving an Free Trade Agreement (FTA) between the three countries. Preliminary RIS simulations suggest that a FTA between the three countries has the potential of increasing mutual trade but the distribution of gains would be asymmetric and Brazil and South Africa would benefit more than India (keeping in mind the existing tariff structures and the potential of trade creation). Furthermore, a trilateral FTA between India-Brazil-South Africa may not be technically feasible as Brazil and South Africa are members of customs unions (*viz.,* MERCOSUR and SACU respectively) and hence are bound to maintain common external tariffs with other partners. Therefore, we may consider evolving an *Free Trading Arrangement between India-MERCOSUR-SACU*. This FTA could subsume the ongoing negotiations between India-MERCOSUR, India-SACU and SACU-MERCOSUR PTAs. This way we could have a framework for mutual trade taking place on a preferential basis besides giving access to even other members of the respective customs unions.

An FTA covering India-MERCOSUR-SACU by giving access of markets of other SACU and MERCOSUR countries, other than Brazil and South Africa, may also neutralise some of the asymmetries in trade with respect of Brazil and South Africa. The scope of FTA could be extended to cover trade in services and investments on positive list basis so that some asymmetries in the goods trade can be neutralised in the services trade. However, in view of asymmetric benefits resulting from FTA, as suggested by the preliminary study indicated above, it may be prudent to move in a cautious manner. It is important that a detailed analysis is conducted of the gains and losses in terms of market access expected and given so that an attempt can be made to maximise the gains and minimise the adverse effects.

Generally, the launch of negotiations of FTAs are preceded by setting up of Joint Study Groups (JSGs) involving academics and officials of the partner countries. The JSGs are able to make detailed studies of the trade potential and also suggest the framework for a potential agreement. *Therefore, India may suggest setting up of an IBSA Joint Study Group to examine the relevance and prepare a blue print or elements of an IBSA FTA within an agreed time frame*. The JSG Report after adoption by the member governments could provide a basis for launching negotiations.

The JSG could have broad terms of reference, e.g. detailed feasibility of an FTA, scope and coverage of an FTA, elements of a proposed FTA, the negotiating group (whether limited to IBSA countries or also the representatives of other MERCOSUR and SACU members). JSG should also examine the possibility of a comprehensive economic partnership agreement besides FTA and hence examine and propose other areas of cooperation, e.g. in trade facilitation, investment facilitation, promotion of trade in services, potential of sectoral cooperation and institutional mechanisms for their promotion and exchange of experiences in development and networking of think tanks, framework for cooperation in multilateral forums, among others, as summarised in this Study.

2. IBSA Trade Facilitation Framework (IBSA TFF)

The IBSA FTA may be supplemented by an IBSA TFF focusing on identifying and eliminating the non-tariff barriers (NTBs) and evolving a framework for trade facilitation. RIS study finds that significant NTBs impede mutual trade in the grouping. Some of the NTBs identified by the study are as follows:

2.1. Harmonising Conformity Assessment Procedures and Standards

India, Brazil and South Africa have their own regulatory import controls based on standards and conformity assessment procedures, specifically from the standpoint of health and safety. In this context, mutual recognition of conformity assessment procedures between them for the purposes of meeting their respective regulatory requirements represents convenient method of reducing NTBs to trade. This will call for assessing the present situation with respect to the compatibility of each other's standards and enter into mutual recognition arrangements with regard to standards and conformity assessment activities. Hence, there is also the need for the standards and export inspection bodies of IBSA to work together for harmonisation and mutual recognition of conformity assessment procedures.

2.2. Customs Procedures

There is need for harmonisation of customs procedures regarding tendering, importer registration, shipment, customs and port-clearance, etc. This in turns calls for bringing together the customs authorities of IBSA to discuss ways and means of standardising their procedures.

2.3. Addressing the Lack of Business Information and Perception Gaps

Very often a major factor that stands in the way of trade is the lack of information or presence of misinformation. The Indian products, especially in Brazil, are perceived to be of low quality. To overcome this constraint, there is the need for bringing together the trading communities of the three countries. Much could be achieved in this direction by initiating annual IBSA trade fairs with the location rotating among them. An **IBSA Business Forum** could also be set up to bring together the business community in the three countries to promote trade and investment. Such a business forum may be complemented with sectoral bodies especially covering those industries/sectors where the trade and investment potential is higher. Such bodies would facilitate formation of strategic alliances between the enterprises of the region to exploit their synergy for not only the regional markets but also for third country investments and trade opportunities. This Business Forum could also deal with trade disputes with respective governmental bodies involved in IBSA trade and also take up the other issues such as problems concerning LCs, and high cost of insurance, as observed in Brazil or certain anti-dumping or other discriminatory practices as observed in South Africa.

3. Facilitating Trade in Services

In all the three countries, service sector has emerged as the leading sector of the economy, accounting for more than 50 per cent of the GDP. However, with the possible exception of IT software services in India, and travel in South Africa, the services trade is an area wherein IBSA is found to be relatively weak in terms of comparative advantage. Also, the service imports of Brazil and South Africa recorded negligible or negative growth rate during the recent past. The only service sectors of Brazil wherein imports showed a significant increase are insurance, computer services and other business services. The service imports of these countries are subject to a number of barriers such as job quotas and barriers for commercial presence in select sectors. These barriers can be addressed within the framework of IBSA Comprehensive Economic Cooperation Agreement (CECA) in select sectors of mutual interest.

4. Facilitating FDI Flows within IBSA

There have been significant two-way flows between India and South Africa, but potential of investment between India and Brazil has hardly been exploited. A number of measures, as mentioned below, can be taken within the IBSA framework to facilitate mutual investment flows between them:

4.1. An IBSA Investment Agreement (IIA)

A trilateral IIA signed within the framework of IBSA could be a useful component of the IBSA CECA, as proposed in this Report. The IIA could provide a framework for post-investment national treatment, non-discrimination, investment protection and dispute settlement to promote mutual investment flows. It can also be complemented by an IBSA Double Taxation Avoidance Agreement (DTAA) to further promote mutual investment agreements.

4.2. Cooperation among the Investment Promotion Agencies

All the three countries are having their respective investment promotion agencies. These agencies may cooperate between themselves and set up their representative offices in other member countries. Such representative offices could be instrumental in the dissemination of information about the policies, rules and procedures of the respective countries, linking the potential investors with local entrepreneurs, facilitating approvals, among other initiatives.

5. Strengthening the IBSA Transport Network

Given the geographical location of India, Brazil and South Africa, distance acts as a major constraint resulting in high transportation cost between them. The estimated transport cost accounts for more than 12 per cent of the value of trade between India and Brazil and about 10 per cent in case of trade with South Africa. Therefore, the outcomes of initiatives outlined above are likely to be sub-optimal unless the air and shipping connectivity between the three countries is strengthened. Maritime and air linkages between India and South Africa, and between South Africa and Brazil are stronger than that between India and Brazil. The low volume of trade makes the business relatively unattractive to the main-line shipping companies. Competition for business is therefore weak leading to high costs. To improve the transport links between IBSA, following measures may be considered:

5.1. Common Feeder Structure and Liner Network

The alleged lack of coordination between the different carriers offering feeder and inter-island services and between these carriers and the mainline services may tend to increase costs and impair service frequencies. One suggestion that has been made is to discuss the feasibility of a common feeder structure as used in the Mediterranean, whereby the mainline carriers agree to use regional feeders and inter-island carriers operating as a pool. Forming a regional shipping network, "IBSA Liner Network", would be helpful to achieve deeper transport integration in IBSA.

5.2. Warehousing Facility in South Africa

The new element in the equation is the emergence of a geographically dispersed range of ports offering transshipment services. This offers the possibility of providing even the smaller destinations with access to increased regional trade. The principal transhipment ports on the basis of geography for the IBSA trade should be at Durban or Cape Town. This might call for making arrangements for the creation of an IBSA Warehousing facility in South Africa which could be used by Indian and Brazilian enterprises for mutual transhipments.

5.3. Improving the Airlinks

The flag carriers of IBSA countries, *viz.* Air India, Varig and South African Airways (SAA), could join hands to launch code-shared direct flights connecting Delhi/Mumbai, Johannesburg and Rio on a daily basis. This way the connectivity within the IBSA will improve tremendously. The other option is to provide a regime of Open Sky Policy between the IBSA economic space for the national carriers.

6. Sectoral Cooperation and Sharing of Expertise and Experiences

IBSA countries can fruitfully cooperate in the following areas and share their knowledge, expertise and experiences within the framework of the trilateral cooperation.

6.1. Experience Sharing in Transportation Sector

The study holds the view that IBSA have immense opportunity to learn from each other. For example, India's expertise in automation of railways can be extended to South Africa and Brazil. Similarly, India and South Africa can also learn from the Brazilian experiences in introduction of private capital in improving railway efficiency. It would be advisable to form a commercial venture among three leading logistics operators from these three countries; say for example, formation of any commercial venture among Container Corporation of India (CONCOR from India), Transnet Ltd. (from South Africa), and Companhia Vale do Rio Doce (CVRD from Brazil) could be of great boost to closer transport integration among the three countries. While CONCOR and Transnet are public sector companies, CVRD is Brazil's largest logistics company in the private sector. Similarly, Air India can learn from the great success of South African Airways and Varig Airways. Here, apart from code sharing to connect Delhi, Johannesburg and Rio, joining together to promote trade and tourism and to exchange technical experiences will certainly pave the way for sustaining closer integration in near future. India, with its renowned maritime training institutes, can offer modern maritime training to seafarers of South Africa and Brazil. Similarly, South Africa's experiences of port management can also be extended to Indian ports. Shipping lines in all the three countries can forge a network to exchange experiences in implementing ISPS code.

6.2 Promoting Joint R&D Alliances

During the last few decades, India, Brazil and South Africa have developed significant technological capabilities in different fields. IBSA cooperation should be instrumental in taking these capabilities to new heights for the benefits of countries in the South, in general, and IBSA in particular. In pursuing this objective, an *IBSA Fund for Promoting Joint R&D* could be set up to support joint R&D projects with active involvement of private sector and academia in IBSA. This may facilitate creation of strategic alliances between business enterprises of the three countries. It could also facilitate joint research on common problems of IBSA countries such as development of medicines for tropical diseases, AIDS drugs, Hepatitis vaccines, agricultural research. It could also facilitate joint initiatives for processed food safety, quality standard, quality harmonisation, market research and joint marketing, among others. Other areas of cooperation in technology may include capacity building and harmonisation of bio-safety guidelines, IPR regulations, and other regulatory frameworks in tune with the international protocols. To facilitate flow of technology between IBSA a *Technology Transfer Network* could also be set up which may pool information on technologies availabile with the enterprises/R&D organisations in the region.

6.3. Cooperation in SMEs

SMEs not only contribute a substantial proportion of industrial output, employment and exports, but they are breeding grounds for entrepreneurship. All the three countries have very rich experience and exchange of these experiences in promotion of SMEs and micro enterprises is likely to have profound development implications. It is also worth exploring what India could learn from the Black Economic Empowerment programme being implemented by South Africa. The cooperation might take the form of bringing together the small-scale industry promotion agencies and SME Associations of IBSA to establish liaison with each other and learning from each other's experience and technology sharing.

6.4. Energy

About 62 per cent of energy requirements of Brazil is met by renewable sources of which ethanol from sugarcane accounts for as much as 10 per cent.[1] Given the fact that India is the largest producer of sugarcane in the world and is facing booming oil import bill, the returns from India-Brazil cooperation in this field cannot be over emphasised. At the same time, India's capabilities in the field of solar photovoltaic could be of considerable interest for Brazil given the vastness of country and its settlement pattern. South Africa has a highly developed synthetic fuels industry, which takes advantage of the country's abundant coal resources with coal liquefaction technology. With the oil prices ruling at around US$ 60 p.b., this technology may be commercially viable and could be explored by Indian companies. India has some expertise in harnessing solar energy and biofuels that may be of interest to Brazil and South Africa.

6.5. Agriculture and Food Processing

There is a vast potential of cooperation in the agriculture and food processing. IBSA could conduct joint research on products of common interest and share their genetic resources in plant breeding programmes. Brazil is known for its capabilities in the food processing industry. Brazil has developed a wide variety of value-added products from root crops like cassava and other horticultural crops. Both India and South Africa may share these capabilities. Cassava is cultivated on a large-scale in some of the South Indian states. Yet, we have not been able to develop any market value-added products from Cassava. Cassava is also cultivated on a large-scale in some of the African countries. But their success in terms of productivity per hectare is low as compared to India and Brazil. They could also benefit from developing value-added products. Hence, cooperation between IBSA in horticulture and root crops could be beneficial to all

1. In April 2002, India and Brazil signed a memorandum of understanding (MoU) for technology sharing in blending of petrol and diesel with ethanol.

the three. In addition, IBSA countries may share their expertise, capability and experiences in complying with SPS measures applicable to processed foods in the developed country markets.

6.6. E-Governance and IT for Development

This is a case of cooperation among equals. Focus needs to be on exchanging experiences and learning from each other. There is also need for creation of a forum of different stakeholders in IT, like private sector, civil society organisations and government for sharing experiences/expertise in the field of e-governance, harnessing ICT for development, and strengthening capabilities in Free or Open Source Software. They could also work towards an e-South framework agreement to pool together their capabilities to address the common challenges.

6.7. Gems and Jewellery

It is understood that bulk of trade between India and South Africa is in gold, gems and jewellery. However, today this trade is routed through Europe. This leads to a situation wherein neither South Africa nor India has a significant role in the value chain. Therefore, there appears to be an immense potential for investment, which enables these countries to capture a significant position in gold, jems and jewellery value chain. The abundant supply of coloured stones in Brazil and the rich craftsmanship of India in polishing stones provides yet another investment opportunity for the third country markets.

6.8. Tourism

India with its vastness and geographical diversity could be an attractive location for tourist from both Brazil and South Africa. It is found that tourism is one of the vibrant sectors in the South African economy accounting for about 7.1 per cent of the GDP and contributing significantly to job creation as a result of substantial investment made by both public and private sectors. Indian companies also have invested in the tourism sector of South Africa. Cooperative efforts among the three countries could reap rich dividends. For instance, Goa, a well-known beach with large Portuguese population, could be of substantial interest to Brazilians. The low cost of healthcare in India is yet another fact that promotes health tourism. Initiatives to train tourist guides in the languages of three countries, relaxing visa regulations for travel within IBSA are needed to promote tourism besides improving the airline connectivity. Launch of IBSA Packages combining select locations of India-Brazil-South Africa, for instance, Goa, Cape Town and Rio in a single package could be very attractive for western tourists seeking variety in a compact package. An Association of Tour Operators of IBSA could also be formed to explore such possibilities.

6.9. Entertainment and Animation Industries

To leverage the markets in Entertainment and Animation Industries, it may be advisable that the TV and Radio broadcasting companies of IBSA join hands to launch an *IBSA Channel* covering news as well as entertainment content from the entire region. Indian entertainment industry (*a la* Bollywood), which is the largest producer of feature films in the world, could provide a backup for the Channel. It would also help in promotion of tourism and people-to-people contacts.

6.10. Financial Sector and Banking

India and South Africa have considerable experience in development of capital markets with the Bombay Stock Exchange being one of the oldest and well performing stock exchanges in the world. This expertise could be shared among IBSA especially given the fact that the Brazilian capital market needs further strengthening. In addition, integration of the capital markets of IBSA by facilitating cross-listing of securities with minimum standards of listing rules to help the flows of capital across the region may be beneficial to all the three countries. As of now, the presence of Indian banks is limited in Brazil and South Africa. The situation appears to be not much different with respect to the presence of Brazilian and South African banks in India. Hence, for promoting trade and investment, there is a need for intensive commercial banking links by facilitating setting up of branches of commercial banks of IBSA in the partner countries.

6.11. People to People Contacts

One of the key problems in promoting trade and investment between IBSA and especially with India and Brazil appears to be the lack of information. One of the possible ways to address this issue is through strengthening the people-to-people contacts. People-to-people contacts between IBSA are possible only through airlinks. Yet, the air connectivity between India and Brazil is especially weak. In this context, code shared flights and an open sky policy, as outlined above, might be helpful in strengthening the links between the three countries. An initiative like *IBSA Games* could also provide rich dividends in facilitating the people-to-people links. There could be IBSA Soccer and Cricket Tournaments to promote visibility of each other country mutually.

6.12. Media

Greater interaction between media of IBSA is crucial for reducing the information gap. There is very little reporting on India in Brazil and South Africa and vice versa. To bridge this gap, some exchange fellowships for media persons and journalists could be set up to allow journalists from Brazil and South Africa to spend some time in India and vice versa.

6.13. Sharing Development Experiences

RIS study notes that more or less similar policy reforms undertaken in the three countries have yielded quite different outcomes across them. Hence, there is an enormous potential for sharing development experiences between IBSA in managing globalisation and for providing constant policy inputs for promoting mutual cooperation. To facilitate such a process an **IBSA Network of Think Tanks** could be created to facilitate such exchange of development experiences and studies on promotion of mutual cooperation. The Network could comprise national focal points from each member country, and have fund at its disposal to draw upon for launching studies, annual conferences and for instituting fellowships for exchange of scholars.

7. IBSA Cooperation in Multilateral Forums

The strategic importance of IBSA cooperation in shaping the outcome of multilateral negotiations cannot be overemphasised. As emerging powers they can provide leadership to the developing world in these negotiations and thus help in evolving more development-friendly framework for multilateral trade and financial architecture. If the recent experience of their cooperation in multilateral trade negotiations is any guide, this partnership is going to have a major influence on the shape of multilateral negotiations in future.

7.1. Cooperation in Multilateral Trade Negotiations

Over the past year IBSA countries have already cooperated within the framework of the G-20 of developing countries at the Cancun Ministerial Conference of WTO and subsequent negotiations in a very fruitful manner. Later on in the negotiation of the July framework, India and Brazil represented G-20 in the Five Interested Parties (FIPs) that hammered out the agreement. Given the fact that the G-20 was led by Brazil, India and South Africa, it can be said that the trilateral engagement by India with Brazil and South Africa under the IBSA framework has facilitated coalition-building on WTO issues. The Ministerial Meeting of the IBSA Trilateral Commission held in New Delhi in early 2004 emphasised the importance of a common approach with regard to WTO among other priorities. It is important that IBSA countries continue playing such leadership role in the multilateral trade negotiations as they have been over the past. Furthermore, it is important for the longer-term sustainability of the coalition of G-20 in WTO to develop a more constructive proactive agenda. This agenda might cover seeking a reform of the process of decision-making in the multilateral trade negotiations to make it more inclusive, transparent and equitable; setting up a Developing Country Watchdog on the implementation of WTO commitments by developed countries and bringing complaints against any cases of under-compliance; strengthening the provisions of technical assistance for developing countries; strengthening the provisions for special and differential treatment with the help of a framework agreement; seeking a framework agreement on movement of natural persons; and a framework agreement on transfer of technology, among others. G-20 could also become a forum for promoting South-South Cooperation such as mutual cooperation in implementation of commitments, technical assistance for compliance of emerging standards, etc. besides evolving approaches for promoting South-South trade. They could discuss ways and means for revitalising the GSTP for promoting their mutual trade besides addressing NTBs to it. IBSA could take lead for making G-20 to pursue these proactive measures.

7.2. Reform of International Financial Architecture and the United Nations

Considering the common development concerns of IBSA countries, they could also coordinate their positions and provide leadership to developing countries in pushing reforms of international financial architecture including reform of IMF conditionalities to prevent reoccurrence of financial crisis and making it more development friendly and sustainable. Both Brazil and South Africa have suffered from mild crises in the past. The reform of the UN with expansion of the UN Security Council is also a common agenda and Brazil and India have announced support of their candidature for permanent membership of the UN Security Council on a mutual basis within the framework of G-4.

Thus, the IBSA comprehensive partnership could be of an immense strategic importance for the countries involved and a trail-blazer for South-South Cooperation. A Comprehensive Economic Partnership Arrangement (CEPA) including an FTA in trade in goods, services and investments could provide an institutional framework for exploiting the potential of their partnership and their synergies for mutual benefit.

Chapter 1

IBSA in the Context of Re-emergence of South-South Cooperation

1.1 Introduction

South-South Cooperation (SSC) received considerable attention as a philosophy for development during the 1960s, 1970s and 1980s.[1] These were the times when developing countries, having coming out of the yoke of colonisation, were struggling with the poverty and underdevelopment. Lack of financial and technological resources and the western apathy forced them to look to collective self-reliance as an engine of growth. The Non-aligned Movement (NAM) also came into being. Initiatives taken by developing countries also led to creation of UNCTAD, and the Group of 77 in the 1960s. The South Commission was set up in the mid-1980s. A more compact Group-15 of developing countries with annual Summits was also set up in the late 1980s.

Besides these forums for dialogue, the institutional infrastructure for promoting SSC included setting up of the agreements for preferential trade regimes between developing countries including the Bangkok Agreement and the GSTP (Global System for Trade Preferences), in addition to several institutions set up to contribute to capacity building. In the 1990s, however, globalisation took the centre stage and SSC was put on a backburner. The process of globalisation was promoted by the Brettonwoods institutions and GATT and its successor, WTO. A large number of developing countries which faced financial crisis in the 1980s and 1990s against the backdrop of declining resource flows were forced to approach the Brettonwoods institutions for assistance which generally came with the conditionalities binding them firmly with the Washington Consensus. The latter required the borrowing countries to liberalise their trade and investment regimes to integrate themselves more firmly with the world economy.

1. An indicative list of earlier studies include; Pavlic *et al.* (1983), UNCTAD (1986), RIS (1987), The South Commission (1990), Mytelka (1994).

Under the Uruguay Round of trade negotiations within the framework of GATT, developing countries were pushed to undertake substantial commitments to liberalise their trade policy regimes. A number of policy interventions that were hitherto subject to decision-making at the national level came under the purview of WTO discipline such as the intellectual property regime (IPRs) or the industrial policy. Many instruments of development policy that developed countries of today extensively employed in the phases of their own development such as soft IPP regime or local content regulations on foreign investors were denied to developing countries under the new trade rules. While preaching the virtues of free trade and multilateralism, developed countries continued to practice protectionism.[2] This 'selective' globalisation has generated much 'discontent'. Studies have documented that the growth rates in the 1990s have been lower than those in 1980s, the terms of trade of developing countries have declined and inequalities have widened.[3]

Recent trends suggest that developing countries are revitalising SSC as a new engine of growth in the new millennium, partly as a result of their growing discontent with 'selective' globalisation.[4] Developing countries in different regions are also establishing their own schemes of regional economic integration, e.g. MERCOSUR, COMESA and SACU, AFTA, SAFTA and BIMSTEC FTA. The Bangkok Agreement and the GSTP are being revitalised. Developing countries are coordinating their positions at the WTO Ministerial Conferences by forming coalitions such as Group of 20 (on Agreement on Agriculture).

During the last decade there has also been a continued growth in the South-South trade. The share of South-South trade in global trade increased from 34 per cent in 1990 to around 43 per cent by the end of the decade and it is growing at a rate of 10 per cent per year, which is more than twice that of the recorded rate of growth in global trade. Such unprecedented growth in South-South trade may be seen against the fact that during the last few decades developing countries have built up substantial industrial-technological capabilities which in turn provided scope for exploiting synergies among themselves by sharing of knowledge and technologies on the one hand and investment on the other.

---

2. The tariff rates were brought down by them in a manner that discriminated against the exports of developing countries. Therefore, the tariffs imposed on US$ 2 billion worth of exports by Bangladesh to the US were higher than those imposed on the US$ 30 billion exports of France. Developed countries have been slow in liberalising trade of textiles and agriculture and movement of natural persons which were used to lure developing countries into accepting substantial commitments of trade liberalisation. There has been a proliferation of the non-tariff barriers, regional trade blocs and antidumping duties in the developed world as a part of the growing protectionist sentiments as the recent legislations banning the business process outsourcing. See RIS (2003) for a detailed analysis of emerging asymmetries.

3. See RIS (2003) for evidence. Also see Wade (2004) for a critique of the neo liberal view that the distribution of income between all the world's people has become more equal over the past two decades as a result of increased economic integration between countries.

4. See Kumar (2004).

An UNCTAD study concludes that almost all South-South (S-S) RTAs are not only trade creating, but also trade expanding, increasing overall trade with third countries outside the RTA. Further, the study suggests that S-S RTAs could be used as a mechanism for the gradual integration of developing countries into the global economy. The impetus for domestic reforms and the political will for reforms may be further strengthened by the openness initiated through RTAs, particularly S-S ones (Winters and Schiff, 2003). Furthermore, beyond these economic effects, RTAs are very much part of a larger framework for regional cooperation aimed at promoting regional stability, sound and coordinated economic policies and a better regional economic infrastructure. Although difficult to quantify, all these improvements would have led to positive spillover effects that should be taken into account when assessing the overall impact of RTAs (Cernat, 2003). In the absence of major tariff preferences, S-S integration could lead to the removal of several invisible trade barriers such as border norms, customs formalities, testing and other trade facilitation measures. According to Hoekman and Konan (1999) testing costs could account for at least 5 per cent of the total value of the traded product. In addition removal of these invisible barriers do not carry welfare costs, as tariff revenues are not affected (Baldwin, 1994).

1.2 IBSA: The Trinity of the South

One of the latest developments with respect to SSC and forging powerful trading arrangements within the developing world has been the coming together of three leading countries in the South—India, Brazil and South Africa—representing three major democracies in three different continents of the globe to explore the possibilities for close economic cooperation.

India, Brazil and South Africa are not strangers. They share a common economic and political history and have stood together in different multilateral fora on more than one occasion for the cause of developing world. The relations between India and South Africa dates back to 1860 when the first group of indentured labourers arrived on the shores of South Africa from India. India's contribution to South Africa's struggle against apartheid has been widely acknowledged.[5] India was the first country in the world to isolate Apartheid South Africa in 1946 and also the first country outside African continent to recognise African National Congress (ANC) and allowed ANC to set up a mission in Delhi. Also, India has the credit to raise South African question in the United Nations. India and Brazil, though separated by geographical distance, are found close to each other on various issues of concern for the developing countries and have worked together in the GATT/WTO negotiations. As an important member of

5. See in this context Reddy (1985).

MERCOSUR, Brazil provided valuable assistant to India for signing a framework agreement with MERCOSUR in June 2003 in Asuncion.[6]

Apart from shared political and economic history, there are significant synergies between these countries that offer fertile ground for economic cooperation. Over the years these countries have built up a substantial capability in different spheres. Thus, South Africa, for example, has a highly developed synthetic fuels industry, which takes advantage of the country's abundant coal resources and offshore natural gas and condensate production in Mossel Bay and is one of the world's largest manufacturer of oil from coal, with coal liquefaction technology. Brazil is known for its capabilities, among others, in the sphere of aircraft manufacture and non-conventional energy. India, of late, has emerged as a major player in the field of information technology, drugs and pharmaceuticals among others. Yet the capabilities of these countries in different spheres are yet to be shared among themselves and fully utilised for the development and the South in general.

These three countries, that were instrumental in the setting up of the G-20 group of developing countries in the WTO at Cancun Ministerial, set up the IBSA Forum in June 2003 to promote mutual cooperation and to voice jointly the demands and concerns of the South.[7] The leaders of the three countries formally launched IBSA at the UN General Assembly in September 2003. Since then there has been an increased interaction between leaders of the three countries. These include, among others, a meeting of the Defence Ministers in South Africa, Co-operation at WTO's fifth ministerial at Cancun, Mexico on agricultural issues and a state visit by Brazilian President Luiz Inacio Lula da Silva to India in January 2004 where the need for exploring "new trade geography" was highlighted, this was followed by the Ministerial meet in Delhi on 4-5 March 2004.

1.3 Context of the Study

The Ministerial meeting of IBSA held in March, 2004 in New Delhi, in tune with Brasilia declaration, emphasised the importance of concrete trilateral cooperation in civil aviation, infrastructure, job creation and small medium and micro enterprises, science and technology, information technology, tourism, energy, defence and social sectors covering health, education, etc.[8] The Ministers agreed that the IBSA countries can reinforce the economic strength of each other by synergising their complementarities in area of industry, services, business and

6. During President Lula's visit to India, MERCOSUR signed a Preferential Customs Duty Accord on 25th January 2004. This accord expands on the framework agreement signed in June 2003. The Customs Duty Accord is expected to eventually lead to a free-trade agreement.

7. It was agreed that all the three countries should cooperate in opening up of their market to each other and not depend entirely on developed countries for investment and export. Agriculture, defense, aeronautics, IT, biotechnology, civil aviation, etc. are identified as areas of cooperation.

8. See Appendix 1 for details of IBSA Dialogue Forum and Plan of Action.

technology which in turn could create a market of 1.3 billion people, 2 trillion dollars of GDP and foreign trade of 550 billion dollars. It was also decided that each countries could conduct studies to examine the potential for economic and commercial partnership and the ways and means for increasing trade and investment flows among the three countries. It is against this background the present study intends to explore the possibilities of strengthening trade (goods and services) and investment relations between these countries.

1.4 Organisation of the Report

The rest of the study proceeds as follows. The second chapter presents a broad profile of IBSA where an attempt has been made to present recent trends and reform initiatives in these economies in a comparative perspective. The third chapter presents a detailed analysis of trade between these three countries and explores the trade complementarities against the backdrop of the trade policy reforms and tariff-non tariff regimes. The fourth chapter against the backdrop of the growth and structural change focusses on the potential for trade in services in IBSA. The fifth chapter reviews the investment relations between countries concerned and draws the broad contours for intensifying the flow of investment between these countries including the possibilities of joint productions. The benefits of trade and investment liberalisation cannot be reaped fully unless there is an enhanced connectivity between these countries. Therefore, chapter six reviews the present state of connectivity (air and shipping) between these countries and comes up with a future action plan to enhance the connectivity as a means of trade and investment facilitation. The last chapter discusses the potential of strategic cooperation in shaping the international trade and financial architecture.

CHAPTER 2

Growing Regionalism in an Era of Multilaterlism

The Response of IBSA

2.1. Introduction

One of the noteable inter-related developments in the world trading system during the last decade has been a sharp increase in the number of Regional/ Bilateral Trading Arrangements (RTAs) and an unprecedented growth in South-South trade. Most of these were in accordance with article 24 of GATT where in RTAs are allowed if trade barriers after integration are not on the whole higher or more restrictive after the formation of the RTA or custom union than they were before.[1] In tune with the above provision, by October 2003, 285 RTAs have been notified to GATT/WTO. It is also been estimated that an additional 60 RTAs are likely to be in operational but not reported to WTO and another 70 trade arrangements are at varying stages of negotiations.[2] As will be discussed in the last part of this chapter, the countries in the South especially India, Brazil and South Africa have not lagged much behind the developed world with respect to negotiating RTAs. Thus, regional integration among countries in the South has emerged as an effective tool for broadening markets, diversifying exports and achieving economies of scales, which, in turn, are decisive factors enabling the countries to enhance their productivity, generate employment, attract capital and stimulate investment. UNCTAD (2004b) attributes following factors to the growing South-South trade as well as the interest in South-South trade agreements:

---

1. Article XXIV, therefore stipulates that all tariff and other regulations of commerce are removed on substantially on intra-regional exchange of goods within a reasonable length of time namely ten years and they are notified to the Committee Regional Trade Agreements. Article V of GATS also has similar provisions which make possible the formation of RTAs.
2. See UNCTAD (2004a) for a detailed account on the recent trends in bilateralism and regional trading arrangements.

- Despite liberalisation under GATT/WTO in a number of sectors, exporters from developing countries continued to face market access barriers and entry problems in developed countries, which in turn induced exporters in South to explore southern options.
- South-South RTAs offer opportunities for economic of scale and specialisation and provide an avenue for smaller developing countries to overcome the constraints set by their small domestic market.
- Exploring opportunities for trade in other developing countries especially with those having high growth rates makes developing countries less vulnerable to market fluctuation in their traditional market in developed countries.
- A number of developing countries have witnessed major changes in their industrial and market structure that in general have made them more competitive *vis-àvis* developed countries including developing countries market at regional and global levels.
- Market dynamisms in the South for both capital goods and consumer goods along with demographic factors would indicate that growth in demand for goods and services is expected to come from new growth centres in developing countries.
- Enhanced South-South trade may be seen as a means of strengthening capacity in developing countries in dealing with challenging of globalisation and trade liberalisation. This could also serve as a basis for co-coordinating negotiating positions and advanced issues of interest to developing countries in multilateral forum such as the WTO.

In general, there are both demand and supply side factors that are at work as inducement mechanisms for South-South cooperation. While the demand side factors pertains mostly to the world trading environment emerged at the instance of WTO, the crucial factor from the supply side relates to the substantial industrial/technological capabilities built in the South during the last few decades. These capabilities as well as the output emanating from therein are more attuned to the demand conditions and factor endowments of the South and thus giving rise to greater market in the Southern countries.

The recent initiative between India, Brazil and South Africa to strengthen economic cooperation also has to be seen in the context of the emerging global trading environment wherein there has been a mushrooming of bilateral and regional trading arrangements. How has these three leading Southern countries responded to growing bilateralism and regionalism? An answer to this issue forms the basic premise as well as the background for the proposed economic cooperation between these countries. The response of these countries to growing regionalism, apart from the global trends, has to be seen against the backdrop of the recent changes in the policy regime as well as the return to such reform initiatives as manifested in their economic performance in the recent past. Therefore, the section 2 of the present chapter undertakes a quick overview of the recent trends in policy reforms and resultant performance of the countries under consideration. Against this background, section 3 highlights the behaviour of these countries with respect to bilateral/regional trading agreements and highlights the limits and opportunities for trilateral economic cooperation between the three countries.

2.2 Reforms, Recent Performance and Challenges of IBSA

India, Brazil and South Africa are not only the leading economies from their respective continents but they also play a dominant role in three major free trade agreements in the three continents: India in SAFTA, Brazil in MERCOSUR, South Africa in SACU. Hence, any attempt at building bridges between these countries is expected to contribute significantly to enhancing the interface between the respective FTAs that these countries represent. It may also be noted that India and Brazil are among the four countries that are expected to lead the global economy the next 50 years (Wilson and Purushottaman, 2003).

India

The beginning of 1990s marked a profound change in India's economic policies with the twin objectives of stabilisation and structural adjustment. While the former dealt mainly with short-term demand management through correcting fiscal, external and monetary imbalances, the latter focused on addressing the rigidities associated with the supply side of the economy by liberating it from the fetters state control and promoting an open and market friendly economy. The structural adjustment measures, aiming at enhancing efficiency, productivity and competitiveness of the economy; *inter alia* included industrial deregulation, liberalisation of foreign direct investment, trade liberalisation and reforms in public sector, infrastructure and financial sector.

The wide-ranging economic liberalisation of 1991 and its outcome may be seen against the backdrop of the reform initiatives of the decade prior to 1990s and the earlier development strategies. While the strategy of import substitution and the associated state interventions in different spheres of the economy helped establishing a diversified industrial structure and human capital base, by the late 1970s there was a felt need for doing away with series of government controls. This in turn was manifested in the initial attempts at liberalisation of 1980s focusing mostly on the domestic sectors of the economy and expansionary fiscal policies along with selective reduction in tariff barriers and managed floating of Indian Rupee. While there has been acceleration in the rate of output growth, the growth momentum could not be sustained as is evident from the mounting fiscal and current account deficits leading to a liquidity crisis towards the end of 1990s. It was against this background that India embarked on the far-reaching economic reforms in 1991. Given the crisis that prevailed in the external sector, the initial focus of reform was on the external sector and later the reforms were extended to other sectors of the economy.

Reforms: The Highlights

The New Industrial Policy of 1991 has dismantled the industrial approval or licencing system except when it is required for environmental or security reasons. New sectors such as mining, banking, insurance, telecommunications, construction and management of ports, roads and highways, airlines and defence equipment have been thrown open to private including foreign owned companies.

The partial convertibility of rupee on the trade account was announced in the 1992-93 budget that was subsequently broadened to full convertibility on current account by August 1994. India is cautiously moving towards the full capital account convertibility.

Reforms in the trade sector included the progressive reduction in the customs tariff rates from peak rates of 150 per cent in 1991-92 to 45 per cent by 1997-98 to 13.4 per cent in 2005-06. In February 2007, these were further brought down to 12.5 per cent for non-agricultural goods. The import licencing system has been dismantled and quantitative restrictions on imports have been phased out two years ahead of schedule. India has bound over 3298 of the 4701 (i.e. 70 per cent) of her tariff lines (at 6 digit level HS classification). Of these, 99 per cent of the bound lines have been bound at rates 40 per cent or lower. The applied rates are much lower than the binding rates for most of the products.

The Capital Issues Control Act was repealed and the Securities and Exchange Board of India (SEBI) was set up as a watchdog for regulating the functioning of the capital market. SEBI has focused on regulatory reform of the capital market as well as on market modernisation. Online trading and dematerialised trading have been introduced. Companies have been allowed to buy-back their own shares subject to the regulations laid down by SEBI.

In September 1992, the government announced guidelines for investments by foreign institutional investors (FIIs) in the Indian capital market. FIIs were now allowed to invest in all types of securities traded on the primary and secondary market with full repatriation benefits and without restrictions on either volume of trading or lock-in-period. In January 1993, a package of financial sector reforms was announced that included permission to new private sector banks including foreign joint ventures. The government has also established a policy regime for functioning of private non-banking finance companies (NBFCs) and agencies for rating their credit worthiness.

With a progressive liberalisation of FDI policy, foreign ownership of up to 100 per cent is permitted in most of the manufacturing sectors (except for defence equipment and for items reserved for production by small scale industries). A system of automatic approval of FDI proposals fulfilling the conditions laid down has been put into effect. Dividend balancing requirements imposed on consumer goods industries have been withdrawn.

Along with policy measures to integrate the Indian economy with the world market, a conscious attempt was also made to intensify the economic integration with the South Asian countries and the East Asian neighbours as a part of the 'Look East' policy adopted in the early 1990s. Reforms have led to a perceptible change in India's image in outside world as an economy with large domestic market and open trade and investment regime. Moreover, India has been recognised as a major player in some of the knowledge intensive areas like information technology—a new core technology considered as instrumental in facilitating transformation of economies in the new millennium.

Trends in Macroeconomic Performance and Challenges Ahead

The reform initiates have had rich dividends. During the last two decades there has been major structural change in the economy wherein the share of primary sector declined by almost 14 per cent from 39 per cent in 1980 and that of the service sector increased by almost 15 per cent to reach 54 per cent in 2005. The process of structural transformation got momentum during the last decade. Along with structural change, the Indian economy has sustained an average rate of growth of about 6 per cent over the past two decades. With the GDP growth of 9.2 per cent in 2006-07, India has emerged as one of the fastest growing economies in the world second only to China. During 1991-2003, India's trade with rest of the world recorded a little over three-fold increase. Rapid growth in exports of goods has helped in increasing India's share of world trade by nearly 50 per cent during the 1990s to reach a level of 1.1 per cent in 2006-07. With the healthy growth of exports of goods and services and growing capital inflows, India has accumulated foreign exchange reserves of the order of $ 225 billion at present (July 2007) as compared to $ 800 million in 1991. While there is an underestimation on account of different procedures followed, the FDI inflows have recorded more than 15 fold increase. Its stock market has been booming and its currency has appreciated in the last one year by about 13 per cent in relation to the US dollar. India's food reserves are comfortable and the inflation rate remained well below 5 per cent. The large pool of highly talented human resources have enabled India to emerge as a global hub for knowledge-based services such as, research, design and development (RD&D), business process outsourcing and high quality manufacturing such as pharmaceuticals and automotive. Also, India is widely recognised as a major player in the field of software exports that accounts for nearly 20 per cent of total exports. What is more, India also displayed remarkable ability to withstand external shocks despite growing outward orientation; India has been almost unaffected by the "Asian Flu" that humbled even the star performers of Asia. On the whole, India has the inherent strength and the potential to sustain high economic growth and emerge as a leading economy in the world in the near future. In a recent study, Goldman Sachs projects India to emerge, along with Brazil, among the top three economies in the world by 2050. According to Goldman Sachs, "India has the potential to show the fastest growth over the next 30 and 50 years." Recent empirical studies[3] in RIS have observed that growth of IBSA countries along with China would not only complement each others growth process but also significantly influence development process of Developing and LDCs.

Significant achievements notwithstanding, India still has more than 25 per cent of its people below poverty line and the rural population, which accounts for nearly 70 per cent of the total, are having limited access to basic services. Also, there is evidence of growing regional disparities in the levels of development and the extent of success in containing the fiscal deficit has been limited. Thus, though much has been achieved, much more remains to be done. The performance also falls well short of India's potential and its aspirations as formulated in its Tenth Five-Year Plan (2002-07)[4] and its Vision 2020 document. The Tenth Five Year Plan has set the target of 8 per cent annual growth rate. This target is marginally lower than what was accomplished in 2003-04 but considerably higher than 5-6 per cent achieved during the last five years. India's Vision for 2020 seeks to quadruple real per capita income to enable her to join the ranks of upper middle-income countries, eliminating poverty and building the fourth largest economy in the world. The Vision places heavy emphasis on human resource development and job creation to ensure employment for all through small and medium enterprises (SMEs), commercial agriculture, agro-industries, IT and IT-enabled services, among other sectors. Moreover, it is envisaged that by 2020 India would evolve into a knowledge economy *inter alia* by doubling the share of expenditure on education in GDP, increasing the national expenditure on R&D activity and investments in communication infrastructure.

Brazil

Brazil, the largest country in South America and the 10th largest economy in the world is representing about half of South America in population, territory, and economy. With GDP of US $ 706 billion in 2005, shared among its 186 million people resulting in a per capita income of US $7,600[5] , Brazil is placed

3. Mohanty, 2007 and Kumar and Chaturvedi, 2007.
4. Five Year Plan: 2002-07, Vol. I & II Planning Commission, Govt. of India.
5. *http://www.cia.gov/cia/publications/factbook/geos/br.html*

among the upper middle-income countries. The country is rich in agricultural, mineral, manufacturing, and service sectors. It is the largest producer of commodities like coffee and sugarcane, second largest producer of sugar in the world and is one of the leading countries to produce bananas. The country is rich in minerals and the largest producer of high quality iron ore (68 per cent iron), the 3rd largest producer of bauxite, and produces 13 thousand tonnes of tin, 66 million tonnes of petroleum (proven reserves 1200 million tonnes) in 2001. The country has a large and diversified industrial base; the major industries being automobiles, steel, metallurgy, paper, cement, textiles, chemicals, leather, sugar and food & beverages. Exploiting vast natural resources and a large labour pool, Brazil has emerged as the largest economy of South America and a regional leader.

Reforms in 1990s and the Outcome

Brazil experienced a miracle growth of double-digit figure in the late 1960s and maintained the average of 9 per cent growth rate over the period 1965-1980 and 8.6 per cent during the 1980s. The observed economic growth was mainly facilitated by high levels of external borrowing as reflected in the high current account deficit of the order of over 4 per cent during 1980s. Brazils external debt increased almost 1000 per cent during 1970s amounting to US $ 71.5 billion accounting for about 29 per cent of the GDP in 1980. Thus, the higher output growth, financed mostly by external borrowing, could not be sustained and the growth rate during the 1980s was only of the order of 1.6 per cent accompanied by high rate of inflation,[6] current account deficit and depreciating currency. An inefficient state apparatus, an economically isolated and non-competitive economy and repressed financial markets, further fueled the macro economic imbalances and instability. In the context of gloomy performance of the economy in the 80s, wide-ranging reforms were undertaken in the 1990s with a view to bring back the economy to rails.

While the reforms left hardly any sector of the economy untouched, the prominent among them related to dismantling heavy handed regulation, removal of tariff and non-tariff barriers, privatisation of public sector enterprises and emphasising greater role of the markets forces and thus lifting many of the price controls and liberalising the financial sector.

The National Privatization Program (PND), launched in 1990, involved the sale of federal and state companies to the private sector including the foreign firms. Throughout the 90s, the federal and state governments withdrew from sectors such as steel, petrochemicals, fertilisers, railroads and

6. Implicit deflator climbed up from 39.7 during 1970s to 330 during 1980s and further increased to over 2200 in 1994.

telecommunications, and sold off majority and minority holdings in dozens of companies from hotels to textiles. Part of the energy and gas industries was also transferred to the private sector, as were most government banks. Thus far the sale proceeds from the sale of more than 90 companies amounted to US$105.3, of which 62 per cent was accounted by the sale of telecommunications and electricity companies and about 16 per cent from the sale of mining and steel companies. This has dramatically reversed the situation of the 70s where in almost 70 per cent of GDP was in the hands of the government. Privatisation sales are by public auction, with foreign companies allowed to participate via local subsidiaries and the foreign companies have been major players in many of the privatised sectors.

With respect to stabilisation, an ambitious programme called Real Plan (*Plano Real)* was launched in 1994 along with the introduction of new currency. The programme used exchange as a nominal anchor effectively undoing the *de facto* indexation of the exchange rate that existed since the late 1960s. Other elements of the Real Plan included capital and trade liberalisation, elimination of price and salary indexing, strict fiscal control, privatisation, banking reform and a more or less fixed foreign exchange rate.

During the 1990s, fluctuations in output growth rate notwithstanding; there has been an average annual growth rate of 2.7 per cent as compared to 1.6 per cent in the previous decade. The inflation rate fell to 3 per cent by 1998 before rising in 1999 due to currency depreciation. The main factors underlying good growth and inflation performance were the stability already provided by the Real Plan, progress on fiscal reforms, adoption of an inflation-targeting monetary policy in mid-1999, and fiscal stringency.[7] Though the emerging market crisis in the late 1990s interrupted the progress, Brazil consolidated its stabilisation programme, and went well along the way of a liberalisation programme with increased emphasis on economic opportunities for the private sector through increased competition. The major economic stabilisation programmes, like switching over to a floating exchange rate regime and an inflation targeting regime along with tight fiscal policy measures reinforced by a series of IMF programmes seems to have helped the country to recover from the depression phase.[8]

7. A number of factors were responsible for this better than expected performance. First, contrary to prior expectations, Brazilian industrial and individual consumers proved highly resistant to price increases and quickly switched to domestic substitutes or off-brands, thus holding exchange rate pass-through to a minimum. Second, the government continued to make progress on fiscal reforms and to run quarterly primary surpluses in compliance with the agreement with the Fund. Third, the Central Bank initiated an inflation-targeting monetary policy in mid-year that established an explicit link between monetary policy and prospective inflation, thus stabilising inflationary expectations. Finally, improvement in other overseas markets and continuing strong growth in the U.S. economy stimulated an export-led recovery.

8. For details, See U.S. Department of State, *FY 2001 Country Commercial Guide: Brazil.*

The last decade also witnessed a dramatic increase in the inflow of FDI into the country. During 1990-96, the annual average inflow of FDI was only US $ 17 billion. Thereafter, FDI inflows increased to a peak of US $ 31 billion in 2000, but it declined thereafter to reach a level of US $ 14.6 billion in 2004.[9] Nonetheless, in the developing world Brazil's record has been second only to China. The economy showed the clear sign of recovery in 2004 with a real GDP growth rate of 5.7 per cent. With increased exports and reduced imports[10] during 2000-2002, the economy recorded positive trade balance in 2001 and 2002. Since 2000, rate of growth of the economy once again slipped with a negative growth rate (-0.2%) in 2003, which was preceded by 2.9 per cent and 3.7 per cent respectively in 2005 and 2006. As compared to the second half of the 1990s wherein the inflation was kept under control, it remains high at present 7.2 per cent in 2005.

The Challenges Ahead

If the available empirical evidence is any indication, the overall returns to multilateral trade liberalisation and other reform initiates have, at best, been modest in Latin America in general[11] and Brazil in particular. One of the major challenge before the government was to maintain economic growth over a period of time to generate employment and make the government debt burden more manageable. While economic management has been good, there remain important economic vulnerabilities. A more realistic exchange rate acts as a stimulus to exports, but countervailing factors in Brazil's case included increased economic uncertainty, exchange rate volatility, scarcity of export credit, weak demand in key foreign markets, and a sharp decline in basic product prices in the past years. Brazil's trade position underwent a radical transformation under the Real Plan due to market opening, an overvalued exchange rate, and pent-up demand for capital and consumer goods. At the same time, lack of export finance, lag effects, weak demand in Asia and Latin America, and declining basic product prices undermined the overall performance of the economy. While price stabilisation undeniably benefited the poor, lifting an estimated 13 million people above the official poverty line, Brazil still has one of the most unequal income distributions in the world. In other words, highly unequal distribution of income remains a pressing problem.

Since 1998, Brazil has made significant progress on structural fiscal reforms. Notable successes include introduction of an actuarial factor into calculation of public pensions for private sector workers (INSS), passage of the

---

9. See in this context *http://www.investebrasil.org/html/view_Economia_2Politica_303.htm*

10. Brazil's global imports reduced from US $ 57.6 billion in 1998 to US $ 62.8 billion in 2004. The export is estimated to increase to US $ 51.0 billion f.o.b. while import US $ 48.25 billon f.o.b. in 2004.

11. See in this context Sanchez, 2003.

budget guidelines and fiscal responsibility laws, limitation of public worker social security benefits, and completion of a massive debt rescheduling with state and municipal governments. Although Brazil has made immense progress towards fiscal discipline in recent years, it still faces significant challenges. These include: the government-run pensions system requires further reform to reach actuarial balance in the schemes for both public and private workers. Brazil's tax collection agency has been radically modernised in recent years. Virtually all the annual tax declarations are now filed via the Internet, for example. However, the fiscal structure remains complex and burdensome, and the new government has pledged to make tax reform a high priority. There is general consensus that reform must stimulate production, investment and exports, spreading the burden more widely and closing loopholes.[12]

In the external front, the most alarming concern is that, the government's domestic debt increased steadily from 1994 to 2003, straining government finances, while Brazil's foreign debt (a mix of private and public debt) is large in relation to Brazil's modest (but growing) export base. However, export performance continues to be impressive. The government's sound policies have contributed to increase international reserves, helped improve the composition of public debt, and fostered a swing in the external current account. These accomplishments are helping to limit the impact of increased uncertainty and recent volatility in international financial markets on Brazil.

Reforms in South Africa

With a surface area of over 1.2 million square kilometers, a coastline of nearly 3,000 kilometers, and a population of around 47 million,[13] the Republic of South Africa is the biggest country in southern Africa. With GDP of US $ 240 billion in 2005 and per capita income of around US$ 4960, South Africa is placed among the upper middle-income countries. It is also an economy with significant growth potential; enjoys easy access to other markets in Africa, has sophisticated financial institutions and capital markets, a good communication infrastructure and inexpensive electrical power and raw materials. Since 1994, when the first democratically elected government came into power, South Africa has developed into a politically stable country with a more open and outwardly oriented economy.

The transformation of the South African economy over the years has been on par with those of larger and more mature economies leading to the

---

12. See in this context *http://www.investebrasil.org/html/view_Economia_2Politica_303.htm*

13. The average population growth rate was 1.6 per cent per annum over the period 2000 to 2005. The average density in South Africa is 39 people per sq. km. The fertility rate is 3.0 births per woman. Life expectancy in 2005 is down to 48 years compared to the estimate in 1996 of 56.5 years. It was anticipated that life expectancy would drop due to HIV/AIDS deaths taken up in the statistics. Urbanisation has increased, with 59.0 per cent of South Africans now living in urban areas.

establishment of a relatively diversified economic structure where in industry (31 per cent) and services 67 per cent in 2005, accounts for a sizeable share of total GDP. Mining and quarrying account for a large part of South Africa's total exports. The agriculture sector that comprises large modern firms as well as tiny individual holdings using traditional methods on a subsistence basis, remains an important provider of employment (11 per cent), especially in the rural areas though its contribution to GDP is only of the order of 3 per cent in 2005.

In the past, state involvement was seen as the most effective way to develop an indigenous base for the economy, either through parastatal enterprises or through ownership of joint ventures in firms. State enterprises were reorganised to perform specific functions in the economy, such as the diversification of economic activities. Nationalised banking systems assisted in allocating credit to the highest-priority sectors. By the 1980s, however, it became clear that parastatals were not achieving desired results. They were incurring large losses through their lack of administrative and managerial capacity, bloated payrolls and inefficient operations. Government-controlled credit subsidised these losses and diverted resources away from more efficient uses. Unable to sustain such policies, the governments moved toward privatising these state enterprises at the urging of the IMF and World Bank.

The "big four" parastatals are Eskom (power generation and distribution), Denel (defence), Transnet (transportation) and Telkom (telecommunications). Eskom supplies nearly 98 per cent of South Africa's electricity, makes substantial profits and has a turnover of nearly R30 billion per year. Transnet dominates the transport sector and contributes more than 3 per cent of South Africa's GDP. It comprises 13 companies involved in multi-modal transport and includes railways, an airline, ports and a pipeline. The Swiss Air Group bought a 20 per cent stake in Transnet's South African Airlines for R1.3 billion in 1999, but the South African government bought it back in 2002 after the Swiss company experienced financial difficulties. Telkom enjoyed a monopoly until May 2002 on certain international and fixed line telecommunications services. It was already partially privatised in 1997, when 30 per cent of its shares were sold to an US/Malaysia consortium. A further 20 per cent was sold in March 2003 through an initial public offering (IPO).

With a view to addressing the inequality in the country and to ensure black participation in the economy, the SAG has recently become more involved in the economy in certain sectors. For example, all mineral rights have always been in private hands. In terms of new legislation these rights revert to State custodianship within 5 years. The purpose of this is to allow the previously disadvantaged part of the population the right and opportunity to obtain a licence to mine minerals. In terms of Black Economic Empowerment (BEE) objectives, the target ownership of assets or other meaningful involvement and control for blacks in the mining industry has been set at 15 per cent in 5 years and 26 per cent within 10 years. Government has also set similar objectives in other sectors in order to address the inequality between the racial groups and to advance black participation in the economy. Government procurement policies have, for example, been designed to give preference to black businesses.

With the election of Nelson Mandela in 1994, the new government undertook its economic reform plan with great expectations after the long years of apartheid. The Reconstruction and Development Programme (RDP) outlining proposals for jobs, housing, healthcare and social amenities for all was announced along with related reform in education and training, social protection and the promotion of SMEs and the development of black entrepreneurship. In terms of macroeconomic policy, the Growth, Employment and Redistribution (GEAR) programme was developed along with proposals for Central Bank independence. In trade policy, South Africa joined the new World Trade Organization (WTO) and opted for openness in terms of trade and foreign direct investment (FDI).

Recent Economic Performance and Challenges

The South African economy is getting adjusted to the challenges posed by the reform initiatives and the changing global economy. The foundations are being laid for improved long-term economic growth and a series of growth-oriented microeconomic reforms were put into place to complement and sharpen the broader structural changes that have taken place throughout the economy.

Nonetheless, if the available empirical evidence is any indication, the overall returns to multilateral trade liberalisation have at best been modest. Real GDP grew only at an average annual rate of 3.7 per cent during 2000-05. Given the global recession the same rate of growth (3.7 per cent) was recorded in 2002 while there has been steady rise in the growth movementum of output since 2004 (RIS, 2007).[14] Thus, the observed GDP growth during the last decade (2.8 per cent) has been well short of the 4-5 per cent per year required to substantially reduce the country's unemployment rate.[15] However, growth prospects of the country has been moderate (IMF, 2007).

The official unemployment rate increased to 29.4 per cent in February 2002 (from 26.4 per cent in February 2001 and 19.3 per cent in 1996).[16] The September 2002 labour force survey measured an even higher unemployment rate of 30.5 per cent even though many industries in the formal sector have reported growth in

14. For growth performance of the IBSA countries, see RIS (2007).

15. See *IMF Staff Country Report* No.00/42.

16. The economically active population has increased to 16.1 million (11.5 million in 1996), while the total employed rose only to 11.4 million (9.29 million in 1996), with the total unemployed at 4.7 million (from 2.22 million in 1996).

their employment numbers during 2002. A range of factors have contributed to South Africa's persistently high unemployment rate, including the legacy of the apartheid capital-intensive production structure, chronic skilled labour shortages, low investment, rigidities in the labour market, and the increase in urban population since the 1994 political change.

There has been considerable success in containing inflation during the period since 1998 as is evident from the decline in inflation rate from 9.1 per cent in 1998 to 6.6 per cent during 2000-2005. But, driven by rising food and fuel prices, inflation took off in 2002. By the year-end, the government's target of reducing inflation rate to 3-6 per cent was unattainable and the inflation rate for the year averaged rate at about the level that prevailed in 1998 (9.1 per cent). In an effort to contain inflationary pressures, the Reserve Bank raised interest rate four times pushing prime lending rates from 13 to 17 per cent. Inflation rate showed downward trend during 2003 as a result of moderation in food and energy prices, as well as the effects of a stronger Rand. Thus, the central policy challenge facing South Africa seems to be to increase the level of economic activity in a manner that raises living standards across the country.

One of the positive features of the South African economy in recent years has been the Government's commitment to monetary and fiscal discipline. The overall budget deficit of South Africa was reduced from a peak of 9 per cent of GDP in 1993-94 to 1.0 per cent of GDP in 2002-03. This has been achieved by firm control over government expenditure growth along with improved tax collection during these years. By containing the budget deficit, and helped by the downward revaluation of its foreign-currency debt, the South Africa succeeded in reducing the ratio of its debt to GDP from 42.9 per cent in March 2002 to 37.9 per cent at the end of March 2003. These measures are expected to contain the interest cost of servicing government debt and freeing up resources for improved service delivery.

During the recent past South Africa has also made major strides in reducing external imbalances. Trade liberalisation efforts have contributed to eliminate the current account deficit of South Africa's balance of payments. The current account increased from a deficit of 1.7 per cent of GDP in 1998 to a surplus of 3.8 per cent of GDP in 2005 for the first time since 1994. The marked improvement in the current account balance resulted from a substantial increase in merchandise exports and net gold exports.[17] However, in 2002 this trade surplus decreased, resulting in a current account deficit estimated at 1.4 per cent of GDP, due in part to higher oil prices.

---

17. South Africa's terms of trade (the ratio of export prices to import prices) increased by 2.5 per cent from 2001 to 2002.

South Africa has also made steady progress in reducing its external debt exposure, a key source of external vulnerability in the past. Total external debt as percentage of total exports of goods and services decreased from 107.3 per cent in 1997 to an estimated 96.4 per cent in 2001. South Africa's net international reserve position has also improved considerably, from US$ 5.4 billion at the end of 1998 to US$ 20.6 billion in 2005 (*World Development Report*, 2007).

The Reserve Bank considers interventions in foreign exchange market to maintain exchange stability as undesirable and sound economic policy considered as the best policy to protect the national currency. Sound micro policy initiatives not withstanding, Rand has shown substantial volatility in the recent past which had its beginning by the end of 2000. The dollar value of the Rand which remained at 3.55 in 1994, reached at 6.36 in 2005 and further to 7.08 in 2007.[18] In 2002, the Rand became one of the best performing currency in the world. The trade surplus, however, started to narrow during 2003 mainly due to a setback in exports. A much-welcomed development was, however, the fall in the rate of inflation since the end of the first quarter 2003. This was helped by a downward revision to some housing rental data previously released by Statistics South Africa. On June 19, 2003, the South African Reserve Bank (SARB) announced a 1.5 per cent reduction in its interest rates and indicated that further reductions during the course of 2003 may be possible (US Department of Commerce, 2004).

Major achievements in different spheres of the economy notwithstanding, several decades of apartheid coupled with less than potential performance of the economy has left the South African Government with many challenges, which include a highly distorted and unequal income distribution. At one extreme, about 13 per cent of the population is "first world", with high-school education, low childhood mortality rates, and minimal poverty. At the other extreme, is about 53 per cent of the population, half of which have less than a primary school education, over a third suffer from chronic malnutrition, and poverty is maximal.[19] In addition, there are challenges in other socioeconomic spheres relating to ever-increasing crime, high unemployment, poor quality schools, skills shortages, inadequate social services, HIV/AIDS, poverty and corruption. Regarding South Africa's experience with global trading environment, Holden (2001) observed that although export oriented companies have increased investment rates, exports have not proved to be a growth engine for the economy in terms of output and employment. The policy makers hence are at the crossroads; they are reluctant to embrace any further multilateral liberalisation for

18. For details, see *http://www.x-rate.com/d/ZAR/USD/data120.html*

19. Hoddinott, Adato and Besley (2000).

fear of triggering employment losses from imports in the labour intensive industries. They see little response in employment and output to increased exports. The question that must be asked is whether the regional preferential arrangements that are being pursued will address these issues and whether they are viewed as a substitute for liberalisation and will achieve growth and a more equitable distribution of resources for the economy'

To sum up the discussion, though India, Brazil and South Africa have undertaken wide ranging reforms during the last decade, the outcome of the reform initiatives appears to be found varying from one country to another as is clearly evident from different indicators presented in Table 2.1.

While the per capita income of India has been less than one-third that of South Africa and one-half of Brazil, the recorded growth rate in GDP has been significantly higher and on a sustained basis as compared to other two. It is also evident that India depicted growth dynamism induced more by domestic resources with very limited recourse to FDI whereas in the case of Brazil and South Africa despite high inflow of FDI, output growth in a sustained manner is yet to take place.

The performance in the external sector of all the three countries have improved during the last decade but here again India appears to have fared better as compared to other two. This is particularly evident from its turnaround in current account balance and the built up of huge foreign exchange reserves of the order of US$ 140 billion at present by India. Though Brazil, known for its vulnerabilities in the exchange rate and prices, witnessed remarkable stability during the last decade along with South Africa the question, however, remains as to how sustainable the observed stability is? On the whole, the realised returns to multilateral trade liberalisation coupled with various other reforms have not been substantial especially in the case of Brazil and South Africa. Each of the three economies faces several developmental challenges. Hence, the rationale for economic cooperation between these countries is not too far to seek.

2.3 The Response of IBSA to Regionalism and Bilateralism

India

As a founding member of GATT and WTO, India has demonstrated a strong commitment to multilateralism in her trade policy all along while taking a keen interest in schemes of regional economic cooperation in Asia. India has been the founding member of the Bangkok Agreement, one of the first preferential trade arrangement evolved in Asia in 1975. However, until recently, India had a few bilateral trade agreements. India is currently negotiating RTAs with other developing countries, but is not involved in North-South RTAs.

TABLE 2.1

IBSA: Macroeconomic Fundamentals of IBSA Countries

Indicators	Brazil		India		South Africa	
	1995	2005	1995	2005	1995	2005
Area ('0000 sq. km)	8,459	8,459	2,973	2,973	1,214	1,214
Population (million)	161	186	932	1,095	39	47
Population Density (per sq. km)	19	22	314	368	32	39
GDP ($ mill)	704,168	796,055	355,163	805,714	151,113	239,543
GDP Growth	4.2	2.3	7.6	9.2	3.1	4.9
Agriculture Growth	4.1	0.8	-0.9	6	-19.9	5.4
Industry Growth	1.9	2.5	11.6	9.4	3.2	4.1
Manufacturing Growth	1.7	..	14.9	9.1	6.5	4.1
Services Growth	5.7	2.5	10.5	9.9	4.5	5.2
Agriculture (% of GDP)	9	8	28	18	4	3
Industry (% of GDP)	37	38	28	27	35	30
Manufacturing (% of GDP)	..	..	18	16	21	19
Services (% of GDP)	54	53	44	54	61	67
Exports ($m)	54,395	133,520	39,083	165,489	34,412	64,904
Imports ($m)	66,815	98,634	43,334	194,796	33,386	68,412
Merchandise Exports ($m)	46,506	118,308	30,630	95,096	27,853	51,876
Service Exports ($m)	6,135	16,095	6,775	..	4,619	11,157
Merchandise Imports ($m)	54,137	77,585	34,707	134,831	30,546	62,304
Service Imports ($m)	13,630	24,243	10,268	..	5,971	12,155
Trade (% of GDP)	17.2	29.2	23.2	44.7	44.9	55.7
Inflation Rate (%)	77.6	7.2	9	4.4	10.3	4.7
Exchange Rate (Per $)	0.92	2.43	32.43	44.1	3.63	6.36
CAB ($m)	-18,136	14,199	-5,563	..	-2,493	-9,142
Current A/c (% of GDP)	-2.6	1.8	-1.6	..	-1.6	-3.8
Total Reserves ($m)	51,477	53,799	22,865	137,825	4,464	20,624
Reserves (Months of Imports)	7.9	5.1	5.1	..	1.4	3.2
FDI, Net Outflows (% of GDP)	0.20	0.32	0.03	..	1.65	0.38
FDI, Net Inflows (% of GDP)	0.69	1.91	0.60	0.82	0.83	2.61

Source: RIS based on *World Development Indicators 2007 CD-ROM,* World Bank, Washington DC.

India has been a member of the South Asian Association for Regional Cooperation (SAARC) which evolved a South Asian Preferential Trade Agreement (SAPTA) in 1993. In January 2004, the Member States of the South Asian Agreement on Regional Cooperation (SAARC), i.e. Bangladesh, Bhutan, India, Maldives, Nepal, Pakistan and Sri Lanka, signed the South Asia Free Trade Agreement (SAFTA) that will bring down tariffs to 0-5 per cent in next 7-10 years. The Free Trade Area will be operational by January 2006. It will also provide for a list of sensitive items for member countries to safeguard national interests.

India also participates in another regional grouping in the region namely BIMST-EC combining seven South and Southeast Asian nations that has also adopted a Framework Agreement for a Free Trade Arrangement between its members. India has had free trade and transit treaties with Nepal and Bhutan, India's landlocked immediate neighbours.

India signed a bilateral free trade agreement with Sri Lanka in December 1998 and became operational in March 2000. The agreement, envisages gradual phasing out of tariffs on all products, except for certain items included in a negative list. Imports into India of tea and garment are subject to tariff rate quotas.[20] Two-way trade increased from $695 million during 2000-01 to $1088 million during 2002-03. India is one of the largest exporters to Sri Lanka. The balance of trade, which favoured India 15 to 1 when the agreement was signed, has now come down to about 5 to 1. India and Sri Lanka have recently signed a Comprehensive Economic Partnership Agreement (CEPA) which will include services and facilitate greater investment flows between the two countries.

Since 1991, India has pursued a policy of "Look East" in her foreign economic relations. As a part of this, India became a dialogue partner of ASEAN. At the Second Summit of ASEAN-India held in Bali in October 2003, a Framework Agreement on Comprehensive Economic Cooperation has been signed.[21] The parties agreed to enter into negotiations in order to establish an ASEAN-India Regional Trade and Investment Area (RTIA), which includes a FTA in goods, services and investment, and to strengthen and enhance economic cooperation. The free trade is likely to be evolved with 5 ASEAN countries by 2011 and with the CLMV (Cambodia, Lao PDR, Myanmar and Vietnam) countries and the Philippines by 2016.

India signed a free trade agreement (FTA) with Thailand in October 2003 for setting up of a free trade area covering goods, services and investment in 10 years. The Indo-Thai FTA covers many items and several areas in the first phase

---

20. Imports should take place through specific ports (Calcutta and Cochin in the case of tea and Mumbai and Chennai in the case of garments).

21. *http://www.asean.or.id/15278.htm*

including services, investment, economic cooperation and goods like food items, tourism, auto parts, electronic goods. As per the "Early Harvest Scheme (EHS)," under the agreement, a common list of 84 items for exchange of tariff concession at 6-digit level and tariff is slated to be phased out by March 1, 2006. As per the agreement, negotiations on goods are scheduled to be concluded in March 2005 and the FTA for zero duty imports will be put into effect by 2010. Similarly, negotiations on investment would start in January 2004 and is expected to be completed within two years. Currently, discussions are continuing on the framework of 'Rules of Origin'.

In addition, recently initiated negotiations for a Comprehensive Economic Cooperation Agreement with Singapore is at the advanced stage. Similarly, as part of the Look East policy, India is also engaging with China, Japan and South Korea to strengthen economic cooperation between the two countries.

During the state visit of Brazil's president to India,[22] on 25 January 2004, the India-MERCOSUR Framework Agreement was signed. On 25 January 2004, MERCOSUR and India signed a Preferential Trade Agreement (PTA), which would be followed by "subsequent negotiations for the creation of a Free Trade Area".[23] The parties would also negotiate Rules of Origin, Safeguard Measures and Dispute Settlement. The agreement provides for cooperation on technical standards and regulations and SPS measures. The Parties agreed to create a Joint Administration Committee composed by the MERCOSUR Common Market Group and Secretary of the Department of Commerce in India (or their representatives). One of the functions of the Joint Administration Committee is to encourage the active participation of the private sectors in areas covered by the agreement. MERCOSUR presented a request list of over 900 products with an average *ad valorem* import tariff of 33.1 per cent, whereas India presented a list of over 500 products with an average *ad valorem* tariff of 12.5 per cent. During negotiations carried out in Buenos Aires in March 2004, MERCOSUR and India made initial offers covering about 200 products. The lists have subsequently been expanded to cover between 300 and 400 products.

Framework for Preferential Trade Agreement between India and SACU (South African Customs Union whose members include South Africa, Swaziland, Namibia, Lesotho, Botswana) has also been signed and expected to give a push to India's quest for finding new partners for exchanging trade preferences, concession and enlarging cooperation.

---

22. India and Brazil also signed five agreements that include bilateral cooperation in peaceful uses of outer space, tourism, culture and other diversified areas. The two were also keen on cooperation in the areas of information technology, railways, pharmaceuticals and biotechnology.

23. See in this context, Government of India, *India's Current Engagement with RTAs*, Ministry of Commerce and Industry. Available at *http://commerce.nic.in/india_rta.htm*

Brazil

During the last decade, the Latin American countries realised the need for and advantages of regional integration and moved decisively to create new trade blocs and revitalise those created earlier. All the countries have become part of one or other trade blocs. Even those few countries, which were not full-fledged members of any trade blocs have also signed Free Trade Agreements with other countries and blocs within as well as outside the region.

There are five sub-regional groups in Latin America of which Brazil is a leading member of MERCOSUR (Mercado Comun de Sur-Southern Common Market), a South American trade bloc. MERCOSUR was formed in 1991 with the original members, Argentina, Brazil, Uruguay and Paraguay; and it became a custom union in 1995.[24] Within the trading bloc countries, the intra-regional trade is duty-free, and there is a common external tariff (CET) for imports from other countries. It is a third largest integrated market after EU and NAFTA. However, the Customs union is not working perfectly and there are still some NTBs and problems reflecting the turmoil in the markets of the member countries in the last few years.

Brazil, within the framework of MERCOSUR, has been in the process of diversifying its trade relations with other trading blocs as well as individual countries. The two important regional blocs in Latin America, the Andean Community and MERCOSUR signed an agreement to establish a "South American Free Trade Area (SAFTA)". The SAFTA is progressing and there are number of issues such as rules of origin, deadlines and timetables for reducing tariffs on sensitive products, sanitary and phytosanitary regulations, technical standards, NTBs, dispute settlements, etc. are on board.

MERCOSUR is making progress in their trade relations with the associate members. Within MERCOSUR, the member countries are largely dependent upon MERCOSUR for a large part of their trade, while Brazil's trade with MERCOSUR's partners is very limited.

The EU on a constant basis remains Brazil's main trading partner and Brazil remains the EU's main trading partner in Latin America. It has signed a cooperation agreement with MERCOSUR and is negotiating a Free Trade Agreement. The EU-Brazil Framework Inter-Regional Co-operation Agreement of 1995 provides the institutional setting for the political ties between the EU and Brazil and a framework for their cooperation. Brazil is also an important destination for EU investment. Certain important market access problems persist, partly in terms of tariff and NTBs. The development of bilateral relations is likely

24. Chile and Bolivia are the associate members of Mercosur, and Venezuela has sought associate membership of Mercosur.

to be substantially influenced by the outcome of the current EU/MERCOSUR negotiations on an association agreement. Negotiations are scheduled for finalisation by 2005 and an important element of an eventual agreement will be the agreement in relation to creating an EU/MERCOSUR free-trade area.

On July 3, 2002, Mexico and Brazil signed a preferential trade agreement within the framework of the Latin American Integration Association (LAIA). This new agreement will broaden trade between the two largest Latin American economies by eliminating tariffs on 800 industrial and agricultural products. MERCOSUR has signed an agreement for consultation and cooperation with China, and is considering cooperation agreements with ASEAN, Japan and South Korea.

MERCOSUR has been exploring a preferential agreement with the Southern Africa Customs Union (SACU), comprising Botswana, Lesotho, Namibia, the Republic of South Africa and Swaziland.[25] A Framework Agreement was signed in December 2000 during South Africa's President Mbeki's state visit to Brazil. In October 2001, a first meeting of negotiators took place in Montevideo, Uruguay, where proposals on modalities and a timetable for the negotiations were discussed.[26] Progress, however, has been very slow. In accordance with 2002 SACU arrangements, negotiations would only be possible with SACU as a whole, implying a need to involve the other SACU Members. MERCOSUR is currently analysing information on trade and tariffs provided by on SACU as well as issues in the area of standards, in particular sanitary and phytosanitary (SPS) measures.

The Central American Integration System (CIAS), an extension of the Central American Common Market, has plan to open trade negotiation with MERCOSUR along with other trading blocs.

Brazil's trade orientation has been in the direction towards developing countries. It believes that poor countries can stand up to rich ones and achieve development by cooperating with each other. Brazil has also proposed a full-fledged free-trade agreement among the G20 developing countries, a Brazilian-inspired grouping formed ahead of the World Trade Organization (WTO) meeting in Cancún. Brazil has shown very keen interest in developing South-South Cooperation and promoting India-Brazil-South Africa (IBSA) economic cooperation. The partnership with South Africa and India helps to press the claims of all three for permanent seats on the UN Security Council, while the G20

25. Bi-regional trade between MERCOSUR and SACU amounted to around US$ 1 billion in 2002, with an important surplus in favour of MERCOSUR.

26. MERCOSUR and the Republic of South Africa signed an agreement aimed at creating a free trade area in December 2000. During the third meeting of the MERCOSUR-South Africa Negotiating Commission (Pretoria, December 2002) MERCOSUR presented a request list of 4175 items, whereas the Republic of South Africa presented a list of 1157 items, corresponding to 782 items of the NCM.

aspires to take on the rich countries in the WTO's Doha round of global trade talks.

South Africa

South Africa, a founding member of the GATT, is an active member of the WTO. Apart from this, it participates in a number of preferential trade relationships, both regional and bilateral. South Africa's economic outlook has been for a new "relationship of partnership between Africa and the international community" under the broad objectives of the New Partnership for Africa's Development (NEPAD), an African-led initiative released in October 2001.

South Africa is the member of Southern African Customs Union (1968) and hence having free trade among the SACU members.[27] In 1994, South Africa became a member of the SADC.[28] With the key policy objective to strengthen trade and investment linkages with these countries, South Africa has made a free trade offer to address the trade imbalances in the region. The offer was made in terms of the proposed SADC free trade agreement. South Africa has offered to remove its tariffs faster than the other members and could begin reducing its tariffs as soon as other SADC countries ratify agreements.

Over and above these agreements, South Africa has also unilateral preferential trade arrangements with some countries. In these arrangements, other countries unilaterally provide access to their markets through lower tariffs and increased/removed quotas. These arrangements are not negotiated and can be unilaterally amended by the providing country, and are therefore not agreements. The US provides such market access opportunities to a number of African countries, including South Africa, through the African Growth and Opportunity Act (AGOA). A number of countries such as, EU countries, Norway, Switzerland, Hungary, Japan, Canada, USA, Czech Republic provide market access to South Africa through the generalised system of preferences (GSP) mechanism.[29]

Europe is South Africa's biggest source of investment and accounts for almost half of South Africa's total foreign trade, and 7 of South Africa's top 10 trading partners are European countries. The recently concluded trade agreement between the EU and South Africa removes 90 per cent of all trade barriers over the next decade—95 per cent of SA goods (including agricultural products) and 86 per cent of EU imports. However, the agreement provides for the

27. SACU members are South Africa, Botswana, Lesotho, Namibia, and Swaziland.

28. SADC comprises 14 sub-Saharan African countries, Angola, Botswana, Lesotho, Malawi, Mauritius, Mozambique, Namibia, South Africa, Swaziland, Seychelles, Tanzania, The Democratic Republic of Congo, Zambia and Zimbabwe.

29. For details, see South African trade relationships, *http://www.southafrica.info/doing_business/sa_trade/agreements/traderelations.htm*

establishment of a bilateral free trade area between the EU and South Africa in conformity with WTO rules and its combination of free trade, development, co-operation, finance and technical assistance.[30]

South Africa is a member of the Indian Ocean Rim Association for Regional Co-operation (IOR-ARC).[31] Currently, South Africa is involved in two projects: a regional ports initiative and a financial systems harmonisation initiative. The country has built its strongest ties with Malaysia and has attracted a lot of foreign investment (Malaysia is the second largest investor on a cumulative basis in South Africa since 1994).

South Africa has also given importance in its foreign policy[32] for increased trade relationship with two giants in North East Asia, namely Japan and China. Japan is South Africa's largest trading partner in Asia and its fourth largest overall trading partner and the fifth largest investor with cumulative investment since 1994 amounting to approximately R2 billion, and also a substantial aid donor to South Africa. The economic and trade relations with the People's Republic of China have grown rapidly since the formal establishment of diplomatic relations.

In North America, US is one of its key trading partners for both South African export promotion and inward investment mobilisation. The trade and investment relationship between the two countries has been growing since 1994. Since the introduction of AGOA, South Africa is allowed to have a duty-free access of exports into the US.

Brazil is South Africa's largest trading partner in Latin America, with bilateral trade reaching R5.3 billion in 2001. Trade between South Africa and Mexico has grown to R1.2 billion in 2001 and continues to grow.

South Africa is a member of (Africa Caribbean and Pacific (ACP) group of countries. It is a signatory to the EU-ACP Partnership Agreement signed in Cotonou on 23 June 2000.

South Africa has also good bilateral trade relationship[33] with Cuba, Libya, Iran Syria and other countries. Recently, South Africa has turned its attention to

---

30. South Africa was refused to be given as a full member of the Lomé Convention, however, was granted qualified membership in April 1997. Under this, South Africa is excluded from the benefits of duty- free market access to the EU. (For detail, please refer, *The European Union-South Africa Trade Agreement: Implications for Post-Lomé Trade Relations*, 14 April, 2000, *http://www.sacc-ct.org.za/ppu_lome.html*).

31. IOR-ARC is a project-based regional economic grouping of 15 countries in the rim of the Indian Ocean, covering the eastern coastline of Africa, the Arabian Peninsula, southern Asia and Singapore, Indonesia and Australia.

32. For a detailed study on South Africa's earlier foreign policies and the problems associated with, see Henwood (1997).

33. For detail, see *Bilateral Trade Relations and Agreements: South Africa*, September 2002, *http://europa.eu.int/comm/trade/bilateral/southafrica/index_en.htm*

pursuing agreements for greater South-South cooperation. The move to establish trade relations with MERCUSOR through a free trade agreement with Brazil, and also with India, is top of the government's export-oriented trade agenda. This will facilitate greater trade with South America and the East.

Summing Up

The last decade witnessed concerted efforts at the instance of multinational organisation like WTO to promote multilaterlism as a means of promoting world trade and more equitable distribution of its benefits. Inspired by the virtues of multilaterlism, developing countries in general have initiated series of policy measures to liberalise their trade and investment regime leading to a shift in the policy pendulum from import substitution to export orientation with increasing role for market forces. However, inspired by many factors including the sub-optimal performance under multilaterlism, there has also been a proliferation of regional/bilateral trading arrangements both in the developed and developing world. At the same time, formidable alliances have been formed in the WTO forum at the instance of India-Brazil and South Africa that in turn made possible the reflection of LDC concerns in the WTO negotiations than ever before.

In tune with the developments in the rest of the world, India, Brazil and South Africa have also undertaken wide-ranging economic reforms, which included unprecedented policy liberalisation with respect to trade and investment. In this respect, both Brazil and South Africa appear to be ahead of India. Significant policy reforms in the spirit of multilateralism notwithstanding, countries in Latin America and Africa in general and Brazil and South Africa in particular have been disenchanted with the returns to their reform process. This in turn made these countries to explore new trade geographies and foster closer economic cooperation as manifested in a number of regional/bilateral trading arrangement that they have entered into. India's approach towards regionalism also has undergone sea change as manifested in a number of regional/bilateral trading agreements that India has signed during the last decade. It is against this background that India-Brazil and South Africa, three leading countries representing three continents, came together to explore the possibilities of strengthening economic cooperation between them.

CHAPTER 3

Merchandise Trade between India, Brazil and South Africa

Policies, Performance and Potential of Cooperation

3.1 Introduction

The IBSA partner countries have shown resilience in their economies in the new millennium following sustained economic reforms over a long period of time. The global economic situation has been favourable towards the middle of the present decade as a result of bolstering of the growth performance of developing countries and fast recovery of industrialised nations. The IBSA countries have outperformed many of the emerging countries in the developing world during the corresponding period. In this context, analysis of the recent trends and patterns of merchandise trade between India, Brazil and South Africa are important while these countries are seriously thinking of engaging themselves in deeper level of economic cooperation. Based on highly disaggregate analysis, the present study comes up with estimates on trade potential with respect to each of the countries, and highlights certain areas for mutually beneficial cooperation. In addition, there is also a comparative analysis of tariff structure in these countries and reflects on the plausible tariff reduction commitment of the respective countries in case of an FTA. These analyses have been undertaken against the background of the recent trade policy reforms undertaken by these countries.

3.2 Trade Policy Reforms in IBSA

India

From the early 1990s, India adopted policies aiming at liberalising trade and capital flows combined with domestic privatisation and deregulation. These reforms have been based on a fundamental shift in strategy from state-led import substitution to a market-led approach to development. What follows is a brief account of the major trade policy reforms.

Tariff Reforms

Since import duty has been a major source of revenue for the central government, and served as a means of protecting the domestic industry from foreign competition tariff rates in India, in general, have been very high by international standards.[1] As part of the economic liberalisation of the nineties, attempts were made towards bringing down the tariff rates and its rationalisation. The main thrust of tariff reform, as stated in the interim report of the Tax Reform Committee (1992) were:

- reduction in the general level of tariff,
- reduction in the spread or dispersion of tariff rates,
- simplification of the tariff system
- rationalisation of tariff rates, along with the abolition of numerous exemptions and concessions, and
- abolition of the practice of making changes in effective rates through notifications.

India has adopted a policy of tariff reduction and rationalisation of its tariff structure, notably by reducing the number of tariff bands[2] and by removing a special duty (of 5 per cent) and a surcharge (of 10 per cent).[3] In accordance with its Uruguay Round commitments, India agreed to (with a few exceptions) bind tariffs at a ceiling of 40 per cent *ad valorem* on finished goods and 25 per cent on intermediate goods, machinery and equipment. This has to be implemented over a 10-year period and to be completed before January 1, 2005. The trade weighted average tariff declined from 87 per cent in 1991 to around 30 per cent by 2000 (and 26.4 per cent in 2002).[4] Following recent tariffs reductions (April 2004), the average applied tariff was further reduced to around 17 per cent.

The EXIM Policy 2002-07, which came into force from April 1, 2002, provided for easing the procedures applicable for imports and exports. The focus of the EXIM policy has been on trade facilitation and export promotion through

1. In 1980-81, the import weighted average rate of nominal tariff (with quantifiable exemptions) was 38 per cent. In 1989-90, it rose to 87 per cent. The collection rate of duty increased in this period from about 20 per cent to about 44 per cent. For manufactured products the increase in this period was from 38 per cent to 87 per cent (Tax Reform Committee, Government of India).
2. Certain industries and end users continue to benefit from tariff exemptions.
3. However, a special additional duty (SAD) of 4 per cent was introduced apparently in place of state taxes, which applied only to domestically produced goods.
4. Since import duties represented 23.8 per cent of tax revenues in 1994-1996, it was feared that with tariff reductions the revenue base of India would be adversely affected thus impairing India's ability to implement social reforms that are key to poverty reduction. However, the volume of imports has grown and, despite lower tariffs, revenues from import duties have increased marginally,

greater automation in procedures and steps like removal of quantitative restrictions on all products except certain sensitive items. The new trade policy (2004), further simplified the complexities of import regulations maintained in India.

Exchange Rate Reforms

On July 1, 1991, RBI effected downward adjustment in the value of rupee by 8.7 per cent to 9.7 per cent in relation to four major currencies (Pound Sterling, US dollar, Deutsche Mark, and Japanese Yen) and further by 10 to 11 per cent in relation to five major currencies (including French Franc) resulting in an overall appreciation of these currencies in relation to rupee by about 21 to 23 per cent. In the context of exchange rate reforms, an important development has been the introduction of current account convertibility. To begin with, the system of partial convertibility was introduced in 1992, which established dual exchange rates for the rupee, by creating a free market rate and an official rate. Then in 1993-94, the government adopted full convertibility of the rupee on current account. Since then the exchange rate was determined by demand for and supply of foreign exchange in the market, and floating freely in the FOREX market.

Other Trade Policy Measures

Recognising the critical role of capital goods in augmenting productive capacity, the procedures for capital goods imports have been highly simplified. The coverage of the products under Open General License (OGL)[5] were widened to include a number of capital goods. In 1991, it was announced that new units and units undergoing substantial expansion would automatically be granted licences for import of capital goods without any clearance from the indigenous availability angle.[6] According to the Exim Policy (1992-97), all items including capital goods were permited to be imported without any restriction except to the extent that imports are regulated by the negative list.[7] Also, second hand capital goods were permitted to be imported with or without licence depending on the cases. The introduction of a new scheme—Export Promotion Capital Goods (EPCG) Scheme[8]—

5. Items under OGL are subjected to tariffs but not to quantitative restrictions. In July 1991, out of 5021 H.S tariff lines (6 digit) 80 per cent i.e, 4000 lines were subject to import licencing restrictions. As of December 1995, more than 3000 tariff lines covering raw materials, intermediates and capital goods are free of import licencing requirements (Source: *Economic Survey*).

6. This was provided by the condition that the import of capital goods is fully covered by foreign equity or the import requirement is up to 25 per cent of the value of the plant and machinery subject to a maximum of Rs. 2 crore.

7. Since 1992, imports are regulated through a negative list. The negative list of imports (export) may consist of goods, the import (export) of which is prohibited, restricted through licencing or otherwise, or canalised. As of 1996-97, the negative list of imports consists of 3 prohibited items, 65 restricted items and 8 canalised items.

8. Under the scheme manufacture exporters are permitted to import capital goods at a concessional import duty subjected to some stipulated export obligation. This duty was first 25 per cent, and then reduced to 15 per cent of c.i.f value of capital goods imported. The scope of the EPCG scheme was widened on March 31, 1995, by providing for zero duty import of capital goods of value of at least Rs. 20 crore.

in 1992, further enhanced the accessibility of exporters to imported capital goods.

Under the modified Import Replenishment (Rep) Scheme,[9] announced as a part of the Import Export policy (1988-91), the scope of export products qualifying for Rep scheme has been widened to include new items. In July 1991, the Rep has been enlarged and restructured to make it the principle instrument for all categories of exports and came to be called as Exim scrips which can be freely traded.[10] In March 1992, the system of Exim scrips was abolished,[11] and the incentive aspect of this scheme was sought to be incorporated through the partial 'convertibility' of the Indian Rupee.

The Advance Licencing Scheme[12] was liberalised to include all imported inputs and the procedures for grant of advance licences were simplified. In July 1991, a system of value based advance licences has been introduced. A large number of items including consumer goods whose imports otherwise restricted were allowed to be imported freely. Special Import Licences were granted to the export houses/star trading houses and super star trading houses.

The Duty Drawback Scheme[13] has been under continuous review, and changes have been effected from time to time to compensate for increase in import duties, exchange rate variations and movements in international prices.[14] The 1992-97 Exim policy under the Duty Exemption Scheme has allowed selective duty free imports, which are, required for the purpose of export production under five categories of licences[15] subject to the fulfillment of a time bound export obligation and value addition as may be specified.

---

9. Replenishment Licences were issued to exporters to replenish imported raw materials required for the production of exportable. Replenishment licences were granted on the basis of rates which were in the range of 10 to 20 per cent of the f.o.b. value of exports.

10. The Exim scrip scheme brought rationalisation to the Rep licence scheme, by granting to all exporters, to cover even those who were not using imported inputs, a standard rate of import entitlement at 30 per cent of the f.o.b value of exports (which was revised to 40 per cent to some import intensive sectors). This represents a substantial improvement over the previous rate, which ranged between 10 to 20 of the f.o.b value exports.

11. It was for two reasons: first, the premium on the scrips dropped, from about 45 per cent to 10 per cent, which made them an unattractive proposition. Second, the scheme could be misused since the scrips were in the bearer form.

12. An Advance Licence is granted to a merchant exporter or manufacturer exporter for the import of inputs required for the manufacture of goods without payment of basic customs duty.

13. Duty drawback scheme compensates exporters for import duties.

14. On June 1, 1989, a new drawback schedule was introduced which included more items and all-industry rates were fixed for them.

15. Advance Licence, value based advance licence, quantity based advance licence, advance intermediate licence and special import licence.

Cash Compensatory Support (CCS) Scheme[16] also had been under continuous review and more products were made eligible for CCS.[17] However, following the downward adjustment in Rupee exchange rate, CCS was suspended with effect from July 3, 1991. The redundancy of the CCS scheme was felt after the devaluation, because after adjusting the removal of CCS, there was a net devaluation gain to exporters. Decanalisation of imports,[18] introduction of the Export Import Passbook scheme, opening of foreign currency accounts etc., are some other measures adopted to enhance exporters' accessibility to imported inputs.

Brazil

Brazil has seen impressive progress over the past few years towards macro-economic stabilisation, trade liberalisation and a more open investment regime. Its participation in the global trading system had expanded as indicated by higher ratio of total trade to GDP. The economy has emphasised the irreversibility of the liberalisation process, as well as its strong commitment to the 'multilateral process' and 'open regionalism' (Trade Policy Review Body, 1996). Brazil has recently eliminated the state value-added tax for primary and semi-manufactured goods with the objective to increase the competitiveness of Brazilian exports. Brazil has now moved unequivocally away from the import substitution model of earlier years.[19] The state involvement in the agricultural sector through minimum prices and rural credit had decreased sharply during the 1990s. Brazil abolished the Brazilian Coffee Institute, and created Deliberative Coffee Council. The council, with government and private sector representation, had been recently created to define technical, research and financial policies and programmes for the coffee industry. It has also undertaken phytosanitary measures affecting certain banana imports. Brazil was prepared to allow banana imports as soon as there was scientific proof that they did not represent a risk. In general, Brazil has successfully completed its autonomous liberalisation programme. The domestic laws have been adapted to WTO rules, including such areas as anti-dumping, countervailing, safeguards, and intellectual property.

The major anchor of trade policy reform was a revamping of tariffs. The simple average tariff rate was reduced from 57.5 per cent with a standard

16. CCS scheme allows a remission of un rebated indirect taxes on inputs of exported products.

17. The disbursement under the scheme was Rs. 1271 crores in 1987-88 whereas it was only Rs. 900 crores in 1987-88. The 1989-90 Union Budget made a provision of Rs. 1500 crores for the scheme. By 1989, 283 items were eligible for support under the scheme (Source: RBI, *Currency and Finance, Economic Review 1988-89*).

18. In 1985, there were 68 canalised items, in 1989 it was reduced to 49 and by 1992 to only 8.

19. Press Release (2000). Trade Policy Reviews: Second Press Release and Chairperson's Conclusions, PRESS/TPRB/141, 1 November 2000. *http://www.wto.org/english/tratop_e/tpr_e/tp141_e.htm*

deviation of 21.3 in 1987 to 11.2 and 5.9 respectively in 1994. Simultaneously, CACEX, the powerful trade control agency, was disbanded with its functions redefined and farmed out to other Government agencies. A number of other Government regulatory bodies within the Government were closed including the Brazilian Coffee Institute and Sugar and Alcohol Agency (Ferreira, Velez and Barros, 2004).

General Measures Affecting Trade

Despite the liberal policies, Brazil has been adopting protective measures like high applied tariff rates[20] than the binding rates, the relatively frequent resort to anti-dumping actions, recent safeguards measures, and continuing restrictions in the services sector. But still Brazil has complex domestic tax system and restrictions on trade and remittances.[21] Some applied tariff rates were still seen as relatively high, bound rates were considerably higher than applied tariffs, and frequent ad hoc changes had been undertaken since 1992 to protect particular products.

According to Brazilian laws, all import products are required to obtain import licences, which fall into 2 categories, namely voluntary and non-voluntary import licences. About 15 per cent of total imported products are subject to non-voluntary import licences, higher than international average. While import-licencing procedures had been streamlined, concerns were raised about the level of licencing fees and reduction of the validity of licences. Concerns were also expressed about the practice of considering payments terms as a factor in granting licences.

Imports are subject to a number of taxes and fees in Brazil.[22] In addition to these taxes, several smaller taxes and fees are applied to imports, and most taxes are calculated on a cumulative basis.

Brazil has adopted MERCOSUR's common external tariff (CET)[23] which had led to a number of WTO bindings being broken, but Brazil had offered to enter into negotiations with affected parties. It can be noted that the actual tariff rate under the MERCOSUR CET was lower than the pre-existing tariff averages.

---

20. Brazil's average applied tariff on goods was 8.5 per cent in 2005 (RIS, 2007) as compared to 32 per cent in 1990. All tariffs are *ad valorem*, rates between 0-35 per cent, levied on the Cost Insurance Freight (CIF) value of the import, with the exception of some telecommunication goods. (*US Commercial Service Guide to Brazil*, July 2004, p.22).

21. For detailed study on different trade laws, regulations and prevention measures, see *Country Commercial Guide 2001, 2004*.

22. There are three taxes—Import duty, Industrialised product tax and Merchandise and service circulation tax—that account for the bulk of importing costs which are usually paid during the customs clearance process. For details on these tax rates and application procedures, see *US Commercial Service Guide to Brazil*, July 2004, p.23.

23. MERCOSUR CET is currently full of exception rather than a strict rule as the member countries unilaterally adjust their tariffs in response to their economic developments.

In 1997, Brazil established a computerised information system to monitor imports and to facilitate customs clearance known as Foreign Trade Integrated System (SISCOMEX). This has facilitated and reduced the amount of paperwork previously required for importing into Brazil, but customs clearance still remains as a time consuming and frustrating process.

Measures Affecting Sectors[24]

Brazil is a competitive, major producer and exporter of agricultural products. Nevertheless, agriculture received considerable financial support through minimum price supports and rural credits, while large subsidies were given to the National Alcohol Programme (PROALCOOL).

Brazil's automotive régime, containing high tariff as well as TRIMs measures such as local content and export performance requirements, was of great concern. The régime afforded high effective protection to the industry and appeared inconsistent with WTO rules. Brazil also introduced tariff quota system for vehicles. In Brazil's view, such a regime was required to harmonise investment conditions and avoid distortions within MERCOSUR during the transition period allowed by the TRIMs Agreement. The regime, including changes introduced in December 1995, was leading to the industry's modernisation, increased competition, lower production and investment costs and a higher import content of vehicles. As a result, effective protection for vehicles was being reduced.

As per Brazilian laws, commodities imported by sea, maritime transportation insurance contracts should be made by the importers, in which case the insurance premium should be 1.5 per cent of the total import value. Such premium level runs far higher than the international average, 0.3 per cent, which subsequently discouraged the price advantage of the imported commodities.

Difficulties exist for foreign citizens to obtain working visas in Brazil. It was decided by the Ministry of Labor in June 2002 that more rigorous criteria should be enforced in issuing visas to foreigners working in Brazil, especially foreign technicians. A complexity of supporting documents, as many as 12 kinds, are required in application for a working visa. The above practices are likely to have its implications on promoting trade in services especially software and services.

South Africa

South Africa's trade policy witnessed a paradigm shifts towards the end of 1980s from import substitution to export promotion. It has been liberalising the economy and it is now more open to global trade. There is free exchange of trade

---

24. Heavily drawn from *Trade Policy Review* (1996) and *Country Commercial Guide: Brazil* (2001).

between South Africa and the other four countries (Botswana, Lesotho, Namibia, and Swaziland) comprising the Southern African Customs Union (SACU). Once the Southern African Development Community (SADC) Free Trade Agreement comes into full effect, there will be free exchange of goods among the 14 countries of the region. The EU-SA Free Trade Agreement introduced during 2000 will result in substantially freer trade between South Africa and the EU by 2008. The US and SACU are currently in negotiations on establishing a free-trade agreement.

Tariff and Non Tariff Reforms

Given its commitment to multilaterlism and being a member of WTO, South Africa has substantially opened its market since 1994; tariff rates have generally declined and other non-tariff barriers have been reduced. As a matter of government policy, the South African Government is aiming to open its market still further in order to increase trade and to develop more competitive domestic industries.

As a result of its market access offer for the Uruguay Round, South Africa has significantly reduced its number of tariff lines and bound most (95 per cent) tariffs to WTO binding levels. It has cut back tariff lines from the 80 different levels of the past to 8 levels ranging from 0 to 30 per cent with a few exceptions—notably in clothing and textiles and for motor industry manufacturers. The general trend has been for tariffs to be reduced to encourage industries to become more competitive and also to reduce cost structures. The value-added tax (VAT) is 14 per cent. VAT is payable on nearly all imports. However, goods imported for use in manufacturing or resale by registered traders may be exempt from VAT.

In the Uruguay Round, South Africa agreed to a 12-year phase down in duties on clothing and textiles, but since then has unilaterally moved to a 7-year phase down process. As of September 1, 2002, the following rates, which are also end rates, apply to the textile and clothing industries: apparel 40 per cent, yarns 15 per cent, fabrics 22 per cent, finished goods (household goods) 30 per cent and fibres 7.5 per cent.

Barriers to Trade

In spite of these reforms, South Africa's tariff schedule remains complex and can create uncertainty. Traders are subjected to exchange control approval, administered by the South African Reserve Bank. The Department of Trade and Industry (DTI) is empowered to regulate, prohibit or ration imports to South Africa in the national interest but most goods may be imported into South Africa without any restrictions. The International Trade Administration Act of 2002, established a modern and independent regulator of international trade for the entire SACU—the International Trade Administration Commission (ITAC). On June

1, 2003 the ITAC took over the functions from the Board of Tariffs and Trade (BTT).

Each year a list of goods requiring import permits is specified in an annual Import Control Program, and is valid for imports from any country. The Directorate of Import and Export Control within the DTI administers the issuance of permits, though for some imports additional and prior authorisation may be required from other departments (for example the Departments of Agriculture, Health or Environmental Affairs). Most new goods are exempt from import control measures but all used goods, waste and scrap are subject to import control measures. A phytosanitary certificate is required for shipments of living plants, seeds, fresh fruits and vegetables. Special regulations are required for the importation of lard, bacon, ham, hides and skins, animal hair and bristles and honey products. The other products that require import permits include: fish and fish products (residues), petroleum products, ozone-depleting chemicals, firearms and ammunition, gambling equipment, and radioactive chemical elements. According to the DTI, the purpose of the remaining import control measures is to enhance control for environmental health and security reasons, and for safety and quality compliance. Imports of second hand goods are prohibited in order to protect the local industries in SACU.

It is understood that Indian companies are faced with anti-dumping duties from South Africa. For example, anti-dumping duty on exports of Amoxicillin and Ampicillin by Indian pharmaceutical companies including Ranbaxy was imposed in 1997, basically on the grounds of low-cost of these medicines facilitated by the incentives given by the Government of India. On expiry of the five year term of the duty, there is again a sunset review of the duties being made by the Board of Tariffs and Trade on the complaint of Pharmacare, a South African company, that these medicines are still being dumped in South African market to the detriment of South African producers. Ranbaxy's appeal against the duty imposed by BTT to the Ministers of Finance and Trade and Industry did not bring much relief.

In addition, it is understood that the South African Board of Tariffs and Trade had imposed anti-dumping duty on garden tools from India supplied by Gardex on 11.10.1995 at 57.7 per cent/38 per cent/4.6 per cent rates depending on the source of exports from India. The BTT is now again examining review of the imposition with a view to re-impose the duty that expired recently

In general, there are 17 anti-dumping/anti-subsidy cases under investigation by the Board on Tariffs and Trade against India at present in many cases without going through the process of consultations. The items include ampicillin and amoxylin, PVC and PVC rolled goods, garden picks, footwear and shoes, steel wires etc. The number of cases has gone up since the Board was restructured in July 2000 to gear up for protecting the domestic industries. Even some cases in which anti-dumping duty are due to expire, the South African Board on Tariffs and Trade has initiated procedure to continue it beyond the expiry dates. A number of such cases lack in substantive proof of nexus between the prices of Indian goods and the injury caused to the South African industries. The second problem is that South Africa has not yet issued any procedural regulations for handling the anti-dumping/anti-subsidy complaints. There are other discriminatory practices being followed by South African Board against Indian goods, such as carpets by reducing duty on Iranian carpets.

Though there is substantial number of trade complaints from Indian companies, absence of any South African authority dealing with trade complaints from Indian businessmen has put some of the Indian companies in prolonged correspondence without any results. A number of trade disputes arise due to lack of quality control, shortages in packing and supply and non-payment by buyers.

South African High Commission and Consulate has been keeping deposits of Rs.40,000 per person for business visas from Indians whereas there is a visa fee abolition agreement between the two countries. The delay and redtapism in refund of these deposits as well as the very concept of these deposits detracts some of the Indian businessmen doing business with South Africa.

3.3 Overall Trade Performance

The overall trade performance of the IBSA countries has been very gratifying in recent years. The external sector of the proposed regional group is booming rapidly in the late 1990s, and the positive impact of the merchandise trade is felt on their balance of trade. In 2005, the total trade of the proposed IBSA countries was close to US$ 550 billion and there is a marked improvement in the balance of trade position of the proposed countries. The overall growth of the regional export is exceedingly well and imports are catching up steadily, leading to a marked improvement in the overall trade balance of the group. The IBSA countries have shown their biasness towards developed countries, as they have been continuing with sizeable trade with them. But these countries are also strongly engaged with developing countries for trade. While the intra-regional exports are increasing rapidly, the growth in the intra-regional import has shown much improvement during 2000-05. The intra-regional trade imbalances between the three IBSA countries are significant during the period 2000-05. The present level of intra-regional trade has been striking, almost reaching the level of US$ 7 billion in 2005. The share of intra-regional trade in the total trade of the proposed group has been around 2.6 per cent in 2005.

The broad trend in the overall trade performance of the IBSA region is presented in Table 3.1. As mentioned earlier, noticeable performance of the caucus is due to the fact that overall exports and imports grew at the rate of

TABLE 3.1

Overall Trade Performance of IBSA with Major Destinations: 2000-2005

	Exports			Imports			Trade Balance		
	Value 2005 ($ '000)	Share 2005 (%)	CAGR 2000-2005 (%)	Value 2005 ($ '000)	Share 2005 (%)	CAGR 2000-2005 (%)	Value 2005 ($ '000)	Share 2005 (%)	CAGR 2000-2005 (%)
A. IBSA's Trade performance									
DOTS World Total	267948.7	100.0	15.1	275270.9	100.0	14.2	-7322.2	100.0	-3.8
Developing Countries	132324.4	49.4	20.1	111623.7	40.6	15.8	20700.7	-282.7	-312.2
Industrial Countries	127927.8	47.7	13.2	122359.5	44.5	10.0	5568.3	-76.0	-195.6
Africa	17974.6	6.7	20.9	13825.1	5.0	15.2	4149.5	-56.7	94.2
Asia	49619.0	18.5	25.9	56307.3	20.5	24.2	-6688.4	91.3	14.8
Europe	8991.1	3.4	22.6	7188.0	2.6	21.9	1803.1	-24.6	25.3
Middle East	22178.6	8.3	23.1	16467.7	6.0	9.3	5711.0	-78.0	-216.1
Western Hemisphere	33561.1	12.5	11.7	17835.7	6.5	4.3	15725.4	-214.8	26.6
Brazil	1298.6	0.5	26.2	2282.9	0.8	34.8	-984.4	13.4	55.7
India	2319.1	0.9	28.3	2533.4	0.9	31.0	-214.3	2.9	-284.3
South Africa	2779.4	1.0	35.6	2761.9	1.0	12.7	17.5	-0.2	-145.3
IRT	6397.1	2.4	30.7	7578.2	2.8	23.0	-1181.2	-16.1	3.1
B. BRAZIL's Trade performance									
DOTS World Total	118469.0	100.0	14.7	80928.3	100.0	5.5	37540.7	100.0	-275.9
Developing Countries	60755.5	51.3	18.8	39975.8	49.4	9.4	20779.7	55.4	153.4
Industrial Countries	55341.4	46.7	11.1	40738.0	50.3	2.5	14603.4	38.9	-235.0
Africa	4884.7	4.1	35.7	7261.6	9.0	18.2	-2377.0	-6.3	2.6
Asia	15021.8	12.7	31.1	14734.5	18.2	18.8	287.3	0.8	-165.7
Europe	5422.3	4.6	31.7	2036.7	2.5	7.9	3385.7	9.0	-368.8
Middle East	5367.3	4.5	25.4	2832.7	3.5	9.9	2534.6	6.8	-333.7
Western Hemisphere	30059.4	25.4	11.2	13110.3	16.2	0.2	16949.1	45.1	29.2
India	1136.8	1.0	31.0	1323.0	1.6	28.5	-186.2	-0.5	17.4
South Africa	1369.4	1.2	35.3	375.7	0.5	8.5	993.7	2.6	80.5
C. INDIA's Trade performance									
DOTS World Total	97918.1	100.0	18.1	134690.0	100.0	21.8	-36771.9	100.0	36.7
Developing Countries	55237.4	56.4	24.5	49082.1	36.4	22.0	6155.3	-16.7	78.1
Industrial Countries	42352.7	43.3	13.4	44785.6	33.3	17.0	-2432.9	6.6	-202.0
Africa	5972.8	6.1	25.5	4297.3	3.2	7.1	1675.4	-4.6	-208.0
Asia	28265.5	28.9	26.3	28979.8	21.5	27.3	-714.3	1.9	-238.6
Europe	2981.7	3.0	12.4	3590.5	2.7	30.6	-608.8	1.7	-196.8
Middle East	15268.2	15.6	24.2	9889.5	7.3	15.9	5378.7	-14.6	65.2
Western Hemisphere	2749.3	2.8	23.5	2325.0	1.7	24.9	424.2	-1.2	17.2
Brazil	981.6	1.0	37.0	846.1	0.6	34.6	135.5	-0.4	63.4
South Africa	1410.0	1.4	35.9	2386.2	1.8	13.4	-976.2	2.7	0.2

Contd. ...

...Contd. ...

	Exports			*Imports*			*Trade Balance*		
	Value 2005 ($ '000)	*Share 2005 (%)*	*CAGR 2000-2005 (%)*	*Value 2005 ($ '000)*	*Share 2005 (%)*	*CAGR 2000-2005 (%)*	*Value 2005 ($ '000)*	*Share 2005 (%)*	*CAGR 2000-2005 (%)*
D. SOUTH AFRICA's Trade performance									
DOTS World Total	51561.6	100.0	11.1	59652.6	100.0	15.2	-8091.0	100.0	-249.7
Developing Countries	16331.5	31.7	13.1	22565.8	37.8	18.0	-6234.3	77.1	43.5
Industrial Countries	30233.7	58.6	17.5	36835.9	61.8	13.7	-6602.2	81.6	2.3
Africa	7117.2	13.8	12.2	2266.2	3.8	29.9	4851.0	-60.0	7.5
Asia	6331.7	12.3	16.2	12593.0	21.1	25.0	-6261.4	77.4	40.5
Europe	587.1	1.1	21.2	1560.8	2.6	36.2	-973.7	12.0	55.3
Middle East	1543.1	3.0	10.0	3745.5	6.3	-1.6	-2202.3	27.2	-6.6
Western Hemisphere	752.4	1.5	2.1	2400.4	4.0	27.0	-1648.0	20.4	101.0
Brazil	317.0	0.6	9.4	1436.9	2.4	34.9	-1119.9	13.8	56.5
India	1182.3	2.3	26.0	1210.4	2.0	34.1	-28.1	0.3	-178.6

Note: In some places, sums of shares of developing and industrialised countries do not add up to 100 per cent because the gap is contributed by the transitional countries.

Source: RIS based on Direction of Trade Statistics CD, September 2007, IMF, Washington D.C.

30.7 per cent and 23.0 per cent respectively with the world economy during the period 2000-2005. These countries have achieved high growth in their external sector along with volatility in their trade performances during the period mentioned above. The volatility of the external sector performance of the Caucus is mostly contributed by South Africa followed by Brazil and India. The pattern of trade of the group with developed and developing countries are different in recent years. While growth of exports of the Caucus to industrialised countries has increased moderately, growth of imports has been not very impressive with them during the period 2000-05. On the other hand, growth rates of export and import of the group with developing countries have been striking during the aforesaid period. While the group is dependent more on exports rather than imports on developing countries, and the situation is almost balanced in case of their trade linkages with developed countries.

The trade structure of the IBSA countries indicates that the group has a tendency towards further expanding its trade with developing Asia in recent years. The Group has priority for developing countries in other continents for trade in the order of Western Hemisphere, Middle East, Africa and Europe taking total volume of trade in 2005. Taking into account the share and growth of continental trade, Asia is emerging as the most attractive geographical space for the group as compared to other continents in the world for trading. Traditionally, the Western Hemisphere is a strong trading destination for IBSA countries, but the region is losing its importance gradually because of surging Asia in the context of IBSA. The growth rates of exports and imports of IBSA have been low with the Western Hemisphere as compared to some of the other promising destinations such as developing Europe, Africa and Middle East during the period 2000-05.

One of the important features of the present trade is that intra-regional trade is growing rapidly despite having any formal arrangement between IBSA countries. It may be noted that the initial level of trade is very low as compared to total trade of these courtiers with the rest of the world. Between 1998 and 2005, the share of the intra-regional trade to total trade of the group improved from 1.7 per cent to 2.6 per cent. The average annual growth in intra-regional trade is perceptibly faster than overall external sector performance of the Group. While intra-regional exports increased at the rate of 30.7 per cent, the overall growth rate of imports increased by 23.0 per cent during the period 2000-05. The import behaviour of the group indicates that member countries have followed a common strategy of import compression as most of the member countries are passing through economic reforms.[25] At the intra-regional level, the trade balance has come down from 1556.9 US$ million in 2003 to 1181.2 US$ million in 2005. In the present setting, Brazil has been the most important beneficiaries from the proposed IBSA intra-regional trade, and has generated maximum trade surplus from its partner countries within the group. Among the three countries, South Africa's overall trade linkage with the Group has been the least, but it has registered largest unfavourable trade balance with the group, as its growth rate of imports from the group is positive and significantly larger than its exports. However, India's trade linkages with the region are consistent in recent years. The results show that over 36 per cent of region's exports and near 35 per cent of imports are contributed by India.

India has been maintaining adverse trade balance in her trade account where the total exports and imports are estimated at US$ 97.9 billion and US$ 134.7 billion respectively in 2005. While exports to the rest of the world are growing at the rate of 18.1 per cent per annum, the imports are expanding at the rate of 21.8 per cent during the period 2000-05. India is more dependent on developed countries for its trade in recent years. It is important to note that growth rate of India's exports and imports are much better with developing countries than with developed countries. India's most attractive destination for trade is developing Asia, which is followed by other geographical areas in developing world such as Middle East, Africa and Europe. India's two-way trade with IBSA countries is over US$ 4.8 billion in 2005, and has registered unfavourable trade with South Africa. Between the two IBSA countries, South Africa is emerging as the most important partner for India. India's bilateral trade

---

25. IMF (2007) has observed that many Latin American countries revived along with world economy from global recession in 2003 excepting a few. Brazil is one or these counties, and it is yet to recover fully.

with South Africa is not only nearly twice that of Brazil, but also the growth rate of bilateral trade with South Africa is exceptionally higher than that of Brazil. India's close trade engagement with South Africa has been a recent phenomenon.

The total trade of Brazil exceeded US$ 118 billion with the rest of the world, and it maintained a surplus of US$ 37.5 billion in 2005. The external sector performance of Brazil has been robust where average growth rate of country's exports has been impressive and imports growth rate becoming low. The country has been depending on developing and industrialised countries for its exports and imports in a balanced manner. The Western Hemisphere has been emerging as the most important destination for the country followed by Asia, Middle East and other broad destinations in order of their trade linkages. The two-way intra-regional trade of Brazil with IBSA is almost close to US$ 4.2 billion in 2005. The net trade balance of the country with the IBSA countries is significant as surplus with one country is more than compensated by adverse balance of trade with another country. It is interesting to note that growth rate of intra-regional trade is much stronger than overall growth performance of the external sector of the country.

In the Group of IBSA countries, external sector of South Africa is the smallest among others. Total exports of the economy were estimated at US$ 51.6 billion in 2005, keeping a sizeable trade deficit of over US$ 8 billion with rest of the world. The external sector of the country is moderately dynamic in recent years. Despite the fact that South Africa has come out from the apartheid regime, it has continued to have strong trade ties with industrialised countries. About 58.6 per cent of exports and 61.8 per cent of imports of the country are sourced from developed countries. Moreover, country's exports to developed countries are expanding at a faster rate than developing countries. Distribution of South Africa's trade to different continents indicates that Africa and Asia are the major export destinations for the country, but its import from Africa has been very low. Other important trade destinations of South Africa are Europe, Middle East, Western Hemisphere, etc. Country's current level of trade with IBSA countries has improved significantly. The country's two-way trade with the IBSA Group is US$ 4.1 billion in 2005. It has registered trade deficit with both Brazil and India; and more importantly trade deficit with Brazil alone has exceeded US$ 1 billion in 2005.

The aggregate trade performance of IBSA countries presents the following results:

- IBSA is a large expanding economic space where its total two-way trade is close to US$ 543 billion with the world in 2005.
- There is strong preference among associated countries to concentrate their trade with developing countries and also with Asia.

- The current intra-IBSA trade is expanding at a much faster rate than the overall growth performance of the sector, though the total volume of intra-regional trade is very low.

The trends in bilateral trade show that partner countries are coming closer to each other in a significant manner. A close scrutiny of the composition of trade and their trade policies may suggest the possibilities of having a comprehensive economic cooperation between these countries.

Structure of Trade in IBSA

Before examining details about the relative competitiveness of each member country of the proposed IBSA, it is necessary to understand their composition and structure of trade. This may provide some insight about the possibility of a comprehensive economic cooperation between the proposed member countries. Of course, the level of competitiveness, the extent of trade potentials in the markets of partner countries, the trade regimes in partner countries and gains from the proposed arrangement for individual member countries may form the basis of taking a view on the feasibility of the proposal. But the current level of trade and the bilateral trade practices in different sectors may provide some clue about the preparedness of member countries to engage themselves in the new regional trading arrangement. Preparedness of the members, in this case, refers to willingness of an individual country to prefer Linnemann (1966) type of trade complementarity or intra-industry trade as the basis of comprehensive regional economic cooperation.[26] The sectoral trade of the IBSA countries with the world and also among themselves are presented below.

Trade Linkages with the World Economy

The trade structure of the Group indicates that the overall export basket of the IBSA countries is not matching the overall import basket of the group, particularly among the heavily traded products during the period 2000-2002. While some of the important export product segments are vegetable products (Section II), textile articles (Section XI), base metals (Section XV), and vehicles, aircrafts, etc (Section XVII), some of the vital import product groups are chemical products (Section VI) and gems and jewellery (Section XIV) as shown in Table 3.1. Besides, other key products for export are chemical products (Section VI), gems and jewellery (Section XIV) and base metals (Section XV). The proposed

26. Both the approaches are discussed in the literature. Linnemann (1966) argued that trade possibility arises in a situation where the export vector of one country matches with import vector of another country, so that the one country can meet the import requirement of another country and vice vera. Therefore, export-import similarity is the basis of future trade cooperation, as trade complementarity exists in this case. The protagonists of the intra-industry trade theory contest the argument and empirically demonstrated that trade cooperation is feasible even in a situation of export-export similarity (Greenaway, 1989). The success of the EU and the NAFTA is demonstrating the effectiveness of intra-industry trade theory as the basis of forming successful RTAs.

TABLE 3.2

Total Trade of IBSA Countries with the Rest of World

Section	Description	Brazil's								India's							
		Imports				Exports				Imports				Exports			
		Value 2002 ($ '000)	Gr. Rate 1998-02 (%)	Share 2002 (%)	CV 1998-02	Value 2002 ($ '000)	Gr. Rate 1998-02 (%)	Share 2002 (%)	CV 1998-02	Value 2002 ($ '000)	Gr. Rate 1998-02 (%)	Share 2002 (%)	CV 1998-02	Value 2003 ($ '000)	Gr. Rate 1998-03 (%)	Share 2003 (%)	CV 1998-03
I	Live Animals and Animal Products	640428	-12.7	1.3	3.1	3259096	31.0	5.4	2.9	39707	3.3	0.1	2.9	1786090	10.1	2.5	6.8
II	Vegetable Products	1984882	-9.5	4.0	5.0	5130025	0.4	8.5	12.7	1209150	5.1	2.0	4.2	3712923	-0.6	5.1	9.9
III	Animal or Vegetable Fats & Oils	186295	-13.8	0.4	2.4	880026	-2.3	1.5	3.7	1861845	-0.7	3.0	7.1	152944	-2.4	0.2	4.3
IV	Prepared Foodstuff, Beverages, etc.	717387	-8.8	1.4	4.7	7845032	0.0	13.0	10.5	191602	-13.0	0.3	2.2	1209649	9.3	1.7	4.9
V	Mineral Products	8062469	7.9	16.2	5.2	6431598	15.1	10.7	4.1	2E+07	34.2	33.5	3.5	4255376	105.9	5.9	1.6
VI	Products of Chemicals	8722608	-0.1	17.5	31.0	3022460	0.7	5.0	19.6	5205964	1.8	8.5	12.9	5371804	19.8	7.4	4.5
VII	Plastics & Articles thereof	2834378	-1.0	5.7	13.3	1587765	1.8	2.6	13.1	1244372	5.8	2.0	9.8	1522872	35.9	2.1	2.8
VIII	Raw Hides & Skins, Leather, etc.	191579	-4.0	0.4	8.3	1072384	11.3	1.8	5.2	212127	9.6	0.3	5.6	1320103	3.8	1.8	8.4
IX	Wood & Articles of Wood	55697	-14.3	0.1	2.9	1766614	14.2	2.9	6.3	412144	1.8	0.7	6.7	48047	24.6	0.1	3.8
X	Pulp of wood or of other Fibers	793643	-12.2	1.6	4.1	2084328	0.9	3.5	10.2	985459	3.6	1.6	14.0	317403	38.7	0.4	2.9
XI	Textile & Textile Articles	1089641	-11.4	2.2	4.3	1183907	1.6	2.0	10.4	1632030	22.9	2.7	4.0	1.2E+07	7.8	16.3	8.8
XII	Footwear, Headgear and Umbrella	73497	-13.4	0.1	2.6	1518758	2.3	2.5	10.3	31144	-1.0	0.1	14.2	677979	2.6	0.9	15.8
XIII	Articles of Stone, Plaster, Cement	353787	-7.8	0.7	7.0	886227	6.5	1.5	10.7	243642	11.0	0.4	5.7	617024	26.0	0.9	3.8
XIV	Natural or cultured pearls, Jewellery	162894	15.1	0.3	3.1	589540	2.8	1.0	18.4	1E+07	4.0	17.0	16.6	9049459	13.3	12.5	6.7
XV	Base Metals & Articles of Base Metal	2242730	-6.9	4.5	7.5	6119432	1.8	10.1	13.3	2648678	1.0	4.3	15.6	5492080	52.1	7.6	2.2
XVI	Machinery & Mechanical Appliances	15724760	-4.5	31.6	10.5	7319232	5.2	12.1	8.4	1E+07	17.5	16.6	4.4	1.2E+07	151.3	17.1	1.0
XVII	Vehicles, Aircraft and Vessels	3577854	-12.2	7.2	4.2	7325887	3.4	12.1	6.4	1889755	33.9	3.1	2.9	5005416	139.8	6.9	0.9
XVIII	Optical, Photograph & Cinematography	1992789	-3.6	4.0	9.9	403740	3.0	0.7	9.1	1380548	11.4	2.3	5.9	1529684	205.6	2.1	0.9
XIX	Arms and Ammunition	9216	-6.1	0.0	1.0	205360	64.6	0.3	1.4	2537	55.3	0.0	1.5	10984	658.1	0.0	0.9
XX	Miscellaneous Manufactured Articles	308198	-12.3	0.6	3.9	676466	9.4	1.1	7.1	186886	25.7	0.3	3.9	1087710	136.7	1.5	1.0
XXI	Works of Art Collectors' Pieces	8086	19.7	0.0	1.8	1046674	16.6	1.7	4.3	708285	-18.6	1.2	1.4	5104100	140.1	7.0	1.0

Contd. ...

...Contd. ...

Section	Description	South Africa's								IBSA's							
		Imports				Exports				Imports				Exports			
		Value 2002 ($ '000)	Gr. Rate 1998-02 (%)	Share 2002 (%)	CV 1998-02	Value 2002 ($ '000)	Gr. Rate 2000-02 (%)	Share 2002 (%)	CV 2000-02	Value 2002 ($ '000)	Gr. Rate 1998-02 (%)	Share 2002 (%)	CV 1998-02	Value 2002 ($ '000)	Gr. Rate 2000-02 (%)	Share 2002 (%)	CV 2000-02
I	Live Animals and Animal Products	148467	-13.0	0.6	6.4	431812	10.4	1.9	10.4	828602	-13.6	0.6	4.7	5476998	16.6	3.5	7.0
II	Vegetable Products	530929	3.7	2.0	4.8	987020	8.3	4.3	11.7	3724961	4.4	2.7	23.1	9829968	8.7	6.3	12.3
III	Animal cr Vegetable Fats & Oils	200098	12.7	0.8	8.2	37824	-4.8	0.2	13.4	2248238	11.7	1.6	8.0	1070794	21.8	0.7	5.2
IV	Prepared Foodstuff, Beverages, etc.	469627	1.6	1.8	34.7	1153483	1.8	5.0	26.5	1378616	2.1	1.0	46.1	1E+07	10.8	6.5	9.2
V	Mineral Products	3437062	-6.4	13.1	14.0	4085435	2.3	17.7	14.1	3.2E+07	-0.1	23.3	22.2	1.5E+07	15.7	9.5	7.0
VI	Products of Chemicals	2903020	-0.6	11.1	28.9	1880404	1.4	8.2	26.0	1.7E+07	1.4	12.3	54.3	1E+07	5.5	6.6	12.8
VII	Plastics & Articles thereof	1095034	1.3	4.2	15.9	549762	6.5	2.4	15.8	5173784	0.8	3.8	72.8	3660399	5.5	2.3	15.0
VIII	Raw Hides & Skins, Leather, etc.	122085	-10.9	0.5	8.2	190465	-10.1	0.8	8.3	525791	-6.4	0.4	11.9	2582952	1.9	1.7	51.2
IX	Wood & Articles of Wood	168002	-1.5	0.6	15.1	363256	5.1	1.6	15.4	635843	-8.3	0.5	9.2	2177917	9.0	1.4	10.2
X	Pulp of wood or of other Fibers	506667	-2.6	1.9	21.3	718232	-11.8	3.1	7.4	2285769	-8.8	1.7	10.4	3119963	-8.5	2.0	10.2
XI	Textile & Textile Articles	835973	-1.4	3.2	19.9	682712	4.0	3.0	22.6	3557644	-2.7	2.6	35.7	1.4E+07	0.2	8.8	18.5
XII	Footwear, Headgear and Umbrella	209968	-3.4	0.8	27.9	30997	0.8	0.1	42.4	314609	-3.0	0.2	31.8	2227734	-2.8	1.4	22.7
XIII	Articles of Stone, Plaster, Cement	352096	-4.2	1.3	18.4	179287	1.9	0.8	29.1	949525	-2.4	0.7	28.8	1682538	5.9	1.1	12.4
XIV	Natural or cultured pearls, Jewellery	523952	2.2	2.0	1.7	1797267	-7.9	7.8	1.5	1.1E+07	2.5	8.1	15.6	1.1E+07	5.8	7.3	7.2
XV	Base Metals & Articles of Base Metal	1096620	0.6	4.2	14.3	4034803	-5.2	17.5	10.5	5988028	0.8	4.4	33.5	1.6E+07	6.8	10.0	7.4
XVI	Machinery & Mechanical Appliances	7303351	-2.0	27.9	26.6	2646013	6.3	11.5	16.0	3.3E+07	-0.5	24.2	46.8	2.2E+07	39.6	14.3	2.8
XVII	Vehicles, Aircraft and Vessels	2533247	6.8	9.7	5.1	2617360	9.0	11.4	6.0	8000856	-1.9	5.8	28.7	1.5E+07	15.9	9.6	5.7
XVIII	Optical, Photograph & Cinematography	1017230	1.2	3.9	57.6	145613	1.2	0.6	80.2	4390567	4.5	3.2	17.3	2079037	60.4	1.3	2.1
XIX	Arms and Ammunition	0		0.0		0		0.0		11753	-42.5	0.0	0.9	216344	100.9	0.1	1.4
XX	Miscellaneous Manufactured Articles	370589	-4.2	1.4	13.7	495272	4.3	2.1	15.0	865673	-5.3	0.6	16.4	2259448	35.0	1.4	3.0
XXI	Works of Art Collectors' Pieces	2381479	4.5	9.1	18.2	26030	-49.6	0.1	1.2	3097850	-0.2	2.3	18.3	6176804	7.1	4.0	15.0

Note: Trade in thousand US$.

Source: RIS based on PCTAS 1998-2002, ITC, UNCTAD,WTO,UNSD, 2003.

regional caucus is also highly dependent on a number of product groups for imports such as chemicals (Section VI), plastic products (Section VII), base meals (Section XV), vehicles, aircraft, etc. (Section XVII) and optical, photography, etc (Section XVIII). The group also witnesses strong intra-industry trade in certain product ranges such as prepared foodstuffs (Section IV), mineral products (Section V), machine and machinery appliances (Section XVI), where the associated member countries exports as well imports similar products. This trend shows that both trade complementarity and intra-industry trade exist in these countries. These are positive signs for the formation of comprehensive partnership.

Since Brazil and South Africa are under the process of economic reforms, these countries have witnessed significant compression in their imports. The reflection of such policies is amply reflected in the overall import performance of the Group. More than half of broad import product groups (at HS Section) is witnessing negative growth rate during the period 2000-2002. Some of the significant imports group including mineral products (Section V), machinery & mechanical appliances (Section XVI), and optical, photograph & cinematography (Section XVIII) have witnessed negative growth during the period 2000-2002. Certain other major import groups have shown signs of recovery in terms of picking up growth during the same period, and they include chemicals (Section VI), plastics & articles thereof (Section VII) and gems and jewellery (Section XIV). Some large export sectors having noticeable growth rate are prepared foodstuff, beverages, etc. (Section IV), mineral products (Section V), machinery & mechanical appliances (Section XVI), and vehicles, aircraft and vessels (Section XVII). The overall position of the IBSA trade indicates that imports are highly unstable compared to exports during the period 2000-2002. Among the three partners, India is positioned in a better situation than others in terms of their external sector performance. In case of India, both exports and imports are expanding simultaneously during the period 1998-2002. But the situation is not similar for other two partners. While export is expanding, the import growth rates are declining in both Brazil and South Africa during the same period.

Brazil's exports are mostly concentrated in a few broad sectors such as vegetable products (section II), prepared foodstuff, beverages, etc. (Section IV), mineral products (Section V), products of chemicals (Section VI), base metals & articles of base metal (Section XV), machinery & mechanical appliances (Section XVI), and vehicles, aircraft and vessels (Section XVII). These products constitute around 72 per cent of country's total exports of the country. Except for mineral products (section V), other product groups have shown low export growth during 1998-2002. Export in the sector also has shown low level of volatility as compared to other large export product groups of the country. Except a few import product groups, others have registered negative growth during the period

1998-2002. Some of important import groups are mineral products (Section V), products of chemicals (Section VI), plastics & articles thereof (Section VII), base metals & articles of base metal (Section XV), machinery & mechanical appliances (Section XVI), and vehicles, aircraft and vessels (Section XVII). Among the Important Import groups, mineral product (Section V) has shown moderate growth during the aforesaid period. Except for a few significant sectors, imports have been stable during 1998-2002.

Exports and imports South Africa are concentrated in a few sectors. Some of the important export earning sectors are mineral products (Section V), chemicals (Section VI), natural or cultured pearls, jewellery (Section XIV), base metals & articles of base metal (Section XV), machinery & mechanical appliances (Section XVI), and vehicles, aircraft and vessels (Section XVII). The expansion of these important exports sectors is mostly between moderate to low level. Moreover, most of the export sectors have shown high degree of instability between 2000 and 2002. Imports are also concentrated in sectors like mineral products (Section V), products of chemicals (Section VI), machinery & mechanical appliances (Section XVI), vehicles, aircraft and vessels (Section XVII), and works of art collectors' pieces (Section XXI). Like exports, country's imports are also subject to high degree of fluctuations in sizeable number of sectors. It is important to note that most of the import sectors have registered either negative growth or stagnation during the period 2000-2002. Excepting sectors like vehicles, aircraft and vessels (Section XVII), and works of art collectors' pieces (Section XXI), imports of other dominant important sectors have experienced negative growth.

Though India has undergone countrywide economic reforms in the 1990s, and the process continued in the new millennium, the experience of India is different from that of Brazil and South Africa so far as the external sector is concerned. With the liberalised policies in India, both imports and exports have expanded in almost all the segments of exports and imports. It is interesting to note that about four per cent of total imports of India suffered from negative growth rates, covering as many as three HS sections of the imports vector. Like others, India's imports are concentrated in a few sectors such as animal or vegetable fats & oils (Section III), mineral products (Section V), products of chemicals (Section VI), plastics & articles thereof (Section VII), base metals & articles of base metal (Section XV), machinery & mechanical appliances (Section XVI), and vehicles, aircraft and vessels (Section XVII). Among the key import sectors, growth rates have been impressive in sizeable number of product segments such as mineral products (Section V), machinery & mechanical appliances (Section XVI), and vehicles, aircraft and vessels (Section XVII). Unlike other trade partners in IBSA, India has witnessed almost no fluctuations in sizeable number of important import products, and the level of instability in various important product segments was minimal as compared to other partner countries during 1998-2002. The performance of the India's export sector is impressive in the early part of the new millennium. India's global exports are concentrated in a few sectors, which are strikingly expanding in recent years. Three product groups, namely textile & textile articles (Section XI), natural or cultured pearls, jewellery (Section XIV), and machinery & mechanical appliances (Section XVI), are contributing about half of India's total exports. Other important product groups contributing to the export sectors are vegetable products (Section II), mineral products (Section V), products of chemicals (Section VI), base metals & articles of base metal (Section XV), vehicles, aircraft and vessels (Section XVII), and works of art collectors' pieces (Section XXI). For number of such product segments, the exports growth rates have been very high during the period 1998-2002. The results show that exports of India in various product segments have been highly stable as compared to performances of other partners in the Group.

Trends in Bilateral Trade

The existing trade pattern among IBSA countries is different from their trade pattern with the rest of the world. The intra-IBSA trade is close to two per cent of the total trade of IBSA caucus, but their intra-regional trade is highly concentrated in a few sectors. Expansion of trade in these sectors has been highly impressive as compared to performance of those sectors with the world economy. Another important feature of the trade relationship between these countries is that the level of fluctuations in trade has been much lower among them than with the world economy as a whole.

A detailed account of the bilateral trade among IBSA countries is presented in Table 3.3. As discussed earlier, performance of the current level of trade within IBSA countries is better than their overall trade performances. Though the bilateral trade between different pairs of IBSA countries show limited trade in specific sectors, the trade in those sectors are impressively growing with low level of fluctuations over a period of time. The present level of bilateral trade in different sectors is indicating that their trade linkages are based on trade complementarities and intra-industry trade.[27]

India's dominant imports from Brazil are mostly concentrated in certain sectors, and they include sectors like animal or vegetable fats & oils (Section III), base metals & articles of base metal (Section XV), and machinery & mechanical appliances (Section XVI). India also imports large amount of products from other product groups including prepared foodstuff, beverages, etc. (Section

27. Greenaway (1989) has observed that trade cooperation under a RTA is more enduring when it is mostly based on intra-industry trade. It is argued that the spectacular surge in intra-regional trade of the EU and NAFTA is the reflection of growing intra-industry trade among the member counties.

TABLE 3.3

Bilateral Trade of IBSA Countries with their Proposed Partners

A: Brazil's Section	Description	Imports from								Exports to							
		India				South Africa				India				South Africa			
		Value 2002 ($ '000)	Gr. Rate 1998-02 (%)	Share 2002 (%)	CV 1998-02	Value 2002 ($ '000)	Gr. Rate 2000-02 (%)	Share 2002 (%)	CV 2000-02	Value 2002 ($ '000)	Gr. Rate 1998-02 (%)	Share 2002 (%)	CV 1998-02	Value 2002 ($ '000)	Gr. Rate 2000-02 (%)	Share 2002 (%)	CV 2000-02
I	Live Animals and Animal Products	240	95.0	0.0	1.6	880	17.1	0.5	3.0	0		0.0		19891	48.2	4.2	3.1
II	Vegetable Products	5481	-9.6	0.9	5.3	578	-15.6	0.3	1.4	2579	166.9	0.4	1.0	16081	155.4	3.4	1.4
III	Animal or Vegetable Fats & Oils	374	-23.6	0.1	0.8	0		0.0	0.6	2E+05	66.6	24.9	2.2	30748	549.6	6.5	1.2
IV	Prepared Foodstuff, Beverages, etc.	235	3.2	0.0	2.0	1746	-41.7	0.9	1.3	13890	-3.9	2.1	0.8	43605	85.3	9.2	2.1
V	Mineral Products	3E+05	7821.7	48.8	0.8	48555	-5.2	25.1	13.3	3E+05	316.4	53.2	0.6	16922	-11.4	3.6	1.8
VI	Products of Chemicals	2E+05	34.4	31.7	2.7	42111	-7.0	21.8	4.2	20481	20.2	3.1	3.4	38071	-2.6	8.1	6.6
VII	Plastics & Articles thereof	17304	9.0	2.8	3.4	1027	0.3	0.5	2.1	8939	277.4	1.4	1.4	21874	55.8	4.6	2.2
VIII	Raw Hides & Skins, Leather, etc.	3647	19.5	0.6	1.8	0	...	0.0	...	5026	1.6	0.8	7.3	10954	1.1	2.3	15.8
IX	Wood & Articles of Wood	459	2.1	0.1	8.2	0	...	0.0	...	1126	138.7	0.2	1.5	4375	1.5	0.9	4.4
X	Pulp of wood or of other Fibers	0		0.0	...	5351	-2.3	2.8	14.4	701	42.1	0.1	1.5	7043	36.2	1.5	3.5
XI	Textile & Textile Articles	29262	-11.3	4.7	2.6	9349	-14.8	4.8	5.8	13408	51.0	2.1	0.8	3186	6.7	0.7	2.1
XII	Footwear, Headgear and Umbrella	60	1475.0	0.0	0.7	17	-25.0	0.0	1.6	269	586.4	0.0	1.1	4362	28.2	0.9	2.4
XIII	Articles of Stone, Plaster, Cement	4375	15.0	0.7	2.3	1459	-1.3	0.8	3.6	2288	19.7	0.4	3.7	23924	55.0	5.1	2.7
XIV	Natural or cultured pearls, Jewellery	742	44.5	0.1	2.3	27775	0.1	14.4	1.6	3085	15.7	0.5	4.2	716	-6.2	0.2	14.1
XV	Base Metals & Articles of Base Metal	11906	-3.4	1.9	3.8	40065	-20.1	20.7	3.6	10801	-7.3	1.7	3.8	13094	-16.6	2.8	3.4
XVI	Machinery & Mechanical Appliances	33886	23.4	5.5	2.4	7467	20.3	3.9	5.1	31912	28.6	4.9	3.1	77028	13.5	16.3	7.6
XVII	Vehicles, Aircraft and Vessels	9007	-5.9	1.5	7.2	5907	14.9	3.1	7.0	22948	340.6	3.5	1.6	1E+05	44.7	29.1	3.0
XVIII	Optical, Photograph & Cinematography	3168	27.2	0.5	2.7	32	-47.4	0.0	0.9	4847	161.7	0.7	1.6	1524	27.0	0.3	2.3
XIX	Arms and Ammunition	0	...	0.0	...	758	74.7	0.4	1.0	0		0.0		376	-3.9	0.1	24.2
XX	Miscellaneous Manufactured Articles	390	6.8	0.1	1.4	71	-34.1	0.0	1.4	292	536.5	0.0	1.8	510	-24.7	0.1	2.1
XXI	Works of Art Collectors' Pieces	0	...	0.0	...	0	...	0.0	...	60	-4.5	0.0	4.9	648	9.1	0.1	3.4

Contd. ...

...Contd. ...

B: India's		Imports from								Exports to							
Section	Description	Brazil				South Africa				Brazil				South Africa			
		Value 2002 ($ '000)	Gr. Rate 1998-02 (%)	Share 2002 (%)	CV 1998-02	Value 2002 ($ '000)	Gr. Rate 2000-02 (%)	Share 2002 (%)	CV 2000-02	Value 2002 ($ '000)	Gr. Rate 1998-02 (%)	Share 2002 (%)	CV 1998-02	Value 2002 ($ '000)	Gr. Rate 2000-02 (%)	Share 2002 (%)	CV 2000-02
I	Live Animals and Animal Products	0		0.0		0		0.0		162	73.8	0.0	0.9	5859	9.7	1.0	9.4
II	Vegetable Products	1784	30.6	0.6	1.4	1874	158.2	0.1	1.5	3989	8.1	0.7	2.8	2E+05	259.9	28.1	1.2
III	Animal or Vegetable Fats & Oils	1E+05	19.4	44.1	2.3	5167	-26.6	0.2	1.4	302	-23.2	0.1	0.6	1313	-7.9	0.2	5.3
IV	Prepared Foodstuff, Beverages, etc.	13925	-13.1	4.5	0.7	137	-39.7	0.0	0.9	124	-16.8	0.0	1.0	5166	69.4	0.9	2.3
V	Mineral Products	16547	2.8	5.3	3.5	140394	-3.5	6.8	14.3	3E+05		43.4	0.5	23465	245.2	4.0	0.9
VI	Products of Chemicals	19244	10.3	6.2	2.4	109758	0.4	5.3	15.4	1E+05	35.4	20.9	2.9	48386	8.6	8.3	8.7
VII	Plastics & Articles thereof	11271	639.6	3.6	1.1	2308	-8.8	0.1	4.9	12567	11.8	2.1	2.4	10560	-8.8	1.8	6.6
VIII	Raw Hides & Skins, Leather, etc.	4641	7.3	1.5	3.7	277	-25.0	0.0	3.1	2128	89.7	0.4	1.3	14655	-9.3	2.5	9.4
IX	Wood & Articles of Wood	1330		0.4	1.3	1060	-41.7	0.1	1.5	0		0.0		111	13.1	0.0	0.9
X	Pulp of wood or of other Fibers	278	-19.9	0.1	1.4	9792	-35.4	0.5	1.8	0		0.0	0.6	3664	26.8	0.6	4.5
XI	Textile & Textile Articles	8539	20.8	2.7	1.0	7865	-19.5	0.4	4.0	27916	-4.7	4.7	5.2	84528	-6.4	14.4	14.0
XII	Footwear, Headgear and Umbrella	162	19.0	0.1	1.5	0		0.0		715	185.3	0.1	1.6	2372	-31.0	0.4	2.2
XIII	Articles of Stone, Plaster, Cement	1446	16.4	0.5	3.0	62	-11.7	0.0	6.8	4515	37.7	0.8	1.8	4888	-7.3	0.8	12.4
XIV	Natural or cultured pearls, Jewellery	8632	3.9	2.8	5.2	1707992	89.2	82.1	2.0	644	33.5	0.1	2.1	6151	59.9	1.1	1.2
XV	Base Metals & Articles of Base Metal	30669	24.5	9.8	3.4	53868	-8.8	2.6	6.3	22056	35.2	3.7	1.8	43378	21.6	7.4	5.6
XVI	Machinery & Mechanical Appliances	33086	15.9	10.6	4.2	36152	32.9	1.7	3.6	80850	183.4	13.7	1.0	69831	100.5	11.9	1.4
XVII	Vehicles, Aircraft and Vessels	15101	2072.4	4.8	1.4	2480	119.9	0.1	1.9	35686	138.4	6.1	1.0	56241	135.8	9.6	1.2
XVIII	Optical, Photograph & Cinematography	4623	165.7	1.5	1.5	561	-24.6	0.0	2.0	5666	278.3	1.0	1.0	9774	279.5	1.7	1.2
XIX	Arms and Ammunition	0		0.0		0		0.0	0.6	0		0.0		0		0.0	
XX	Miscellaneous Manufactured Articles	1029	893.8	0.3	0.7	0	-50.0	0.0	0.6	2962	197.4	0.5	0.9	11881	111.6	2.0	1.4
XXI	Works of Art Collectors' Pieces	1766	-2.3	0.6	1.3	158	-46.8	0.0	0.8	9971	286.2	1.7	1.0	18368	105.1	3.1	1.4

Contd. ...

...Contd. ...

C: South Africa's		Imports from								Exports to							
Section	Description	India				Brazil				India				Brazil			
		Value 2002 ($ 000')	Gr. Rate 2000-02 (%)	Share 2002 (%)	CV 2000-02	Value 2002 ($ 000')	Gr. Rate 2000-02 (%)	Share 2002 (%)	CV 2000-02	Value 2002 ($ 000')	Gr. Rate 2000-02 (%)	Share 2002 (%)	CV 2000-02	Value 2002 ($ 000')	Gr. Rate 2000-02 (%)	Share 2002 (%)	CV 2000-02
I	Live Animals and Animal Products	2456	-22.3	0.9	3.5	18594	45.3	4.0	3.2	0		0.0	0.6	505	-13.2	0.3	2.3
II	Vegetable Products	54544	39.3	20.3	2.4	18617	147.6	4.0	1.7	1111	333.1	0.3	0.9	491	-7.7	0.3	1.7
III	Animal or Vegetable Fats & Oils	1660	-23.8	0.6	2.9	33500	1735.7	7.3	1.0	74	-3.2	0.0	1.2	0	-50.0	0.0	0.6
IV	Prepared Foodstuff, Beverages, etc.	6164	133.8	2.3	1.6	19432	31.0	4.2	4.0	1496	226.0	0.4	0.9	1572	-37.8	0.9	1.4
V	Mineral Products	3455	10.8	1.3	1.3	2012	-11.6	0.4	5.1	87851	2.8	25.2	10.3	50893	13.5	29.1	8.3
VI	Products of Chemicals	48806	10.4	18.1	7.3	38465	-4.8	8.3	7.6	1E+05	-11.6	31.3	7.6	49233	-1.2	28.1	8.4
VII	Plastics & Articles thereof	9994	6.7	3.7	15.7	20063	69.8	4.3	2.1	2127	44.6	0.6	2.4	789	-23.0	0.5	1.8
VIII	Raw Hides & Skins, Leather, etc.	16918	-5.2	6.3	18.1	11098	2.7	2.4	12.5	570	-3.7	0.2	4.3	18	-49.4	0.0	0.9
IX	Wood & Articles of Wood	429	-3.2	0.2	11.5	5378	-14.2	1.2	5.5	1408	10.3	0.4	2.2	585	-29.8	0.3	2.4
X	Pulp of wood or of other Fibers	2216	24.5	0.8	5.1	7792	80.8	1.7	1.9	34809	-8.8	10.0	4.5	5048	-5.2	2.9	4.8
XI	Textile & Textile Articles	36457	-9.8	13.5	7.6	3156	3.5	0.7	2.6	6169	-3.8	1.8	7.9	9269	-14.0	5.3	6.1
XII	Footwear, Headgear and Umbrella	3388	-29.2	1.3	2.5	4168	21.1	0.9	2.4	0		0.0		0		0.0	
XIII	Articles of Stone, Plaster, Cement	4871	2.7	1.8	20.7	19474	53.6	4.2	2.7	200	-22.6	0.1	2.2	70	66.7	0.0	2.5
XIV	Natural or cultured pearls, Jewellery	7344	16.1	2.7	3.8	195	393.2	0.0	1.0	6447	-27.6	1.9	2.7	624	-19.4	0.4	3.0
XV	Base Metals & Articles of Base Metal	20021	-7.6	7.4	8.7	33308	-1.2	7.2	10.8	69340	7.8	19.9	7.0	39034	-18.5	22.3	4.4
XVI	Machinery & Mechanical Appliances	27108	0.9	10.1	106.3	64656	1.3	14.0	30.7	24542	36.0	7.1	3.6	7586	0.5	4.3	8.6
XVII	Vehicles, Aircraft and Vessels	7931	27.3	2.9	3.7	70105	194.7	15.2	1.1	1790	12.3	0.5	0.8	8505	17.7	4.9	0.8
XVIII	Optical, Photograph & Cinematography	4446	47.7	1.7	3.0	1766	14.5	0.4	5.5	1242	30.5	0.4	4.2	677	-21.7	0.4	3.5
XIX	Arms and Ammunition	0		0.0		0		0.0		0		0.0		0		0.0	
XX	Miscellaneous Manufactured Articles	6110	10.3	2.3	6.1	775	-22.0	0.2	3.5	1	-49.8	0.0	0.6	51		0.0	0.6
XXI	Works of Art Collectors' Pieces	4888	26.7	1.8	2.1	89032	27.0	19.3	4.4	0		0.0		0		0.0	

Note: Trade in thousand US$.

Source: RIS based on PCTAS 1998-2002, ITC, UNCTAD,WTO,UNSD, 2003.

IV), mineral products (Section V), products of chemicals (Section VI), plastics & articles thereof (Section VII), and vehicles, aircraft and vessels (Section XVII). In most of these product segments, imports are persistently increasing in a robust manner during the period 1998-2002. Another important feature of India's imports from Brazil is that such imports registered least fluctuations as compared to Brazil's total exports to world during the same period as mentioned above.

As compared to Brazil, India's imports from South Africa are less diversified and heavily concentrated around certain sectors. For example, India's imports of natural or cultured pearls, jewellery (Section XIV) cover more than 82 per cent of the total imports from the country. Other important imports from South Africa cover mineral products (Section V), products of chemicals (Section VI), pulp of wood or of other fibres (Section X), natural or cultured pearls, jewellery (Section XIV), and machinery & mechanical appliances (Section XVI). Imports of most of these products are increasing steadily during the study period.

India's export basket to the IBSA partners is more broader than its imports, though the level of exports is not that promising at present. India's broad export to Brazil covers mineral products (Section V), products of chemicals (Section VI), and machinery & mechanical appliances (Section XVI). Other significant exports from the country include plastics & articles thereof (Section VII), textile & textile articles (Section XI), base metals & articles of base metal (Section XV), and vehicles, aircraft and vessels (Section XVII). Bilateral exports are increasing rapidly in certain product groups with marginal fluctuations.

The current bilateral trade flows show that export of India to South Africa is highly diversified and spread over a sizeable group of products. Exports in most important sectors include vegetable products (Section II), products of chemicals (Section VI), machinery & mechanical appliances (Section XVI), and vehicles, aircraft and vessels (Section XVII). Other priority exports comprise mineral products (Section V), base metals & articles of base metal (Section XV), miscellaneous manufactured articles (Section XX), and works of art collectors' pieces (Section XXI). In most of these product lines, the exports have been increasing steadily with very low level of fluctuations.

Brazil's important imports from South Africa covers broad sectors like mineral products (Section V), products of chemicals (Section VI), natural or cultured pearls, jewellery (Section XIV), and base metals & articles of base metal (Section XV). Other important imports consist of plastics & articles thereof (Section VII), pulp of wood or of other fibres (Section X), textile & textile articles (Section XI), and machinery & mechanical appliances (Section XVI). A large number of product groups have shown considerable level of fluctuations during the period 1998-2002.

About 80 per cent of Brazil's import from India is from two sectors, namely mineral products (Section V) and products of chemicals (Section VI). It also imports significant level of other products from India, covering products like plastics & articles thereof (Section VII), textile & textile articles (Section XI), base metals & articles of base metal (Section XV), and machinery & mechanical appliances (Section XVI). The growth rates have been very significant in number of important import product groups such as mineral products (Section V) and products of chemicals (Section VI). Some of these imported products from Brazil are highly fluctuating in recent years.

Like imports, Brazil's exports to India are concentrated in two broad sectors such as animal or vegetable fats & oils (Section III), and mineral products (Section V). Exports to these two sectors constitute about 78 per cent of Brazil's bilateral exports to India and the volumes of exports in these product categories are currently increasing steadily. Other important broad products exported to India are chemicals (Section VI), textile & textile articles (Section XI), machinery & mechanical appliances (Section XVI), and vehicles, aircraft and vessels (Section XVII). The general trend in the bilateral exports to India has been consistent during 1998-2002.

Brazil's exports to South Africa are restricted to a few sectors. Sizeable exports are reported in specific sectors like prepared foodstuff, beverages, etc. (Section IV), machinery & mechanical appliances (Section XVI), and vehicles, aircraft and vessels (Section XVII). These three sectors constitute about 55 per cent of Brazil's bilateral exports to South Africa in 2002. The growth of exports in these product ranges excluding prepared foodstuff are significant in recent years. There are imports in other sectors also such as animal or vegetable fats & oils (Section III), products of chemicals (Section VI), and articles of stone, plaster, cement (Section XIII). However, there are large-scale fluctuations in the bilateral export from Brazil to South Africa.

The imports and exports baskets of South Africa from India and Brazil are highly diversified. In certain product segments, India and Brazil compete among themselves to gain market access in South Africa, but in other product segments there is nearly no competition between them. As discussed earlier, the external sector of South Africa is currently passing through a phase of stagnancy. But in several core product segments, country's exports and imports are fast rising *vis-à-vis* India and Brazil.

Despite structural disadvantages like geographical distance, the intra-IBSA trade has been significant. The intra-IBSA trade to total trade is hovering around two per cent in 2002.

The coverage of products under the global trade is much wider than the products traded under the regional process. Focused policy may help in expanding intra-regional trade in other areas. The domestic economic reforms in Brazil and

South Africa have compelled them to adopt import compression policies, which have adversely affected the intra-regional trade in recent years.

India being in the second generation of reforms, its external sector policies are liberal as compared to the policy environment existing in the pre-reform period. India's exports and imports from both these countries are growing in large number of sectors. However, bilateral imports of Brazil and South Africa from India are declining in several key sectors where India has it commercial interest.

3.4 Analysis of Tariff Structure in IBSA

Reduction of tariff under FTA is one of the most lucrative forms of incentive for exporters/importers for member countries, and therefore, analysis of tariff structure is important to assess efficacy of Close Economic Relations (CER) on individual member countries. In the Vinerian tradition, trade creation and trade diversion effects are the basis for fostering intra-regional trade, and the current level of tariff in individual countries plays an important role in determining the sharing of welfare-gains between the contracting partners. With the formation of FTA, it is generally believed that combined effects of comparative advantage in trade and level of tariff of individual country, determine the extent to which benefits are shared between individual members in the RTA. A member country having high tariff structure is likely to gain less compared to other members in a regional arrangement. In this context, the analysis of tariff bands, average applied tariffs by broad trade sectors and structure of imports in different levels of tariffs, etc. may be useful in examining the relevance of proposed RTA for an individual member country.

Analysis of Tariff Bands

The experiences of IBSA countries indicate that the number of tariff bands is inversely related with maximum level of tariff. The tariff policies of Brazil and South Africa indicate that their maximum tariff rates are almost similar to each other, but similar rate for India is placed at a higher level. The maximum tariff rate of India is 210, and similar rate for Brazil and South Africa are 55 per cent and 60 per cent respectively in 2001 as shown in Table 3.4. The number of tariff bands is much higher in case of Brazil and South Africa, than that of India. While Brazil has 38 tariff bands, the similar figures for South Africa and India are 37 and 22 respectively. This shows that tariff bands are chosen at a close interval in both Brazil and South Africa.

In regional and multilateral trade negotiations, the number of lines under zero tariffs has special implications.[28] In terms of product lines having zero

28. As zero tariff refers to free trade in specific product segment, such product bands are used for specific mode of negotiation in multilateral trade negotiations, such as zero-by-zero negotiation (for details see Mehta and Mohanty (2001).

tariffs, South Africa is way ahead of both Brazil and India. While over 57 per cent of total tariff lines are subject to free imports in South Africa, about 5.8 per cent in Brazil and 1.0 per cent in India are subject to zero tariffs in 2001.

It is commonly observed that sizeable number of countries maintain in the proposed IBSA large number of tariff bands, but the concentration tariff lines are mostly found in a few tariff bands. In India, 87.5 per cent of total tariff lines are concentrated in two tariff bands (i.e., 25 per cent and 35 per cent). Most of South African's tariff lines are concentrated in zero tariffs, and there is high concentration of tariff lines in five tariff bands, namely 10, 15, 20, 22 and 40. These tariff lines under the selected tariff bands constitute about 87.5 per cent of country's total tariff lines. In Brazil, the distribution of tariff lines in different tariff bands has been less skewed than India and South Africa. About 66.5 per cent of total tariff lines are accounted by six tariff bands in Brazil (i.e., 3.5, 11.5, 14, 15.5, 19.5 and 21.5). It is important to note that tariff band up to 21.5 per cent in Brazil, 30 per cent in South Africa and 35 per cent in India constitute around 95 per cent or more of their total tariff lines in 2001. It may be noted that the impact of FTA may be insignificant for those tariff lines where the tariff rate is at 5 per cent or less. The results show that 61.6 per cent of South Africa's total tariff lines are subject to 5 per cent or less tariff rate, and the similar figures for Brazil and India are 19.0 per cent and 2.7 per cent respectively in 2001. The implication of above figures is that higher being the percentage of lines under 5 per cent *ad valorem* tariff or less to the total tariff lines, less may be the cost of restructuring to an individual country under FTA. Countries under high tariff regime are likely to gain little from FTA despite having large export potential in partner countries. Looking at the relative tariff structures of three countries, it may be concluded that India is placed in a more disadvantageous position than Brazil and South Africa in realising gains from the proposed CER.

TABLE 3.4

Tariff Bands and Composition of Tariff Lines in 2001

Sl.No.	Brazil		South Africa		India	
	Band	Tariff Lines* (%)	Band	Tariff Lines* (%)	Band	Tariff Lines* (%)
01	0.0	5.8	0.0	57.1	0.0	1.0
02	1.5	1.1	3.0	0.1	3.0	0.1
03	2.0	0.3	5.0	4.4	5.0	1.5
04	3.0	0.3	6.6	0.2	10.0	0.5
05	3.5	11.1	7.0	0.0	15.0	2.9
06	4.0	0.2	7.4	0.1	20.0	2.9
07	5.0	0.1	8.0	0.8	25.0	18.7
08	5.5	2.9	9.4	0.1	30.0	1.4
09	6.0	0.1	9.8	0.0	35.0	68.8
10	7.5	3.1	10.0	7.1	40.0	0.1
11	8.0	0.1	12.0	0.0	45.0	0.1
12	9.5	2.2	12.5	0.1	50.0	0.1
13	10.0	0.2	13.0	0.2	55.0	0.0
14	11.0	0.1	14.0	0.0	60.0	0.1
15	11.5	11.4	15.0	7.1	70.0	0.3
16	12.0	0.1	16.0	0.2	75.0	0.0
17	13.0	0.0	17.0	0.1	80.0	0.1
18	13.5	5.5	18.0	0.1	100.0	0.7
19	14.0	9.9	19.0	0.5	105.0	0.3
20	15.0	0.1	20.0	7.7	115.0	0.0
21	15.5	9.4	21.0	0.1	170.0	0.0
22	16.0	0.0	22.0	4.1	210.0	0.2
23	17.5	9.1	22.5	0.1	—	—
24	18.0	0.1	25.0	2.1	—	—
25	19.0	0.4	27.0	0.4	—	—
26	19.5	13.9	28.0	0.0	—	—
27	20.0	0.3	30.0	2.3	—	—
28	21.0	0.1	32.5	0.0	—	—
29	21.5	10.8	35.0	0.0	—	—
30	22.0	0.1	37.0	0.3	—	—
31	23.0	0.1	40.0	4.4	—	—
32	25.0	0.1	42.5	0.3	—	—
33	26.0	0.2	43.0	0.0	—	—
34	27.0	0.1	45.0	0.1	—	—
35	29.0	0.0	50.0	0.0	—	—
36	35.0	0.5	55.0	0.0	—	—
37	36.0	0.0	60.0	0.0	—	—
38	55.0	0.0	—	—	—	—

Note: * As a per cent of total number of tariff lines at 6-digit HS of respective country.

Source: RIS based on TRAINS, 2003, UNCTAD.

Trade-Weighted Tariff across Sectors

Trade-weighted average tariff rates by sectors for different proposed member countries are given in Table 3.5. The results indicate that the levels of protection in three countries are different from each other. While South Africa has the most liberal tariff regime, India is the most protected country among the three. In all broad product segments, South Africa has registered much lower level of tariff as compared to India and Brazil. Except four HS sections, the import-weighted average tariff rates are in single digit in South Africa. On the other hand, the import-weighted average tariffs are in single digit in case of one HS section in India and six HS sections in Brazil. A comparison between average

TABLE 3.5

Traded Weighted Tariff Rates in 2001 by HS Section

(in %)

Section	*Description*	*Brazil*	*India*	*SouthAfrica*
01	Live Animals and Animal Products	6.0	35.6	6.4
02	Vegetable Products	7.3	35.2	1.8
03	Animal or Vegetable Fats & Oils	11.8	88.8	8.8
04	Prepared Foodstuff, Beverages, etc.	17.7	50.6	9.2
05	Mineral Products	0.6	17.2	0.5
06	Products of Chemicals	8.6	28.6	2.0
07	Plastics & Articles thereof	13.3	34.9	8.3
08	Raw Hides & Skins, Leather, etc.	16.3	18.3	13.1
09	Wood & Articles of Wood	10.5	7.0	3.2
10	Pulp of wood or of other Fibers	10.1	19.2	5.7
11	Textile & Textile Articles	16.9	21.5	20.3
12	Footwear, Headgear and Umbrella	20.6	35.0	27.3
13	Articles of Stone, Plaster, Cement	12.6	32.7	6.5
14	Natural or cultured pearls, Jewellery	14.1	35.0	3.0
15	Base Metals & Articles of Base Metal	14.7	32.4	5.5
16	Machinery & Mechanical Appliances	11.0	22.7	2.7
17	Vehicles, Aircraft and Vessels	6.1	26.1	16.9
18	Optical, Photograph & Cinematography	12.1	23.9	0.5
19	Arms and Ammunition	21.5	35.0	—
20	Miscellaneous Manufactured Articles	19.8	34.2	8.5
21	Works of Art Collectors' Pieces	3.1	34.4	0.0

Source: RIS Based on TRAINS, 2003, UNCTAD.

tariffs of India and Brazil indicates that in one HS section (Woods and articles of woods, Section IX), India has lower tariff than Brazil, and in another product range (i.e. raw hides, skin and leather products, HS Section VIII), average tariffs of two countries can be comparable. In other product groups (i.e., at section level), India's average tariffs are much higher than that of Brazil. In two product groups (i.e., textile & textile articles, Section XI, and footwear, headgear and umbrella, Section XII), the average tariffs are high in both Brazil and South Africa. In the product segment of raw hides & skins, leather, etc. (Section VIII), the average tariff levels in Brazil and South Africa are moderately high, but their tariff levels can be compared with that of India. In other product segments, including animal or vegetable fats & oils (Section III), prepared foodstuff, beverages, etc. (Section IV), plastics & articles thereof (Section VII), miscellaneous manufactured articles (Section XX), there is some possibility of benefiting from tariff reduction, though the average level of tariffs in Brazil and South Africa are low.

From India's point of view, the prevailing tariff structure in both the partner countries is not promising to formalise a CER between three countries. In case of sectoral negotiation for intra-regional trade liberalisation, India has to incur higher cost than other two partners. In this background, there is a need for examining the manner in which imports of partner countries are subjected to different levels of tariffs.

Composition of Imports by Structure of Tariff

The economic theory on regional trading arrangements stipulates that probability of gains for exporting partner country increases when the importing partner country has a more protected tariff regime. The most liberal country in a proposed regional caucus has to offer fewer commitments than others in a FTA kind of arrangement. As we have observed that the Member countries of proposed Grouping are in different level of tariff regimes, the structure of imports subject to different levels of tariffs may have some underpinning implications while examining the feasibility of the proposed IBSA FTA. The structure of imports attracting various levels of tariffs by broad sectors in individual countries is presented in Table 3.6. The results indicate that moderate to high tariff sectors are diverse for different partner countries depending upon their accomplishment in their level of economic development. The current trading scenario in the region presents a clear trend that vast trade possibilities exist in the region as substantial trade in each partner courtiers in diverse sectors are subjected to moderate to high tariff. Depending upon the trade competitiveness of the partner countries, trade potential for each member may be quantified to ascertain the course of future trade in the region.

...Contd. ...

Tariff Level	*Section*	*Description*	*Brazil*	*India*	*South Africa*
	14	Natural or cultured pearls, Jewellery	29694.22	—	17692.45
	15	Miscellaneous articles of base metal	529599.12	126360.85	78225.79
	16	Electrical machinery & equp & parts	2698266.64	1850311.38	179061.16
	17	Ships, boats & floating structures	242731.66	—	191350.67
	18	Musical instruments; parts & access	421645.29	40094.23	17758.12
	19	Arm & ammunition; part & access	6622.11	—	—
	20	Miscellaneous Manufactured articles	178792.01	—	106879.29
High Tariff (25≥35)	1	Products of animal orgin	35.78	—	7079.02
	2	Vegetable plaiting materials	1651.58	107.30	309.52
	4	Tobacco & manufactured tobacco	21565.75	—	47085.28
	5	Mineral fuels mineral oils and products	248.98	1114844.38	—
	6	Miscellaneous chemical products	—	303209.71	—
	7	Rubber and articles thereof	—	3399.82	68826.40
	8	Furskins and artificial fur	—	137107.70	40569.89
	9	Manufactures of straw, of esparto, etc.	—	6013.75	2661.71
	10	Printed books, newspapers, pictures	—	188069.88	—
	11	Other made up textile articles	—	265977.78	34447.29
	12	Prepared feathers & down & articles	5019.44	—	168825.68
	13	Glass and glassware	—	33928.63	13197.62
	15	Miscellaneous articles of base metal	—	319862.75	12166.69
	16	Electrical machinery & equp & parts	—	2803972.18	43116.21
	17	Ships, boats & floating structures	3629.99	210016.44	702703.64
	18	Musical instruments; parts & access	—	751906.73	—
	20	Miscellaneous Manufactured articles	—	11927.69	3219.68
Very High Tariff (<35)	1	Products of animal orgin	—	32590.20	73170.88
	2	Vegetable plaiting materials	—	624839.09	67070.38
	3	Animal or vegetable fats & oils	—	1439497.02	—
	4	Tobacco & manufactured tobacco	31.98	146765.31	93969.09
	5	Mineral fuels mineral oils and products	79999.63	1821442.04	664.90
	6	Miscellaneous chemical products	216.99	3077219.09	—
	7	Rubber and articles thereof	—	952742.15	—
	8	Furskins and artificial fur	—	8293.54	—
	9	Manufactures of straw, of esparto, etc.	—	29529.16	—
	10	Printed books, newspapers, pictures	—	186037.51	—
	11	Other made up textile articles	—	315240.41	203718.46
	12	Prepared feathers & down & articles	—	35574.13	—

Contd. ...

...Contd. ...

Tariff Level	Section	Description	Brazil	India	South Africa
	13	Glass and glassware	—	148295.53	—
	14	Natural or cultured pearls, Jewellery	—	9859431.27	—
	15	Miscellaneous articles of base metal	—	1788152.14	—
	16	Electrical machinery & equp & parts	—	1762969.92	—
	17	Ships, boats & floating structures	166833.24	517334.29	—
	18	Musical instruments; parts & access	—	103497.12	—
	19	Arm & ammunition; part & access	—	436.16	—
	20	Miscellaneous Manufactured articles	—	128688.69	—
	21	Miscellaneous goods-Handicrafts, carpets	4424.15	424.21	2512.67

Source: RIS Based on TRAINS, 2003, UNCTAD.

3.5 Export Competitiveness

Measuring Export Potentials: Some Methodological Issues

In this section, we suggest a methodology for analysing the prospects of India for entering into a FTA with Brazil/South Africa. The efficacy of the proposed agreement depends upon the export potential of one partner in other partner's market depending upon the price competitiveness of the exporting country. The tariff and other concessions under the FTA would further support the realisation of the potential exports to actual.

In fact, price competitiveness complements export potential of goods from the exporting country. For instance, the production structure of an exporting country is such that the country can export an item with a price which is lower than the price offered by other competitors in the market of an importing country (see Mohanty, 2002a). In such a case, the importing country can opt for the switching of its source of imports from the high cost to low cost supplier. From the perspective of the exporter, price competitiveness could lead to the creation of an export potential in the importer's market.

The formation of an FTA improves the price competitiveness of the exporting partner, depending upon the tariff structure of importing trade partner and the level of concession offered in the arrangement. The exporting country gets an edge over other competitors in the market of the importing country and the benefits from the FTA increase when the tariff structure is very stringent in the latter country.

There is some sense in initiating negotiations with Brazil/South Africa provided that India has a sizeable export potential in that market, and at the same time if an export item from India is likely to get reciprocate tariff reduction from that country. In case the expected benefit from the proposed FTA is not shared equally between both countries, the country receiving fewer benefits may be extended concessions in other sectors like services and joint ventures. There is a strong perception that Brazil/South Africa has a large export potential (in trade in goods) in India and is likely to benefit substantially from the proposed FTA in view of India's relatively strong tariff regime. There are doubts regarding India's gains in terms of additional market access share in Brazil/South Africa following the signing of the proposed agreement.

Several statistical methods can be used to estimate potential for trade. One approach is to compare Revealed Comparative Advantage (RCA) indexes.[29] Another method is a trade flow analysis to identify complementary products between countries, i.e. products that are exported by one country (or region) towards the rest of the world, and for which there is significant import demand in another country (or region). This method is applied in a recent ITC study,[30] following both a static and dynamic approach.[31] The ITC study also uses the concept of indicative export potential. In the case of MERCOSUR exports to India this would be the lower value of MERCOSUR exports to the world and Indian imports from the world (calculated at the 6-digit HS level). The untapped export potential is defined as the difference between the indicative potential and current trade.

It may be noted that Brazil/South Africa exported about 1386 commodities (at HS 6-digit) to India in 1997. The export basket of Brazil/South Africa to India includes both agricultural and industrial products. In this study, the price competitiveness of either country's export is estimated on the basis of Adam Smith's "absolute cost advantage" theorem. While estimating the price competitiveness of a particular commodity (say 'i'), a comparison is made between the prices offered by an exporting country (say X) with the prices of its competitors (Y's) in an importing partner country (say Z). If the price offered by X is lower than those of others (i.e. Y's), it means that country X has a relative price competitiveness *vis-à-vis* the others. It is not always necessary to presume that the offered price of X to country Z is the lowest among other suppliers to Z in order to ensure that X has price competitiveness in the export of the i-th product. If the price offered by X is lower than some of the suppliers/competitors (if not all) in country Z, then it also means that supplier X has price competitiveness in country Z.

---

29. A measure of relative export performance by country and industry, defined as a country's share of world exports of a good divided by its share of total world exports. (See, Balassa, 1965).

30. International Trade Centre (2003).

31. The same approach is implicitly followed in a press report emphasising that for 20 agricultural products that Argentina is interested in exporting to India, the value of total Indian imports amounted to US$ 4.9 billion, whereas imports from Argentina represented only US$ 272 million, i.e. 5 per cent. *http://www.elpais.com.uy/04/03/03/ultmo_82948.asp*

In the present study, the methodology for the estimation of price competitiveness is the most realistic one. In this measure, we take the actual price offered by country X, and compare it with prices offered by other competitors in the importing country. For examining India's price competitiveness, we have to make a comparative analysis between India's export price with the price of its competitors in Brazil/South Africa for a particular product.

Price Competitiveness and Export Potentials

In the present study, for the estimation of price competitiveness, we consider each product separately at a disaggregate level (i.e. at the 6-digit HS level). In this measure, we compare the export price of India in each product group (at the 6-digit level) with the corresponding prices offered by its competitors in the market of Brazil/South Africa.

Suppose India is exporting i-th product to Brazil/South Africa at a given price (PX_{Nij}) and another competing supplier also exporting the same product to Brazil/South Africa at a different price (PX_{kij}) where,

PX_{Nij} = Export price of India, for the i-th product, in j-th market (Brazil/South Africa).

PX_{kij} = Export price k-th competitor, for the i-th product, in the j-th market.

N = India

i = 1, 2, ..., P (Products)

k = 1, 2, ...l...., K (India's K competitors in the i-th product segment)

For a given product 'i', if India has price competitiveness over other competitors in the j-th market then the export price of India should be lower than those of other competitors. In such case, the condition may be,

$$PX_{Nij} < PX_{kij} \quad (1)$$

If India has price competitiveness in one product, it does not mean that all the competitors in that product category necessarily have higher prices than that of India. In the given product, some of them may also be having lower prices than India. In that case, India should look at the market share of those competitors, whose export prices are higher than that of India. The export market shares of India's inefficient competitors may be considered as India's export potentials.

Suppose in Brazil/South Africa's market, India is exporting i-th product and another K-1 number of suppliers are present in the same product segment. So each competitor holds some portion of market share (Sh_{ikj}) in the import of the i-th product by Brazil/South Africa. Therefore, the total market of the i-th product is shared by all the K suppliers in Brazil/South Africa. It means,

$$\sum_{k=1}^{K} Sh_{ikj} = 100 \quad (2)$$

Where Sh_{ikj} stands for market share of the k-th exporter of the i-th product to Brazil/South Africa.

Suppose India has price competitiveness over a few competitors (but not all of them) in the export of i-th product, and in case India effectively enters the Brazil/South African market as a supplier the combined market share of incompetitive competitors (let us assume the ratio as μ) may be treated as India's potential export share, where,

$$0 > \mu > 1 \quad (3)$$

and μ denotes proportion of the i-th product market, which is covered by the exports of less competitive competitors of India in the markets of Brazil/ South Africa.

The export potential of India (POT_{Nij}) in the exports of i-th product in Brazil/South Africa may be estimated as:

$$POT_{Nij} = \mu \, IM_{ij} \quad (4)$$

Where IM_{ij} stands for total imports of the i-th product by Brazil/South Africa from all sources.

If μ is less than 1, it means that India has a price edge over a few competitors and a part of the i-th import market of Brazil/South Africa would form India's potential export. If μ is equal to 1, it means, that the entire import of the i-th product by Brazil/South Africa would be India's potential export. Jacob Vinner denotes such trade potential as the trade creation effect of a regional trading arrangement.

In this measure, we assume that with changes in the policy environment, India may be able to improve its market share by taking over market segments from less efficient competitors in Brazil/South Africa on the basis of her absolute cost comparative advantage. One of the limitations of this measure is that we cannot identify the products where India has global competitiveness but is yet to tap the export potentials in Brazil/South Africa. This issue is empirically examined in a recent study (for details see Mehta and Mohanty, 2001).

What are the prospects for India, should it go for a bilateral FTA with Brazil/South Africa? To analyse this it is necessary first to estimate the size of the export potential for those commodities where Brazil/South Africa continues to have a high tariff. These tariff peaks include both *ad valorem* and specific tariffs (taking *ad valorem* tariff equivalence). The negotiation would be on the basis of total trade opportunities created by the trade creation and trade diversion effects based on the existing tariff structure. The preferential bilateral tariff reduction would determine the level of trade diversion in both the countries (see Mohanty, 2002b). The sharing of potential benefit from the FTA between the countries would be at the core of bilateral negotiations.

For the negotiations, we have to identify commodities, which are exported or likely to be exported by Brazil/South Africa, and are also facing different levels of tariff (both *ad valorem* and tariff equivalence of specific tariffs) in India. A similar exercise may be repeated for India too. Based on the coverage of identified commodities and their potential exports, recommendations are to be made about the future course of negotiations (See Mohanty, 2002b). In this study, we have extended our analysis to cover commodities of both the agricultural and industrial sectors.

Since India and Brazil/South Africa have decided to consider the possibilities of close economic cooperation, there is a need to examine the potentials of trade in both the countries. In case, the potential exists to augment trade between both the countries, there is a need to examine the extent to which the FTA can help both the countries in providing tariff and other support on a reciprocal basis. The reduction of tariffs under the purview of FTA would provide immense advantage to the exporting partner over other exporting competitors in the market of the importing partner country. This would, in fact, support some of the marginally cost disadvantage products of the exporting partner, which we describe as the 'trade diversion effect' in the framework of Jacob Viner's 'customs union' model. In this context, we would like to examine the competitiveness of Brazil/South Africa's exports in the Indian market and vice versa.

3.6 Export Potential

As discussed in the earlier section, the trade potential of each proposed partner in the markets of other proposed partners are examined empirically based on the Vinerian framework. In this context, two important issues are discussed in this section. Firstly, attempts have been made to estimate the level of export potential at a more disaggregated level of products[32] based on price competitiveness of products. Secondly, feasibility of harnessing such export potentials in the backdrop of existing tariff regimes in partner countries, is examined.

---

32. For the present exercise, we have used trade creation effect to estimate trade potential of individual countries. The results could be more worrying for India as it has maintained a more protected trade regime than other members of the caucus.

Sectoral Distribution of Export Potentials

The economic theory stipulates that the possibilities of trade under the close economic cooperation is primarily depending upon the extent of competitiveness a country has *vis-à-vis* other partners and also the existing suppliers in the market. Various trade theorems including Smith (1776), Ricardo (1817), Heckscher (1919) and Ohlin (1933), have emphasised the relevance of competitiveness as the basis of trade possibilities for trade. Viner (1950) has extended the Ricardian approach of cost comparative advantage to examine the basis for formation of Customs Union in a situation of differentiated tariff regimes among participating countries. Balassa (1967, 1975) empirically examined the implication of a customs union on members of the Europe community, taking note of heterogeneous tariff regimes in member countries. The present study is based on the Vinerian approach. A detailed discussion on the methodology adopted for the present analyses is already discussed in Section 4.

In the context of examining the efficacy of the proposed IBSA, and the relevance of India in the caucus, we are encountered with number of questions, which need to be reviewed. Should we go ahead with the IBSA proposal? What is our specific economic interest, including trade interest from the proposed RTA? If the proposal were through, what would be the size of market access that India might have to offer? In return, what would be the extent of market opening that India is likely to commit based on relative competitiveness of countries?

The analysis of export potentials indicates that distribution of net gains from the proposed RTA would be large for all the partner of propose regional caucus. South Africa's export potential in the IBSA is to the extent of US$ 59.8 billion whereas similar estimates for Brazil and India are US$ 46.2 billion and US$ 17.3 billion respectively. The implementation of IBSA may open floodgate of opportunity for trade in the merchandise sector. If IBSA is launched with its full mandate, the regional partners will be benefiting by opening up several sectors, *viz.*, investment and services. Understanding of export potentials of different contracting parties in various sectors of other partner countries is likely to provide further impetus to ongoing negotiations. Detailed discussions on the sectoral composition of export potentials of each country in their partner countries are presented below.

The details of each member country's export potentials in other partners' markets are presented in Table 3.7. The trend analysis is presented by sectors, and estimations are made for the period 1998-2002 using PC-TAS. The member countries have strong export potentials in wide range of sectors ranging from agriculture to manufacturing sectors and from primary resource-based products to high technology-intensive products. The regional trade is likely to witness spur in export growth in sectors like vegetable products, minerals, gems and jewellery,

TABLE 3.7

Export Potentials of IBSA Countries in their Respective Partner Countries: By Section

Export Potential of India in

Section	Descrption	Brazil			South Africa		
		Export Potential ($ '000) 2002	Annual Growth Rate (%) 1998-2002	Share in Total (%) 2002	Export Potential ($ '000) 2002	Annual Growth Rate (%) 1998-2002	Share in Total (%) 2002
I	Live Animals and Animal Products	231089	-11.6	1.8	39326	-0.8	0.8
II	Vegetable Products	1258342	-6.6	10.0	173692	17.2	3.7
III	Animal or Vegetable Fats & Oils	27386	-11.5	0.2	9840	-11.7	0.2
IV	Prepared Foodstuff, Beverages, etc.	374321	-8.6	3.0	195849	6.2	4.1
V	Mineral Products	607246	13.6	4.8	295368	97.4	6.3
VI	Products of Chemicals	5063947	0.6	40.3	1613572	0.9	34.2
VII	Plastics & Articles thereof	2286205	-0.4	18.2	710985	1.2	15.1
VIII	Raw Hides & Skins, Leather, etc.	127525	-3.0	1.0	16868	-17.3	0.4
IX	Wood & Articles of Wood	21520	-5.7	0.2	74192	14.2	1.6
X	Pulp of wood or of other Fibers	418408	-12.2	3.3	360927	2.0	7.6
XI	Textile & Textile Articles	633519	-10.6	5.0	356937	7.1	7.6
XII	Footwear, Headgear and Umbrella	56018	-8.6	0.4	121236	-4.2	2.6
XIII	Articles of Stone, Plaster, Cement	251928	-3.1	2.0	232979	-5.7	4.9
XIV	Natural or cultured pearls, Jewellery	3406	89.4	0.0	110		0.0
XV	Base Metals & Articles of Base Metal	1197265	-4.0	9.5	517415	6.6	11.0

Export Potential of Brazil in

Section	Descrption	India			South Africa		
		Export Potential ($ '000) 2002	Annual Growth Rate (%) 1998-2002	Share in Total (%) 2002	Export Potential ($ '000) 2002	Annual Growth Rate (%) 1998-2002	Share in Total (%) 2002
I	Live Animals and Animal Products	16911	28.7	0.0	45855	-6.5	0.4
II	Vegetable Products	347095	49.4	1.0	116224	32.8	0.9
III	Animal or Vegetable Fats & Oils	1555589	230.8	4.6	48137	31.3	0.4
IV	Prepared Foodstuff, Beverages, etc.	118135	8.8	0.3	179121	2.5	1.4
V	Mineral Products	18157188	1067.2	53.6	3137298	-3.0	25.3
VI	Products of Chemicals	1612236	6.8	4.8	1791294	-0.4	14.5
VII	Plastics & Articles thereof	634809	4.0	1.9	570550	2.1	4.6
VIII	Raw Hides & Skins, Leather, etc.	81005	-2.3	0.2	33312	-16.7	0.3
IX	Wood & Articles of Wood	388755	3.3	1.1	73170	11.8	0.6

Contd. ...

...*Contd.* ...

Section	Descrption	India Export Potential ($ '000) 2002	India Annual Growth Rate (%) 1998-2002	India Share in Total (%) 2002	South Africa Export Potential ($ '000) 2002	South Africa Annual Growth Rate (%) 1998-2002	South Africa Share in Total (%) 2002
X	Pulp of wood or of other Fibers	634171	5.6	1.9	323618	1.1	2.6
XI	Textile & Textile Articles	546182	21.0	1.6	279947	7.6	2.3
XII	Footwear, Headgear and Umbrella	8168	-9.8	0.0	5290	-19.9	0.0
XIII	Articles of Stone, Plaster, Cement	164434	14.1	0.5	263346	-2.6	2.1
XIV	Natural or cultured pearls, Jewellery	3783557	2.4	11.2	165		0.0
XV	Base Metals & Articles of Base Metal	1415101	6.7	4.2	627948	11.0	5.1
XVI	Machinery & Mechanical Appliances	3020385	9.3	8.9	2453035	7.6	19.8
XVII	Vehicles, Aircraft and Vessels	1152622	48.4	3.4	2180236	13.5	17.6
XVIII	Optical, Photograph & Cinematography	184409	9.5	0.5	143453	-2.1	1.2
XIX	Arms and Ammunition	831		0.0	0		0.0
XX	Miscellaneous Manufactured Articles	66345	19.0	0.2	123910	18.2	1.0

Export Potential of South Africa in

Section	Descrption	India Export Potential ($ '000) 2002	India Annual Growth Rate (%) 1998-2002	India Share in Total (%) 2002	Brazil Export Potential ($ '000) 2002	Brazil Annual Growth Rate (%) 1998-2002	Brazil Share in Total (%) 2002
I	Live Animals and Animal Products	9227	28.5	0.0	256401	-9.4	0.7
II	Vegetable Products	356496	42.9	1.4	1302576	-8.4	3.7
III	Animal or Vegetable Fats & Oils	526606	57.8	2.1	119998	-13.2	0.3
IV	Prepared Foodstuff, Beverages, etc.	99366	15.9	0.4	316963	-10.5	0.9
V	Mineral Products	3561802	41.1	14.3	3381536	51.9	9.7
VI	Products of Chemicals	2965452	3.5	11.9	4949852	1.0	14.1
VII	Plastics & Articles thereof	766712	7.4	3.1	2089674	-1.4	6.0
VIII	Raw Hides & Skins, Leather, etc.	99473	2.2	0.4	153633	-0.6	0.4
IX	Wood & Articles of Wood	21569	12.1	0.1	19461	-4.5	0.1
X	Pulp of wood or of other Fibers	645876	4.5	2.6	558521	-12.2	1.6
XI	Textile & Textile Articles	646443	25.8	2.6	537822	-12.7	1.5
XII	Footwear, Headgear and Umbrella	16293	-3.1	0.1	64761	-7.8	0.2
XIII	Articles of Stone, Plaster, Cement	155171	20.8	0.6	214750	-1.5	0.6
XIV	Natural or cultured pearls, Jewellery	2411146	18.3	9.7	3789	41.0	0.0
XV	Base Metals & Articles of Base Metal	1817681	5.6	7.3	1795996	-4.5	5.1
XVI	Machinery & Mechanical Appliances	7820542	20.5	31.5	14382165	-3.4	41.1
XVII	Vehicles, Aircraft and Vessels	1646925	64.9	6.6	2965173	-11.4	8.5
XVIII	Optical, Photograph & Cinematography	1141725	12.5	4.6	1697313	-3.0	4.8
XX	Miscellaneous Manufactured Articles	113414	30.9	0.5	199629	-12.5	0.6

Source: RIS based on PCTAS, ITC/WTO/UNSD/UNCTAD, Geveva, 2004.

base metals, machineries, transport and photography in the post-FTA. It is because partner countries have strong export competitiveness in certain sectors; and strong demand for these products already exists for these products in the proposed regional caucus. For example, India is likely to benefit from sectors like chemicals, mineral products, base metals, textiles and vegetable products. Similarly, Brazil and South Africa have export interest in various other sectors in the region

Possibility of Harnessing Export Potential

Though the results show that the proposed countries have substantial trade potential in other partner countries, the realisation of such potentials depends upon the tariff structure of the importing partner. If substantial trade potential is subject to low level of tariff in the market of export destination, then the exporting country may not get any advantage from that amount of export potential. For example, India has large export potential in South Africa, but for those products the tariff level is very high in the latter country. In such a situation, India may not benefit from the regional arrangement since India may not receive any preferential treatment *vis-à-vis* other suppliers to South Africa in the export of those products.

The distribution of export potentials of each IBSA member country in other two partner countries is examined in relation to the prevailing trade policies in importing partner countries. These results are presented in Table 3.8. This may provide the basis for trade liberalisation in the region. As complete trade liberalisation is not possible in the short run, this process may be spread over a couple of phases. For achieving impressive effects of the trade liberalisation programme, liberalisation may be initiated in highly protected products first and may be preceded further to cover less protected products in the subsequent phases. Taking into account the export potentials existing in a country for its partners and its tariff regimes, suitable strategy can be adopted for sectoral trade liberalisation. In this regard, 'negative list' approach may be suitable for 'sectror-by-sector' liberalisation. Protection of specific products is often required because of domestic sensitivity, and these products can be kept out of the framework of negotiations under 'sensitivity list'.

3.7 Trade Targets

The New Delhi Agenda for Cooperation and Plan of Action for IBSA has proposed that the current level of intra-regional trade has to be more than doubled from US$ 4.7 billion to US$10.0 billion by 2007. Based on the IMF statistics, we have found that the share of India in the intra-regional trade of IBSA using exports is 35 per cent in 2002. It is assumed that there may not be a structural shift in terms of intra-regional trade between the partner countries.

...Contd. ...

Projection of Exports to South Africa *(Mil US$)*

Sec	Description	Export 2003	Projection 2007	Growth Rate	Share	Rank
IX	Wood & Articles of Wood	0.2	0.9	55.7	0.0	
X	Pulp of wood or of other Fibers	3.8	18.1	75.2	1.0	
XI	Textile & Textile Articles	87.2	408.5	73.7	23.4	1
XII	Footwear, Headgear and Umbrella	2.5	10.7	65.3	0.6	
XIII	Articles of Stone, Plaster, Cement	5.0	19.2	57.0	1.1	
XIV	Natural or cultured pearls, Jewellery	6.3	32.1	82.6	1.8	9
XV	Base Metals & Articles of Base Metal	33.1	154.0	73.0	8.8	4
XVI	Machinery & Mechanical Appliances	25.5	113.2	68.8	6.5	6
XVII	Vehicles, Aircraft and Vessels	25.8	130.6	81.2	7.5	5
XVIII	Optical, Photograph & Cinematography	4.6	22.0	75.1	1.3	
XX	Miscellaneous Manufactured Articles	4.6	20.5	68.4	1.2	
XXI	Works of Art Collectors' Pieces	6.7	31.4	73.4	1.8	9
	TOTAL	475.7	1743.0	53.3	100.0	

NB: Revised Projection Based on DGCI&S Data.

Source: RIS based on PCTAS, ITC/WTO/UNSD/UNCTAD, Geveva, 2004.

The past experience shows that the export basket of India is considerably diversified for both South Africa and Brazil. In 2002-03, India's exports to Brazil and South Africa were US$ 476.9 million and US$ 475.7 million, respectively. The trends of India's bilateral exports to the partners in IBSA suggest that exports are taking place for large number of products to each destination, but there is lack of persistence in bilateral exports in substantial number of products, leading to year-to-year fluctuations in the overall bilateral exports of India to these countries. Moreover, India's bilateral exports are mostly concentrated in selected number of products *vis-à-vis* both the partner countries. In recent times, it is noticed that some of the dominant products are becoming important in shaping the overall magnitude of bilateral exports of India with its partners. For example, India's bilateral export of rice (HS 100630) to South Africa[33] and certain type of petroleum product (HS 271000) to Brazil[34] constitute 30.7 per cent and 53 per cent of total bilateral export to these countries, respectively in 2002-03. While making projection for India's exports to IBSA countries in 2007-08 based on Delhi Action Plan, we have included the above structural factors in the estimation exercise.

33. India exported US$ 146 million worth of semi-milled or wholly milled rice (whether or not polished or glazed, HS 100630) to South Africa in 2002-03.

34. In the same year, India exported petroleum oils and oils obtained from bituminous minerals (other than crude; preparations not elsewhere specified or included, containing by weight 70 per cent or more of petroleum oils, HS 271000) to the extent of US$ 253 million to Brazil for the first time between 1997-1998 and 2002-03.

India's export projection for the IBSA partner countries in 2007-08 is estimated, using bilateral export behaviour of India for the period 1997/98-2002/2003. For projections, all products are grouped into: (a) lead export item (LEI), (b) dominant products (in terms of share in total exports to a partner country) and (c) small export items (SEI). Using these criteria, projections are made separately for individual products at 6-digit HS. For both the countries, we found one product for each partner as India's dominant export. In the bilateral exports of India to both the countries about 76 and 151 products are considered as LEI for Brazil and South Africa, respectively.

For meeting the New Delhi Action goal, India's exports to both Brazil and South Africa would need to double by the year 2007-08. In both the countries, the lead export sectors of India will not be significantly different. While lead sectors in India's export to Brazil are likely to be chemical products (Section VI), mineral products (Section V), textiles (Section XI), plastic products (Section VII), etc, similar sectors for South Africa may be textile & textile articles (Section XI), vegetable products (Section II), products of chemicals (Section VI), base metals & articles of base metal (Section XV), machinery & mechanical appliances (Section XVI), etc. It may be noted that India's export to Brazil is likely to grow in selected sectors, and therefore growth targets are set at a higher level in those sectors than others. However, the situation relating to India's exports to South Africa is different from that of Brazil, and projected growth targets for different export sectors in South Africa are likely to be less skewed than Brazil.

3.8 Non-Tariff Barriers

The study finds significant non-tariff barriers impeding mutual trade in the grouping. Some of the NTBs identified by the study are as follows:

Issues Specific to Brazil

Payment Problems

Despite reforms in the financial sector Indian firms are having payment problems relating to the absence of line of credit and long time taken for clearance while dealing with Brazilian counterparts. While more than 180 day LC exists, counterpart bank normally do not provide credit if the buyers are not credible.

High Cost of Insurance & Transportation

Apart from higher cost of transportation involved in India-Brazil trade, as per Brazilian laws, for commodities imported by sea, maritime transportation insurance contracts should be made by the importers, in which case the insurance premium should be 1.5 per cent of the total import value. Such premium levels run far higher than the international average, 0.3 per cent, which subsequently discouraged the price advantage of the imported commodities.

Perception Gaps and Lack of Business Information

Very often a major factor that stands in the way of trade is the lack of information or presence of misinformation. The Indian products, especially in Brazil, are perceived to be low quality. To overcome this constraint, there is the need for bringing together the trading communities in the three countries. Much could be achieved in this direction by initiating annual IBSA trade fairs, with the location rotating among them.

Issues Specific to South Africa

Anti-dumping Duties

It is understood that Indian companies are faced with anti-dumping duties from South Africa and no procedural regulations have been issued for handling the anti-dumping/anti-subsidy complaints. There are other discriminatory practices being followed by South African Board against Indian goods, such as carpets by reducing duty on Iranian carpets.

Tendering Practices

While Indian pharmaceutical companies are more used to supply on tender basis, South African Government tends to invite bids directly from supplier. Therefore, while Indian pharmaceutical companies would be in a position to supply, they are left out of the supply process.

Lack of Institutional Mechanism

Though there is substantial number of trade complaints from Indian companies, absence of any South African authority dealing with trade complaints from Indian businessmen has put some of the Indian companies in prolonged correspondence without any results. A number of trade disputes arise due to lack of quality control, shortages in packing and supply and non-payment by buyers.

Issues Common to Brazil and South Africa

Harmonising Standards

India, Brazil and South Africa have their own regulatory import controls based on standards and conformity assessment procedures, specifically from the standpoint of health and safety. In this context, recognition of conformity assessment procedures between them for the purposes of meeting their respective regulatory requirements represents convenient method of reducing non-tariff barriers to trade. This will call for assessing the present situation with respect to the compatibility of each other's standards and enter into mutual recognition with regard to standards and conformity assessment activities. Hence, there is also the need for the standards and export inspection bodies of IBSA to work together for harmonisation and mutual recognition of conformity assessment procedures.

Customs Procedures

Also, there is the need for harmonisation of customs procedures regarding the tendering, importer registration, shipment, customs and port-clearance, etc. This in turns calls for bringing together the customs authorities of IBSA to discuss ways and means of standardising their procedures.

Lack of Business Interaction

An IBSA Business Forum could be set up to bring together the business community in the three countries to promote trade and investment. Such a business forum may be complemented with sectoral bodies especially covering those industries/sectors where the trade and investment potential is higher. Such bodies would facilitate formation of strategic alliances between the enterprises of the region to exploit their synergy for not only the regional markets but also for third country investments and trade opportunities.

3.9 Steps Towards Achieving Trade Targets

IBSA Comprehensive Economic Partnership Arrangement

The possibility of having CEC between India, Brazil and South Africa is more of a legal than a policy issue. According to GATT Article XXIV, the basic difference between PTA/FTA and Customs Union is the issue of common external tariff. Under the Customs Union, a member country cannot have the right to change the external tariff, which will put other countries in the caucus in a disadvantageous situation. As individual members are closely linked with other members of the customs union, the group has to negotiate with other countries for preferential trade. The EU has been following the similar practice, while pursuing the policy of preferential trade.

Considering that Brazil and South Africa are members of regional customs unions namely MERCOSUR and SACU respectively, there are constraints in evolving a trilateral FTA within the IBSA framework. That does not preclude, however, evolving a preferential trading regime. India has already signed a framework agreement with MERCOSUR which will provide a preferential trade regime to India-Brazil trade. A similar initiative is being worked out with SACU. With these agreements in place, India's trade with both South Africa and Brazil will have a preferential trading regime.

IBSA constitutes a large and expanding economic space where in the total two-way trade is close to US$ 540 billion currently. The share of intra-IBSA trade in their total trade has been approximately 2.6 per cent (about US$ 7 billion) in 2005. The New Delhi Action Plan has put an ambitious goal for doubling the mutual trade by 2007. To achieve this target several measures will be necessary. To exploit the synergies and potential of cooperation for mutual benefit, IBSA countries can explore an **IBSA Comprehensive Economic Partnership Arrangement** covering the following aspects among others:

An India-MERCOSUR-SACU FTA

At the Ministerial Meeting of IBSA in New Delhi in March 2005, it was decided to work towards evolving an FTA between the three countries. Preliminary RIS simulations suggest that a free trade agreement between the three countries has a potential of increasing mutual trade but the distribution of gains would be asymmetric and Brazil and South Africa would benefit more than India (keeping in mind the existing tariff structures and the potential of trade creation). Furthermore, a trilateral FTA between India-Brazil-South Africa may not be technically feasible as Brazil and South Africa are members of customs unions (*viz.*, MERCOSUR and SACU respectively) and hence are bound to maintain common external tariffs with other partners. Therefore, we may consider evolving an IBSA Free Trading Arrangement (IBSA FTA) between India-MERCOSUR-SACU. This FTA could subsume the ongoing negotiations between India-MERCOSUR and India-SACU PTAs. This way we could have a framework for mutual trade taking place on a preferential basis besides giving access to even other members of the respective customs unions.

An FTA covering India-MERCOSUR-SACU by giving access of markets of other SACU and MERCOSUR countries other than Brazil and South Africa, may also neutralise some of the asymmetries in trade with respect of Brazil and South Africa. The scope of FTA could be extended to cover trade in services and investments on positive list basis so that some asymmetries in the goods trade can be neutralised in the services trade. However, in view of asymmetric benefits resulting from FTA, as suggested by the preliminary study indicated above, it may be prudent to move in a cautious manner. It is important that a detailed analysis is conducted of the gains and losses in terms of market access expected and given so that an attempt can be made to maximise the gains and minimise the adverse effects.

Generally, the launch of negotiations of FTAs are preceded by setting up of Joint Study Groups (JSGs) involving academics and officials of the partner countries. The JSGs are able to make detailed studies of the trade potential and also suggest the framework for a potential agreement. Realising the institutional difficulties in forming IBSA-FTA, the member countries have agreed setting up of an IBSA Joint Study Group to examine the relevance and prepare a blue print or elements of an IBSA FTA within an agreed time frame. The JSG Report after adoption by the member governments could provide a basis for launching negotiations.

The JSG could have broad terms of reference, e.g. detailed feasibility of an FTA, scope and coverage of an FTA, elements of a proposed FTA, the negotiating group (whether limited to IBSA countries or also the representatives of other MERCOSUR and SACU members). JSG should also examine the possibility of a comprehensive economic partnership agreement besides FTA and hence examine and propose other areas of cooperation, e.g. in trade facilitation, investment facilitation, promotion of trade in services, potential of sectoral cooperation and institutional mechanisms for their promotion, promoting exchange of experiences in development and networking of think tanks, framework for cooperation in multilateral forums, among others, as summarised in this study. At present, India is also examining different aspects of a comprehensive economic cooperation within the SACU-India-MERCOSUR framework and the opportunities for other countries of SACU and MERCOSUR in the new trade initiative (RIS, 2007).

IBSA Trade Facilitation Framework (IBSA TFF)

The IBSA FTA may be supplemented by a IBSA TFF focusing on identifying and eliminating the non-tariff barriers and evolving a framework for trade facilitation. This study finds that significant non-tariff barriers impede mutual trade in the grouping. Some of the NTBs identified by the study are as follows:

Harmonising Conformity Assessment Procedures and Standards

IBSA member countries have their own regulatory import controls based on standards and conformity assessment procedures, specifically from the standpoint of health and safety. Mutual recognition of conformity assessment procedures between them for the purposes of meeting their respective regulatory requirements represent convenient method of reducing non-tariff barriers to trade. There is a need for assessing the present situation with respect to the compatibility of each other's standards and enter into mutual recognition arrangements with regard to standards and conformity assessment activities. In this context, the standard and export inspection bodies of IBSA may have to work together for harmonisation and mutual recognition of conformity assessment procedures.

Customs Procedures

Taking into account the ground reality in IBSA, harmonisation of customs procedures regarding the tendering, importer registration, shipment, customs and port-clearance, etc., needs to be given priority. This in turns calls for bringing together the customs authorities of IBSA to discuss ways and means of standardising their procedures.

Addressing the Lack of Business Information and Perception Gaps

The lack of information has been the major impediment for the surge of trade among IBSA countries. The Indian products, especially in Brazil, are perceived to be of low quality. To overcome this constraint there is the need for bringing together the trading communities in the three countries. Much could be achieved in this direction by initiating annual IBSA trade fairs with the location rotating among them. An **IBSA Business Forum** could also be set up to bring together the business community in the three countries to promote trade and investment. Such a business forum may be complemented with sectoral bodies especially covering those industries/sectors where the trade and investment potential is higher. Such bodies would facilitate formation of strategic alliances between the enterprises of the region to exploit their synergy for not only the regional markets but also for third country investments and trade opportunities. This Business Forum could also deal with trade disputes with respective governmental bodies involved in IBSA trade and also take up other issues such as problems concerning LCs, and high cost of insurance, as observed in Brazil or certain anti-dumping or other discriminatory practices as observed in South Africa.

CHAPTER 4

Trade in Services

Potential and Prospects

4.1 Introduction

Trade between developing countries has been growing rapidly in recent years following significant reductions in tariff barriers (UNCTAD, 2007). Services have become the single largest sector in many developing countries (WTO, 2001, 2004, 2006; UNCTAD, 2004c). Developing countries have not only achieved a robust growth in trade in services (23.16 per cent in 2004) but also surpassed the same recorded by the developed countries (15.59 per cent).[1] Services make up a major portion of the world economy. Measured both in terms of growth and share, global trade in services has risen spectacularly during 1981 to 2004. On average, the rate of growth of global trade in services is found to be higher than the rate of growth in goods during the last two decades. Leading role of services in the domestic economy coupled with the recent trends in world trade wherein growth of service trade exceeding merchandise trade point towards the emerging potential of trade in services in IBSA.[2]

During the recent past, there has been major structural change in world economy resulting which service sector has emerged as the leading sector accounting for 2/3rd of world production, 1/3rd of global employment and about 1/5th of world trade.[3] The services sector's expansion has been attributed to demand as well as supply factors. On the one hand, demand for many services is highly income elastic, i.e. as people grow richer, their consumption of services such as tourism, education and health expands more rapidly than their demand for

---

1. Calculated based on UNCTAD (2005)
2. Refer, Gabriele (2004), which provides an excellent illustration of the trends in international trade in services for the last two decades.
3. Calculated based on World Bank (2006)

manufactures and agricultural products. To a certain degree, the growing share of services in GDP also reflects structural changes in an economy. Services sector not only provide the bulk of employment and income in many countries, it also serves as vital input for producing other goods and services. An efficient services sector is not only crucial for the overall economy but also critical to the competitiveness of a country. The importance of services is therefore increasingly reflected in the policy agenda—ranging from liberalisation to promotional efforts to regulation at national and international levels (WTO, 2006).[4]

Countries in IBSA are services-driven; the service sector has emerged as the leading sector accounting for more than 50 per cent of the GDP in IBSA countries. The opportunities in the field of service trade and cooperation between IBSA in different service sectors cannot be over emphasised. Given the policy reforms undertaken by these countries unilaterally and in the context of WTO, the environment today appears to be more conducive than ever before for mutually beneficial cooperation.

Having examined the relative competitive position as well as the potential in merchandise, let us now proceed to explore the trends and patterns in trade in services to identify the plausible areas of cooperation. In the present chapter, we shall begin with an examination of the current policies governing service trade and their commitments under GATS with special focus on Mode 1 and Mode 4. Then, we proceed to explore the potential for service trade among these three countries by analysing the growth of domestic service sector on the one hand and trade in different segment of services on the other. The competitiveness of the three countries is analysed by estimating the revealed comparative advantage in different service segment. Finally, a select number of service sectors have been identified for trilateral cooperation.

4.2 Service Sector Reforms in IBSA

During the last decade, the service sector in all the three countries have been subjected to substantial liberalisation as manifested in the removal of barriers to trade and investment in different segments of the service sector. The underlying economic rationale for these policy reforms are not too far to seek. The removal of barriers to trade in services is likely to result in lower prices, improved quality, and greater variety. As with trade in goods, restrictions on trade in services reduce welfare because they create a wedge between domestic and foreign prices, leading to a loss to consumer surplus that could be greater than any benefit to producer surplus and government revenue. Furthermore, as countries reduce tariffs and other

4. A good numbers of studies explore why it would be beneficial for developing countries to actively participate in the services negotiation associated with the General Agreement on Trade in Services (GATS). For example, one can refer, Chaudhuri *et al.*, (2004), and Charlton and Stiglitz (2005), on global services trade issues, and Sung (2004), on country specific issues.

barriers to trade, effective rates of protection for manufacturing industries may become negative if they continue to be confronted with input prices that are higher than they would be if services markets were competitive. Another major benefit of liberalisation in services is the access to a wider variety of such services and consumers may derive not only a direct benefit from diversity in services such as healthcare, restaurants and entertainment, but also an indirect benefit on account of a wider variety of more specialised producer services, such as telecommunications and finance. This can lower the costs of both goods and services production. Estimates of such benefits vary for individual countries—from under 1 per cent to over 50 per cent of GDP depending on the initial levels of protection and the assumed reduction in barriers (World Bank, 2004a). Moreover, the gains from liberalising services may be substantially greater than those from liberalising trade in goods, because current levels of protection in many countries are higher and could create greater spillover benefits

Certain service industries clearly possess growth-generating characteristics. A competitive and well-regulated financial sector leads to the efficient transformation of savings to investment, ensuring that resources are deployed wherever they have the highest returns; and facilitates better risk-sharing in the economy. Improved efficiency in telecommunications generates economy-wide benefits, as this service is a vital intermediate input and also crucial to the dissemination and diffusion of knowledge. Business services such as accounting and legal services are important in reducing transaction costs.

Service Sector Reforms in Brazil

As part of the liberalisation process that swept the Brazilian economy during the last decade, there has been wide ranging reforms in almost all segments of the service sector. This in turn has had the effect of attracting substantial foreign investment into the service sector mainly as a part of the privatisation programme of the government. However, privatisation and liberalisation programmes are yet to reach some sectors. The constitutional changes to open partially the activities such as telecommunication and maritime transport were appreciated but concerns were raised on remaining constraints to foreign investment, particularly in banking and insurance. The examination and approval procedures for foreign banks to establish a branch are quite complicated. The lowest statutory capital requirement for foreign banks or foreign companies to control a Brazilian multifunctional bank or commercial bank is two times as that for a Brazilian bank. The access to the local market by foreign firms in both sectors is considered on a case-by-case basis. Brazil has made a constitutional amendment ending the monopoly on insurance and opening it to private participation, as well as the Government's interest in promoting foreign participation in health insurance. In telecommunication, a new law had been approved allowing foreign participation, rising to 100 per cent from

July 1999, in cellular, satellite and cable services; new contracts awarded in early 1997.

Remaining Barriers

The reforms notwithstanding there are certain explicit barriers to trade that exist today. In a sense, barriers to trade in services are more complex and less visible than tariffs. These barriers include quantitative restrictions on provision of services by foreigners—ranging from cargo sharing in transport services, limits on number of suppliers in telecommunication and banking to restrictions on the movement of service providing personnel that effect trade in all services. Sometimes, these quantitative restrictions prevent entry by a new supplier (both foreign and local) where a public monopoly exists.

In addition, there are a number of explicit discriminations against foreign providers through taxes and subsidies as well as by allowing less favourable access to essential services such as ports, airports and telecommunications networks. It has also been shown that there are certain measures that require specific types of legal entity through which a foreign service provider may supply a service, and limitation on the participation of foreign capital and foreign nationals in entities supplying services in Brazil.[5]

In general, following World Bank (2004b), the sectoral policy regime for different categories of services may be grouped as follows.

The first category consists of those sectors where few expressive barriers to foreign participation exist. This includes telecommunication and distribution system, and various business services such as management consultancy, advertising, software, database and data processing services.

The second category covers sector with uncertain policy environment but that are *de facto* quite liberal. This includes financial services, where participation by foreign financial institution is constitutionally prohibited, but where liberal exits for foreign providers have nevertheless been granted on the basis of an exception specified in the constitution.

The third category includes sectors where explicit barriers are pervasive. This includes transport services where market access is generally determined by bilateral original agreements between trading partners, Audio visual services—subject to restrictions on cross border provision, foreign investment and employment of foreigners; constructions services—subject to nationality and technology transfer obligations; and professional services—subject to quotas on foreign professionals.

The final category, which is closed, includes postal and reinsurance services

5. See for a detailed discussion World Bank (2004b).

which are provided by public monopolies services, although express mail and courier services are open to domestic and foreign competition.

Service Sector Reforms in South Africa

There has been a historical legacy of concentrated ownership in some sectors of the South African economy. During the apartheid years, a large portion of the South African population was entirely excluded from ownership of business enterprises. Moreover, government policies from 1961 to 1994 prohibited some successful companies such as South African Breweries, Anglo American (including DeBeers) and SASOL from investing abroad. They, therefore, expanded their activities locally. As a result, conglomerates with considerable market power developed in the South African marketplace. This situation has been changing, as many of the major players have been expanding internationally and have listed on foreign stock exchanges. Together, with more effective competition authority and strong sectoral initiatives to enlarge the share of black participation in the economy, South Africa's business environment is becoming more competitive and more open to new entrants.

Sectors such as energy, transport and telecommunication have also historically been controlled or dominated by parastatals. As part of the policy reforms, these sectors are gradually being restructured and opened for competition from the private sector. The privatisation programme of the South African government, although moving slowly, is also starting to bring a change in ownership patterns.

Government purchases are by competitive tender for project, supply, and other contracts. The South African government uses its position as both buyer and lawmaker, however, to promote the economic empowerment of historically disadvantaged individuals (HDIs) through its Black Economic Empowerment (BEE) programme. Regulations set a legal framework and formula for allowing preference points to HDIs when tendering for a government procurement contract. Points are awarded based on such criteria as a percentage of HDI ownership and the percentage of HDI managers.

Financial Sector

South Africa's formal banks comply with international banking standards and offer one of the most sophisticated banking systems in the developing world. Customers have online, real-time, nationwide access to bank accounts 24 hours a day, 365 days a year despite the fact that 80 per cent of the country's economically active population remains un-banked. In May 1995, amendments to the Banks Act permitted foreign banks to conduct banking operations via branches, ending the earlier requirement that they establish subsidiaries. Any person, whether South African or foreigner, may control a bank. There are three alternatives for conducting banking operations in South Africa (all of which require prior approval of the Registrar of Banks, who heads up the Bank Supervision Division): a separate banking company, a branch of an international bank or banking group, and a representative office of an international bank. The participation of foreign banks in the local banking industry has been found to be about 6.9 per cent of the total banking sector assets by the end of December 2002. South African banks maintained adequate levels of liquidity despite liquidity strains experienced by the system during the first half of 2002.

The Financial Services Board (FSB) governs South Africa's sophisticated non-banking financial services industry. The FSB regulates insurance, pension funds, unit trusts (i.e., mutual funds), participation bond schemes, portfolio management, and the financial markets. The financial markets consist of The JSE Securities Exchange SA[6] and The Bond Exchange of South Africa.[7] The JSE is the 16th largest exchange measured by capitalisation in the world. At the end of 2002, the market capitalisation stood at around $182 billion (R1.6 trillion) with a total of 472 firms listed. This is much larger than all the exchanges in Africa combined. The Bond Exchange of South Africa (BESA) regulates the fixed-interest securities market and is licenced under the Financial Markets Control Act. Membership includes banks, insurers, investors, stockbrokers, and independent intermediaries. The bond exchange consists principally of government bonds with some bonds from government parastatals also available. There is a growing corporate bond sector, however, as more companies seek to raise capital through this mechanism.

Financial services in South Africa are characterised by extensive interlocking shareholding relationships between the major banks and the large insurance companies. The securities markets are well developed. Total assets held by the financial sub-sector represented the equivalent of about 370 per cent of GDP, with banks accounting for roughly 27 per cent of total assets. Non-residents' participation in the securities and stock markets has increased sharply. The JSE began permitting foreign banks and firms to join its registry in November 1995.

Telecommunications

South Africa has made a series of WTO commitments on value-added telecommunications and basic telecommunication services and has adopted the WTO reference paper on pro-competitive regulatory principles. The South African government is also committed to licence a second supplier no later than January 1, 2004, to compete against the current monopoly supplier, Telkom, in long-distance, data, telex, fax, and private leased circuits services. Despite the end of Telkom's exclusivity period in May 2002, Telkom has been able to continue its monopoly because of the absence of a second network operator. Nineteen per cent of the

---

6. Refer, *www.jse.co.za*

7. Refer, *www.bondex.co.za*

shares of the new operator will be reserved for BEE groups and 30 per cent will be allocated to the telecommunications divisions of Eskom (the state energy utility) and Transnet (the transport parastatal), which already have some infrastructure in place. Equity interest from either foreign or domestic investors in the second national operator (SNO) will make up the remaining 51 per cent and provide capital and technical expertise needed to compete with the incumbent operator.

In November 2003, the Minister of Communications announced that the government would licence the SNO and would name an equity partner by the end of the year. In December 2003, the Minister of Communications announced that 26 per cent of the equity in the SNO would be sold to a combined entity of two consortia. These consortia originally applied separately for the equity stake in the SNO. The remaining 25 per cent is retained by the government and warehoused for the foreseeable future. This decision allowed the SNO to move forward and allowed South Africa to meet the WTO deadline of having a competitor to Telkom in place by January 1, 2004. The initial public offering (IPO) for the partly privatised Telkom took place in March 2003 when it was listed on both the Johannesburg Stock Exchange and the New York Stock Exchange.

Internet Service Providers (ISPs) and value-added network services (VANS) have cited problems with Telkom in the past. Telkom refused to provide new facilities to VANS operators, claiming that VANS and ISPs are resellers of basic services and thus were infringing on Telkom's monopoly. This problem is made even more acute by South Africa's failure to liberalise resale services between 2000 and 2003, as it committed to do under its WTO schedule on basic telecommunications. South Africa's telecommunications regulatory authority, ICASA, has sole authority to determine whether these services are illegal. In the past, service providers have complained about ICASA ineffectiveness in asserting its authority over Telkom and have pursued remedies in the Pretoria High Court. Telkom also often challenges decisions taken by ICASA, leading to delays in implementing rulings. The Amended Telecommunications Act of 2001 allows only Telkom and the SNO to provide voice over Internet protocol (VOIP) services, and it appears to expand the definition of a public switched telecommunications service (PSTS) to include the provision, repair, and maintenance of any other telecommunications apparatus. The Ministry of Communications is considering legislation that will strengthen the regulatory authority of ICASA.

South Africa passed an electronic commerce bill on July 31, 2002, designed to encourage use of the Internet in business transactions. The new law is controversial because of the uncertainty of its impact on the ".za" domain name, Internet retailing, encryption providers, unsolicited e-mail, and government access to private databases. For example, the bill would give the South African government sole control of the ".za" domain name in contrast to international norms, and would require retailers to provide a mandatory seven-day return policy for all products, including music and software.

Electronic Commerce

Effective July 31, 2002, all companies that conduct business in South Africa via electronic commerce must comply with the new Electronic Communications and Transactions Law. The new law was designed to facilitate electronic commerce but may increase regulatory burdens and introduce uncertainty into the future of electronic commerce in the country. The law requires government accreditation for certain electronic signatures, takes government control of the ".za" domain name, and requires a long list of disclosures for web sites that sell *via* the Internet.

Immigration Laws

It has been shown that South African immigration legislation and the application of the law made it extremely difficult to get work permits for their foreign employees. Previously, South Africa relied on the apartheid-era Aliens Control Act, which did not take into account international developments and the opening up of the South African market. A new immigration law entered into force on May 31, 2002. The legislation establishes yearly quotas for granting work permits to foreigners. Local businesses have criticised the new law for creating uncertainty because the quota system sets limit on the number of skilled people in particular categories that may enter the country, and because corporate permits allow investors to make blanket applications for the people they need, it is not clear whether these corporate permits fall in or out of the quota system.

The Trade and Industry Minister suggested that the South African government may need to revise the law to acquire critically needed skills in South Africa. Home Affairs officials oppose moving away from quotas because it might mean reverting to the Aliens Control Act, wherein an employer had to establish the clear need for a skill. The Minister of Home Affairs has said that the new law is an enormous improvement over the previous legislation and places South Africa on a par with other countries, especially with respect to investors and intra-company transfer permits.

4.3 WTO Commitments by IBSA

The GATS service sector commitments of the three countries are: 60 by Brazil, 37 for India, while South Africa has made 91 commitments.[8] Table 4.1 enumerates the commitments of the three countries under the GATS agreement in terms of the horizontal commitments of the countries.

With respect to Mode 1, Brazil has limitations on market access in accounting, auditing and book keeping;[9] architectural services; engineering services;

---

8. See WTO, at *www://stat.wto.org/Country Profiles*

9. Participation of non-residents in legal sectors controlled by Brazilian nationals is not allowed. Special registration requirements for accountants who wish to audit such companies as financial institutions and savings and loan associations in case of national treatment.

TABLE 4.1

Summary of WTO Commitments by IBSA with respect to Mode 1 and Mode 4

		Brazil	*India*	*South Africa*
Mode 4	Movement of Natural Persons	MA: Unbound except for measures related to specialised technicians, highly qualified professionals, managers and directors. NT: unbound except as indicated in the market access.	MA: Unbound except for measures affecting the entry and temporary stay of natural persons such as business visitors; intra-corporate transferees including managers, executives and specialists; professionals. NT: Unbound except as indicated under market access.	MA: Unbound except for temporary presence for a period of up to three years, unless otherwise specified without requiring compliance with an economic needs test, of the services salespersons; intra-corporate transferees including executives, managers, specialists, and professionals; personnel engaged in establishment.
Mode 3	Investment	MA: All foreign capital invested in Brazil must be registered with the Central bank of Brazil. NT: None.	NT: In case of collaboration with public sector enterprises or government undertaking as joint venture partners, preference in access will be given to foreign service suppliers which offer the best terms for transfer of technology.	NT: Local borrowing by South African registered companies with a non-resident shareholding of 25 per cent or more is limited.
	Commercial Presence	MA: Must be organised as a legal entity seen by the Brazilian law. NT: None		
Modes 1, 2		Unbound		

Source: RIS based on WTO.

and advertising services and services related to management consulting.[10] Other limitations on Brazilian markets pertain to insurance; where restriction on market access relate to freight insurance, life insurance, medical care, property insurance, liability insurance and auxiliary services.[11] In case of banking, acceptance of funds from the public in the form of demand deposits, time deposits and financing of

10. Foreign service suppliers must join Brazilian service suppliers in a specific type of legal entity (consorcio); the limitations on market access for engineering services is the same as with architectural services. In case of advertising services, foreign participation is limited to 49 per cent of the capital of companies established in Brazil. In addition, foreign producers must live at least 3 years in Brazil before being authorised to produce films. With regard to services relating to management, consulting companies must be registered with the Regional Council of Administrators.

11. On all of these except auxiliary services (which are open only to natural persons), specific type of legal entity is required. Foreign participation is limited to 50 per cent of the capital of a company and to one-third of the voting stock.

commercial transactions are subject to certain restrictions.[12] Such restrictions are also applicable to participation in public issues of all kinds of securities including underwriting and placement agent and provision of services related to such issues. Limitations on market access also exist in case of rail[13] and road freight[14] and limitations on national treatment exist in hotels and restaurants.[15]

The MFN exemptions enjoyed by Brazil include audiovisual/motion picture and videotape production and apply to all countries; land transport, maritime transport, ocean shipping (cargo), and telecommunication services supplied for distribution of radio or television programming for direct reception by service consumers.

In the case of South Africa, limitations on market access apply to legal services,[16] telecommunications,[17] direct insurance,[18] and in certain categories of banking and other financial services.[19] Apart from that, in auditing, citizenship is required for accreditation.

Commitments of India in WTO

India has been playing a pro-active role in liberalisation of services trade

12. The limitations on market access apply to the establishment of new branches and subsidiaries of foreign financial institutions as well as increases in the percentage of the participation of foreign persons and firms in the capital stock of Brazilian financial institutions that are not permitted. Individual network for ATMs may be set up only by Brazilian banks and minimum requirements for paid-in capital and net worth applicable to branches of foreign banks and those banks controlled by foreign capital are twice those established for Brazilian banks.

13. Government authorisation required and the number of service suppliers may be limited.

14. Foreign participation is limited to one-fifth of the voting shares of Brazilian companies engaged in this activity.

15. While Brazilian firms operating in the Amazon and North-eastern region benefit from certain tax credit incentives, firms with majority of capital held by Brazilian citizen also enjoy other incentives.

16. An advocate is not allowed to form a partnership/company.

17. Foreign investment in suppliers permitted up to a cumulative maximum of 30 per cent in case of packet switched data transmission services and other services like paging services, mobile cellular, and satellite based services. In the case of electronic mail, there are general limitations on the bypass of South African facilities for routing of domestic and international traffic.

18. All insurers need to be incorporated as a public company in South Africa and registered with the supervisory authority to carry on insurance business in South Africa. The acquisition of shares or any other interest in a registered insurer resulting in the holding of 25 per cent or more of the value of all shares or other interest in that business requires the written approval of the Registrar of Insurance. Apart from this the executive chairman, public officer and the majority of directors must be resident in South Africa and life insurance actuaries must also be resident in South Africa.

19. In banking and other financial services accepting of deposits and other repayable funds from the public, all dealings in foreign exchange must be carried out through a dealer authorised by the SA Reserve Bank and national treatment is restricted to branches of bank not incorporated in South Africa which maintain a minimum balance of R 1 million on the deposit accounts of natural persons. In lending of all types as well as payments and money transmission services including credit, charge and debit cards, traveler cheques and bank drafts have limitations on market access for foreigners exist, only banks registered to operate in South Africa with the minimum capital base are eligible to seek authorisation as foreign exchange dealer. Companies involved in asset management, collective investment schemes and custodial services and financial instruments for securities and financial instruments need to be incorporated as public companies in South Africa and registered with the supervisory authority to carry on business in South Africa.

since Doha Round of multilateral trade negotiations under GATS.[20] In services negotiations, one of India's major objectives is to achieve better access for the country's service suppliers. The Modes of supply of interest to India are generally Mode 1 and Mode 4.

India had undertaken commitments at the end of Uruguay Round (1994). In Doha Round, commitments were taken only in 33 sub-sectors and while taking commitments a number of limitations on market access and national treatment were made in the schedules consistent with our national policy objectives. In most cases, these were no more than the autonomously liberalised policies already in force in India.

For India, limitations on market access exist in engineering services, consultancy services, R&D services[21], technical testing and analysis services, data and message transmission services, construction work for civil engineering, hospitals, hotels and other lodging services, travel agencies and tour operators. In all these cases foreign equity can be held through incorporation with an equity ceiling of 51 per cent. Communication services are also subject to limitations on market access; this includes the category voice telephone service, circuit switched data transmission services, facsimile services, private leased circuit services and cellular mobile telephone services. Audiovisual services i.e. motion pictures or video tape distribution services[22] have limitations on market access as also certain categories of insurance[23] and banking and other financial services.[24]

Under the Doha Round of services negotiations, India submitted its conditional Initial Offer at WTO in January 2004. In the Initial Offer, India

---

20. The country has even played a pivotal role in the Hong Kong Ministerial Meeting of 2005 by incorporating Annex C into the main draft of the Agenda (see, Government of India, 2006b).

21. Only on the natural sciences dealing with heat, light, electromagnetism, astronomy, but excluding atomic energy and related matters, engineering and technology including applied science and technology for casting, metal machinery, electricity, communications, vessels, aircrafts, civil engineering, construction, information etc. However this category is unbound due to lack of technical feasibility.

22. Market access limitations exist and such services can be offered by foreigners only through representative offices, which will be allowed to function as branches of companies incorporated outside India. Limitations on national treatment exist and are subject to the prescribed authority having certified that the motion picture has won an award in any of the international film festivals notified by the Ministry of Information and Broadcasting or participated in any of the official sections of the notified international film festivals or received good reviews in prestigious film journals notified by the Ministry of Information and Broadcasting.

23. Insurance intermediation limited to reinsurance, in which case overseas brokers are allowed to have resident representatives and representative offices that can procure reinsurance business from Indian insurance companies to the extent mentioned above. They can also place reinsurance business from abroad with Indian insurance companies. However, except for the business indicated above the resident representatives and representatives cannot undertake any other activity in India. All expenses of the resident representatives and representative offices have to be met by remittances from abroad and no income can be received in India from Indian residents.

24. Acceptance of deposits and other repayable funds from the public and lending of all types including consumer credit, mortgage credit and financing of commercial transactions but excluding factoring are subject to limitations on market access and can operate only through branch operations of a foreign bank licenced and supervised as a bank in its home country. Grant of licence as permissible under existing laws.

substantially improved access in critical service sectors and offered commitments in 47 sub-sectors. India also submitted its Revised Offer at WTO on August 24, 2005. Building further on the improvements in the initial offer, India has offered to undertake extensive commitments in a number of new sectors/sub-sectors and also improved its existing commitments in various service sectors and modes. Under Mode 4, India already made improvements to its commitments by including Contractual Service suppliers and Independent professionals in the Initial Offer, the definitions and conditions of which were later further refined in the Revised Offer.

In the recent past, Mode 3 also appeared as important for India because of overseas expansion of a number of Indian companies (e.g. banking: ICICI, State Bank; Pharmaceutical: Dr. Reddy's Laboratory, Ranbaxy; Non-Conventional Energy: Suzlon; Telecom: VSNL, Reliance; and IT: Infosys, TCS, WIPRO), among others.

India is a proponent of liberalisation of trade in services through Mode 4. In order to promote the liberalisation of Mode 4, India has submitted negotiating proposals at the WTO.[25] The Indian proposal notes that the developed member countries have taken limited commitments in Mode 4, which is of significant interest to developing countries. These commitments are further reduced in scope on account of various measures taken by developed member countries, such as economic needs test (ENT); restrictive visa regimes; non-recognition of qualifications, etc. The proposal suggested various strategies for improving access for Indian service providers such as transparency in the visa regimes, creation of a separate GATS visa different and less onerous from the normal immigration visa, facilitation of mutual recognition agreements (MRAs), etc.

In the area of disciplining of India's domestic regulations, which is important for gaining effective market access for our service providers, India has been playing a pro-active role at the WTO. In this regard, India has put in several proposals for discussions on this subject, including a paper on Development of Disciplines for Professional Services.[26] Later, India along with some other developing countries such as Chile, Mexico, Pakistan and Thailand again tabled a proposal[27] suggesting some alternative approaches for addressing the issue of recognition such as development of disciplines for Professional Services; establishing guidelines for recognition of qualification; possibility of undertaking

25. In November 2000, India submitted a proposal on "Liberalization of Movement of Professionals" (refer, S/CSS/W/12 dated 24th November, 2000, Ministry of Commerce and Industry, Government of India, (Government of India, 2006b)).

26. Refer, JOB (03)/192 dated 30 September 2003, Ministry of Commerce and Industry, Government of India (Government of India, 2006b). Also to be noted that in pursuance of the Hong Kong Ministerial, and to conclude the disciplines in Domestic Regulations, India along with some other countries had submitted a Room Document on May 1, 2006 on Disciplines on Qualification Requirements and Procedures, and Chairman of the Working Party on Domestic Regulation (WPDR) circulated a consolidated working paper based on the proposals submitted by WTO members on July 12, 2006 on the matter.

27. Refer, JOB(05)/50, dated 30 March 2005, Ministry of Commerce and Industry, Government of India (Government of India, 2006b)

Additional Commitments for verifying a foreign service provider's competence to provide the service, etc.

With respect to plurilateral negotiations,[28] it has been agreed that all members making requests will be considered to be deemed recipients of the request except in Mode 4.[29] India is the coordinator of Mode 1 and Mode 4 plurilateral groups. India has also participated as a requesting member in the Computer and Related Services (CRS) group and Architecture, Engineering and Integrated Engineering Services (AEI) group. As a part of the plurilateral process, India has also received a number of plurilateral requests in some sectors/areas except for the Horizontal Request in Mode 3, MFN Exemptions (General) and MFN Exemptions (Financial Services). India has, therefore, received requests in 14 sectors/areas, excluding those sectors/areas in which India is a requesting member and therefore a deemed recipient. India is expected to respond to the plurilateral requests and bilateral requests placed on them by making improved Offers in the second round.

FIGURE 4.1

Service Sector Contribution to GDP

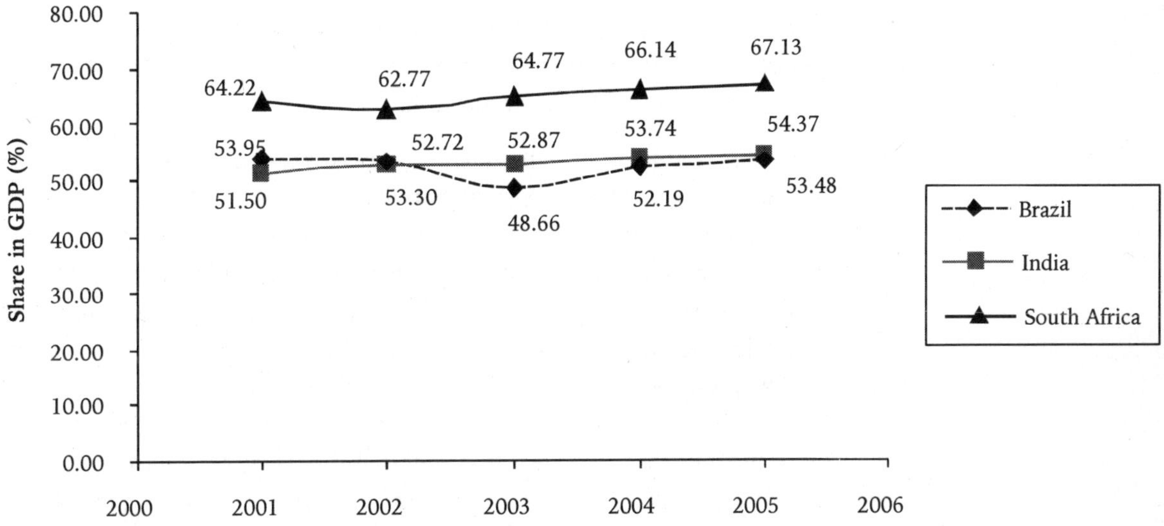

Source: RIS based on *World Development Indicators CD-ROM 2007*, World Bank.

4.4 Growth of Service Sector in Domestic Economy

During the last decade India, Brazil and South Africa have undergone major structural transformation as is evident from significant increase in the share of

28. Adopted in Hong Kong Ministerial, 2005 (as indicated in Government of India (2006b))
29. The first and second rounds of meetings of all plurilateral groups were held from March 28 to April 6, 2006 and May 15-24, 2006, respectively, (see, Government of India, 2006b).

service sector in their gross domestic products. Among the three countries, increase in the share of service sector in GDP was the highest in Brazil—increasing from 41 per cent in 1990 to about 53 per cent in 2005. In case of South Africa, the share of service sector increase was from 55 per cent in 1990 to 67 per cent in 2005 and in case of India the increase in the same period was from 41 per cent to 54 per cent. To date, about 2/3rd of GDP comes from service sector in South Africa, whereas the same in cases of India and Brazil is slightly above 50 per cent (Figure 4.1). This vibrancy in the domestic service sectors may be viewed as an indication of the potential for trade in services. The realisation of this potential however, will depend on the extent of trade orientation by the sectors. This calls for an examination of the trend in export and import of different services sector in these economies.

4.5 Trade in Services: A Comparative Analysis

Any detailed analysis of service trade, especially in developing countries, is handicapped by the paucity of required data. The major source of cross-country data on service trade is the "Balance of Payment (BoP) Statistics", published by International Monetary Fund. It may be useful to keep in mind some of the limitations of this data. To begin with, country level data on service trade is at present available only at very high level of aggregation, which prevents any one to draw meaningful conclusion on competitiveness of specific sub-sectors. Very often even the aggregated data is not comparable across different countries which makes inter-country comparison all the more difficult.

Let us begin with the overall trends in service trade and merchandise in a comparative perspective. Table 4.2 shows that while there is some similarity in the overall trade patterns of Brazil and South Africa, India presents a different picture. To be more specific, while India recorded deficit in merchandise and surplus in services, Brazil has surplus in merchandise, but deficit in services. South Africa is having deficit in both merchandise and services. The difference becomes all the more stark when we compare the trade performance of service sector. In case of India, service exports increased almost 14 folds and imports five times during 1995-2005, reflecting the presence of a highly vibrant trade in services. When it comes to both Brazil and South Africa, services exports and imports have shown negligible growth during the same period (see Table 4.2).

From the above it is evident that notwithstanding a vibrant domestic service sector, the service sector in both Brazil and South Africa has been highly domestic market oriented. The preliminary evidence may therefore tend to suggest that the opportunities for services exports from India may be limited. However, a definite conclusion calls for a more detailed examination of the growth and structure of service exports from these countries.

Structure and Growth of Service Trade

As already noted, India today has substantial trade surplus in services. India's emerging services trade sectors are financial, information and communication technology services. Despite the rise in absolute volume of exports during 1995 and 2005, shares of transport and travel services in country's total services exports have fallen over time (see Table 4.3). Earning from software services (US$ 23.60 billion) in 2005-06 was one of the remarkable achievements by India in recent years.

Growth in India's services imports was very high, particularly during the period 2000-01 to 2005-06, which was mostly driven by communication, construction and insurance services. Even though the decline in transport services

TABLE 4.2

Role of Service Trade in Current Account in IBSA (US$ million)

	India			*Brazil*			*South Africa*		
	Export	*Import*	*Trade Balance*	*Export*	*Import*	*Trade Balance*	*Export*	*Import*	*Trade Balance*
Goods									
1995	31239	-37957	-6719	46506	-49663	-3157	30071	-27404	2667
2002	52743	-65159	-12416	60362	-47219	13143	31085	-26713	4372
2005	104780	-156334	-51554	118308	-73551	44757	55280	-56484	-1204
Services									
1995	6775	-10268	-3493	6135	-13630	-7495	4618	5969	-1351
2002	24859	-18691	6168	9606	-14644	-5038	4486	5321	-835
2005	91481	50539	40942	16095	-24243	-8148	11157	-12155	-998
Income									
1995	1486	-5219	-3734	3457	-14562	-11105	1136	-4011	-2875
2002	2298	-6184	-3886	3295	-21486	-18191	1816	-4507	-2691
2005	5651	-11250	-5599	3194	-29162	-25967	4640	-9569	-4929
Current Transfers									
1995		8382			3621			-645	
2002		14790			2390			-556	
2005		24276			3558			-556	
Current Account									
1995		-5563			-18136			-2205	
2002		4656			-7696			290	
2005		-10612			14199			-9142	

Sources: RIS based on IMF, *Balance of Payments Statistics Yearbook 2006*, and RBI, *Database on Indian Economy 2007*.

import was quite steep, transport and travel services together still share about 1/3rd of country's services imports (see Table 4.3). What is interesting is that with rising import and export of US$ 1.34 billion and US$ 23.6 billion of software services respectively in 2005, intra-industry trade in services is fast emerging in knowledge intensive services (e.g. software services).

The Central Bank of Brazil provides a more disaggregated data on service trade. It is observed that travel accounts for the majority share (24 per cent in

TABLE 4.3

Components of India's Services Trade (US$ million, %)

	1995-96			
	Export	*Share**	*Import*	*Share***
Services	7344		7544	
Travel	2712	36.93	1168	15.48
Transportation	2011	27.38	2169	28.75
Insurance	179	2.44	143	1.90
G.n.i.e.	13	0.18	218	2.89
Miscellaneous	2430	33.09	3847	50.99
	2000-01			
	Export	*Share**	*Import*	*Share***
Services	16268		14576	
Travel	3497	21.50	2804	19.24
Transportation	2046	12.58	3558	24.41
Insurance	270	1.66	223	1.53
G.n.i.e.	651	4.00	319	2.19
Miscellaneous, *of which*	9804	60.27	7672	52.63
Software services	6341	38.98	591	4.05
	2005-06(P)			
	Export	*Share**	*Import*	*Share***
Services	60610		38345	
Travel	7789	12.85	6421	16.75
Transportation	6277	10.36	7394	19.28
Insurance	1042	1.72	985	2.57
G.n.i.e.	305	0.50	480	1.25
Miscellaneous, *of which*	45197	74.57	23065	60.15
Software services	23600	38.94	1338	3.49

Notes: *-Share in total services export. **-Share in total services import. P-Provisional.

Source: RIS based on RBI, *Database on Indian Economy 2007*.

2005) of all services exports. Next comes export of transportation services. While share of transportation services in total services exports has fallen in Brazil during 1995 to 2005, that in case of travel services has increased. In case of services import, there is a steep rise in imports of computer and information services in Brazil, increased from US$ 251 in 1995 to over US$ 1.71 billion in 2005 (see Table 4.4).

Similar to Brazil, South Africa also had near stagnation service trade. The recorded growth in the import of most of the service activities has been either negligible or negative during 1995-2005. Export of travel services from South Africa has increased from US$ 2.13 billion in 1995 to US$ 7.34 billion in 2005. The share

TABLE 4.4

Components of Brazil's Services Trade (US$ million, %)

	1995		*2000*		*2005*	
Export	*Value*	*Share**	*Value*	*Share**	*Value*	*Share**
Transportation	2600.00	42.38	1409.26	14.84	3186.30	19.80
Travel	972.00	15.84	1809.85	19.05	3861.44	23.99
Communications	36.00	0.59	35.73	0.38	239.19	1.49
Construction	14.00	0.23	227.58	2.40	8.03	0.05
Insurance	186.00	3.03	312.21	3.29	134.15	0.83
Financial	827.00	13.48	375.94	3.96	507.17	3.15
Computer and information	43.00	0.70	33.97	0.36	87.73	0.55
Personal, cultural, and recreational	46.00	0.75	63.04	0.66	55.80	0.35
Government, n.i.e.	130.00	2.12	537.42	5.66	1193.83	7.42
Total Services Export	6135.00		9498.35		16095.00	
Import	*Value*	*Share***	*Value*	*Share***	*Value*	*Share***
Transportation	5800.00	42.55	4304.85	25.84	4975.97	20.53
Travel	3391.00	24.88	3894.06	23.37	4719.86	19.47
Communications	53.00	0.39	32.04	0.19	111.87	0.46
Construction	4.00	0.03	0.17	0.00	0.14	0.00
Insurance	308.00	2.26	316.51	1.90	701.84	2.90
Financial	950.00	6.97	669.66	4.02	736.76	3.04
Computer and information	251.00	1.84	1145.36	6.87	1713.26	7.07
Personal, cultural, and recreational	256.00	1.88	362.70	2.18	451.40	1.86
Government, n.i.e.	469.00	3.44	1086.89	6.52	1947.22	8.03
Total Services Import	13630.00		16660.40		24242.90	

Notes: *-Share in total services export. **-Share in total services import.

Source: RIS based on *IMF Balance of Payments Statistics Yearbook 2007*.

of export of transportation services in total services export declined during 1995-2005 (see Table 4.5). However, in case of services import, while the share of transportation services to total services import increased during 1995 to 2005, that for travel services declined.

Export Competitiveness of IBSA in Services

As in manufacturing, the most important potential contribution of competitiveness of services sector is the level and scale of technology. Services industries differ greatly in their hard and soft technology mix. Sectors such as air and rail transport, communications, broadcasting, electricity, gas and water are

TABLE 4.5

Components of South Africa's Services Trade (US$ million, %)

	1995		*2004*		*2005*	
Export	*Value*	*Share**	*Value*	*Share**	*Value*	*Share**
Transportation	1069.61	23.16	1417.25	14.64	1533.39	13.74
Travel	2126.17	46.03	6321.83	65.30	7335.21	65.74
Communications	43.85	0.95	188.54	1.95	230.78	2.07
Construction			27.98	0.29	34.55	0.31
Insurance	438.94	9.50	105.84	1.09	124.47	1.12
Financial			425.63	4.40	534.35	4.79
Computer and information			89.00	0.92	109.39	0.98
Personal, cultural, and recreational			87.86	0.91	113.82	1.02
Government, n.i.e.	204.24	4.42	238.17	2.46	258.91	2.32
Total Services Export	4618.69		9681.75		11157.10	
Import	*Value*	*Share***	*Value*	*Share***	*Value*	*Share***
Transportation	2296.25	38.46	4400.51	42.61	5328.06	43.83
Travel	1849.39	30.97	3156.79	30.57	3373.35	27.75
Communications	123.55	2.07	147.24	1.43	197.85	1.63
Construction			4.97	0.05	6.28	0.05
Insurance	813.54	13.63	391.21	3.79	478.49	3.94
Financial			148.85	1.44	183.60	1.51
Computer and information			84.10	0.81	113.61	0.93
Personal, cultural, and recreational			5.00	0.05	7.54	0.06
Government, n.i.e.	214.72	3.60	265.37	2.57	291.95	2.40
Total Services Import	5970.73		10327.90		12154.90	

Notes: *-Share in total services export. **-Share in total services import.

Source: RIS based on *IMF Balance of Payments Statistics Yearbook 2007*.

highly capital-intensive, whereas construction services is relatively labour-intensive. Nevertheless, most of the developing countries have registered a considerable expansion of total services trade in recent years, but very few of them have been able to sustain their services trade specialisation and not all are having rising competitiveness in services trade (De, 2006a). In general, as in trade in goods, developing countries as service exporters benefit from labour and natural resource abundance. Therefore, in their initial years of development, these countries gain comparative advantage in labour-intensive services (construction services, tourism, data processing, etc.) and, as countries grow, their production and trade specialisation pattern also evolve towards higher-skilled and technologically advanced services.

Having analysed the structure of service trade, the pertinent question is to explore the relative competitiveness of IBSA in the service sector in general and in different sub-sectors. With a view to provide a preliminary answer to this question we have estimated the Revealed Comparative Advantage (RCA)[30] of different service sectors, and for the goods in the three countries. The results are presented in Table 4.6. Some interesting observations with implications for plausible cooperation among countries could be made from the Table. To begin with, Brazil and South Africa have shown comparative advantage consistently during the last decade in the goods producing sector. But in the case of India, there has been a decline in the comparative advantage of merchandise especially since the mid 1990s. However, India has shown steady improvement in her comparative advantage in services export since the mid 1990s, whereas, the estimated RCA indices for the service sector of Brazil and South Africa show that both of the countries are not having comparative advantage in services. More importantly in the case of Brazil, there is hardly any service sub-sector, which has recorded RCA greater than one during the period under consideration, but when it comes to South Africa, travel has shown comparative advantage.

To a great extent, it can be said that India has achieved RCA in financial and computer and information services (falling in the category of others in Table 4.6), whereas the country is losing the advantage in traditional sectors like transport and travel services. In general, with the possible exception of IT software services in India, the service sector is an area wherein IBSA is found to be relatively weak in terms of comparative advantage. This collective weakness however may be construed as providing opportunities for trilateral cooperation in different service sectors with a view to build up the comparative advantage of all the countries. On this premise, what follows is a brief discussion on certain important areas wherein initiatives could be made to foster cooperation among IBSA. We

30. The RCA index calculated by taking the share of a particular sectors exports in total exports of goods and services from the country and dividing this share by the share of all the countries exports in this sector in aggregate global exports of goods and services. If the estimated RCA index of a sector is greater than one, then it is considered as globally competitive.

must also hasten to state that the list of areas specified below need not necessarily be considered all-inclusive. Moreover, even with respect to the areas specified, there is need for more in-depth studies to come up with specific plan of action and to highlight the role of different actors in the three countries.

4.6 Select Areas for Trilateral Cooperation

IT Software and Services

Over the past decade, the Indian software and IT-BPO industry has witnessed significant transformation because of country's advantages in large pool of English speaking skilled population, and supplying capability of low-cost–high-end services. During the last decade, India's has emerged as a major IT software and service provider to the rest of the world. In 2005-06, software services accounted for over 39 per cent of India' services export. There are several factors (both tangible and intangible) which helped India to sustain its software exports. For example, according to Kumar and Joseph (2005), strong base of human capital is widely believed to have been the main force in the growth of the software industry

TABLE 4.6

Estimates of RCA in Select Service Sectors of IBSA

Items \ Year	1990	1995	1996	1997	1998	1999	2000	2001	2002	2003	2004	2005
India												
Goods	1.00	1.02	1.03	0.99	0.93	0.90	0.87	0.86	0.85	0.83	0.84	0.83
Services	1.00	0.91	0.89	1.03	1.26	1.39	1.54	1.58	1.58	1.78	1.89	1.97
Transport	0.76	1.03	1.04	0.94	0.85	0.79	0.68	0.66	0.72	0.63	0.60	0.59
Travel	1.07	1.10	1.09	1.05	1.02	0.93	0.84	0.74	0.66	0.74	0.89	0.92
Others	1.16	0.70	0.65	1.03	1.53	1.98	2.38	2.61	2.63	2.77	2.95	3.12
Brazil												
Goods	1.12	1.10	1.14	1.12	1.09	1.09	1.06	1.08	1.08	1.14	1.17	1.19
Services	0.53	0.59	0.44	0.51	0.64	0.64	0.76	0.69	0.68	0.69	0.63	0.65
Transport	0.71	1.03	0.57	0.52	0.71	0.44	0.49	0.46	0.50	0.51	0.48	0.47
Travel	0.65	0.30	0.22	0.27	0.35	0.46	0.47	0.42	0.48	0.49	0.52	0.54
Others	0.30	0.29	0.39	0.49	0.61	0.71	0.85	0.78	0.67	0.69	0.67	0.68
South Africa												
Goods	1.09	1.08	1.07	1.06	1.06	1.06	1.07	1.09	1.10	1.13	1.14	1.15
Services	0.66	0.67	0.73	0.74	0.75	0.75	0.70	0.64	0.62	0.64	0.61	0.60
Transport	0.85	0.66	0.61	0.66	0.70	0.72	0.75	0.75	0.62	0.63	0.61	0.62
Travel	1.08	0.98	1.16	1.25	1.24	1.22	1.16	1.14	1.28	1.30	1.29	1.31
Others	0.02	0.25	0.21	0.23	0.20	0.17	0.16	0.13	0.09	0.10	0.11	0.10

in India as it has helped the industry to capitalise on the sudden surge in demand for software services that emerged in the world economy in the late 1980s. Down the line, starting with basic data entry tasks in late 1980s, the software and IT-BPO industry graduated to a high proportion of voice-based services and a range of back-office processing activities. According to the National Association of Software and Services Companies (NASSCOM), the Indian software and IT-BPO sector (including the domestic and exports segments) is growing at an estimated 28 per cent in 2007-08, and total revenue aggregate for the software and IT-BPO sector is expected to exceed US$ 47.8 billion in 2007-08, nearly a 10-fold increase over the aggregate revenue of US$ 4.8 billion, reported in 1998-99, and direct employment is likely to cross 1.6 million.[31] The US and UK remain the dominant markets for India, contributing to 67 per cent and 15 per cent of total exports respectively in 2006-07.

While India has a highly export oriented software industry, Brazil has a domestic market oriented software industry which is comparable in size (US$ 8.5 billion in 2003). The focus of Brazilian software industry on the domestic market need not necessarily be considered as an indication of their inability to developed and internationally competitive industry. Instead like China, the domestic market might act as a springboard for future export growth.[32] South Africa is known for wide spread use of IT in different sectors of the economy and its strong commitments towards promoting the use of open source software.[33] The share of South African ICT expenditure per GDP was 7.9 per cent in 2003, which was higher than Netherlands, Japan, Denmark, Ireland, Finland, Brazil, Malaysia, China, Mexico, Egypt, and numerous other high-profile countries with innovative approaches to the information society. However, while there has been a high level of investment, there is still an insufficient level of information and communications infrastructure in rural and peri-urban areas, and within most black communities (Cogburn and Nyaki Adeya, 2001). Given the fact that affordability is the crucial issue that stands in the way promoting ICT use in developing countries in general and IBSA in particular, the cooperation among the three countries towards harnessing open source software could provide rich dividends.

Tourism

We have seen that travel (mostly tourism) is an area where both India and South Africa are having comparative advantage. Besides contributing to the national income, promotion of intra-regional tourism has other beneficial spillovers for trade and people-to-people contacts. India with its vastness and geographical

31. See, NASSCOM (2007).

32. See for details Botelho *et al.*, 1999 and Botelho *et al.*, 2005.

33. See for details "Using Open Source Software in the South African Government: A Proposed Strategy Compiled by Government Information Technology Officers' Council" 2003. Available at *http://www.oss.gov.za/docs/OSS_Strategy_v3.pdf*

diversity could be an attractive location for tourist from both Brazil and South Africa. It is found that tourism is one of the vibrant sectors in the South African economy accounting for about 7.8 per cent of the GDP and contributing significantly to job creation as a result of substantial investment made by both public and private sectors. Indian companies also have invested in the tourism sector of South Africa. Three out of the four tourist hotspots in South Africa reside in Cape Town and infrastructural development aims to link these different venues, both for improved convenience for the tourist, and to elevate Cape Town's image. Though Brazil at present is not having significant comparative advantage in tourism, cooperative efforts among the three countries could have rich dividends. For instance, Goa, a well-known beach in India with large Portuguese population could be of substantial interest to Brazilians. With the growing per capita income in India and with a middle class as large as 300 million, Indian tourist could be attracted to both South Africa and Brazil if three country packages are imaginatively planned and implemented at the instance of tourist operators in these countries. More importantly, to promote tourism however, there is the need for cooperation in facilitation of tourism with easier visa facilities and initiatives to train tourist guides in Portuguese language.

Traditional System of Healthcare

IBSA is known for their unequal distribution of incomes. As a result, majority of the population can ill afford the high cost of allopathic medicines. In South Africa, to ameliorate the situation, the Government has started thinking in terms of promoting alternative systems of medicines. The Parliament passed Allied Health Professions Act, which provided for establishment of professional council to regulate complementary health practice, which will include Ayurveda, Unani Tibb, Homeopathy and Sidha. Indian Ayurvedic and other products had thus far been banned. In the case of Brazil also, Indian traditional medicines, given their effectiveness and low cost, could be of much appeal.

Entertainment and Animation Industries[34]

India is the third largest television market behind China and the United States. The number of broadcasters has zoomed from one public sector broadcaster a decade back to around 300 at present including the 26 satellite cum terrestrial channels run by the state broadcaster. The total revenue earned by the television industry in India is estimated to be US$ 2867 million. These revenues are expected to grow at a compound annual growth rate of 17 per cent and touch US$ 6411 million by 2008.

Total revenue earned by the Indian music industry was about US$ 230 million in 2003. Though a large part of the revenue is lost because of the problems

34. For detailed study, see FICCI and EXIM Bank of India (2004).

relating to piracy it is expected to record marked increase in the near future. In 2003, the revenue of the organised sectors of the live entertainment segment was about US$ 129 million. This is expected to go up to US$ 321 million in 2008.

According to the current projections, the Indian entertainment industry is expected to double in size in the next five years from the current level of US$ 4.3 billion to US$ 9.4 billion in 2008. One of the key factors propelling growth of the Indian entertainment industry is the changing distribution network, which is moving up the technology ladder. These include the introduction of Direct to Home (DTH) services for television distribution, use of digital technology for film distribution in semi-urban and rural markets and the development of FM radio as a new medium.

Over the last five-years the size of the overseas markets for Indian cinema has grown substantially. The large Indian Diaspora of around 25 million people scattered across the globe is increasingly being tapped. It is believed that some films were able to realise 15-20 per cent of their total proceeds from overseas.

India's animation industry offers great potential as a creative hot spot and ideal outsourcing destination. According to the estimates made by the industry bodies the total size of the animation segment in India was closer to half a billion dollars and this is expected to go up to US$ 2 billion by 2008. India's strength in the animation industry is based on multiple factors. One is the availability of infrastructure facilities like the high-tech animation studios, with a dozen or so boasting world-class facilities. Their efficacy is boosted by the presence of quality software, communication infrastructure and skill sets. Content developers are also numerous. Another major factor that contributes to the success of the Indian animation industry is low costs. Cost of production in the segment is far lower than that in the United States, Canada or even Korea and the Philippines.

Currently India's foreign direct investment policy allows for 100 per cent investment on the automatic route with no entry-level conditions for film production, television software production exhibition and distribution, including related services and products. In the case of satellite broadcasting, all television channels irrespective of national or foreign ownership are permitted to uplink from India provided they undertake to comply with the broadcast code. However, no private or foreign operator is allowed in terrestrial transmission. Foreign investment of up to 49 per cent of the paid up share capital is allowed in cable networks. Companies with a minimum 51 per cent of paid up share capital held by Indian citizens are allowed to provide cable television services. In the case of DTH television the foreign direct investment allowed is 20 per cent while the overall share inclusive of portfolio investment by foreign institutional investors and non-resident Indians is 49 per cent. Against this background, it appears that there is immense potential for mutually beneficial cooperation in the field of entrainment.

Financial Sector Cooperation

India has considerable experience in development of capital markets with the Bombay Stock Exchange being one of the oldest and well performing stock exchanges in the world. South Africa also is known for their well-developed financial sector and capital market. But in the case of Brazil, the capital market is yet to be fully developed. As of 1999-2000, the values of equities traded as a proportion of GDP is found to be only 17 per cent in Brazil as compared to 104.7 per cent in case of India. Also, by January 2002 only 424 companies were found listed in Brazil in stock markets. Given such an imbalances in the levels of capital market development in these countries, there appears to be room for cooperation among them.

People-to-People Contacts

One of the key problems in promoting trade and investment between IBSA and especially with India and Brazil appears to be the lack of information and very often the presence of misinformation. One of the possible ways to address this issue is through strengthening the people-to-people contacts. People-to-people contact between IBSA is possible only through airways. Yet, the air connectivity between India and Brazil is especially weak. In this context, an open sky policy, might be helpful in strengthening the links between the three countries. An initiative like *IBSA Games* could also provide rich dividends in facilitating the people-to-people links. There could be IBSA Soccer and Cricket Tournaments to promote visibility of each other country mutually.

Media Cooperation

Greater interaction between media of IBSA is crucial for reducing the information gap. There is very little reporting on India in Brazil and South Africa and vice versa. To bridge this gap, some exchange fellowships for media persons and journalists could be set up to allow journalists from Brazil and South Africa to spend some time in India and vice versa.

IBSA Network of Think Tanks

The study notes that more or less similar policy reforms undertaken in the three countries have yielded quite different outcomes across them. Hence, there is an enormous potential for sharing development experiences between IBSA in managing globalisation and for providing constant policy inputs for promoting mutual cooperation. To facilitate such a process an *IBSA Network of Think Tanks* could be created to facilitate such exchange of development experiences and studies on promotion of mutual cooperation. The network could comprise national focal points from each member country, and have fund at its disposal to draw upon for launching studies, annual conferences and for instituting fellowships for exchange of scholars.

4.7 Concluding Observations

In the context of growing service sector in the domestic economy on the one hand and unprecedented growth in service trade by developing countries on the other, the present chapter undertook an exploration of the policy reforms with respect to service trade in the IBSA and trends and patterns in service trade with a view to come up with areas of mutually beneficial service sector cooperation. It has been observed that, while there has been a number of initiatives, towards liberalising service trade in all the three countries, barriers in the field of telecommunications, financial sector, insurance and others remain in the form of restrictions on both mobility of labour and investment. In the context of slow growth of the domestic economy and mounting trade deficit in services, along with barriers, service trade in general and service import in particular has shown negligible or negative growth rate both in Brazil and South Africa. But, India has a relatively vibrant service sector. On the whole, service sector is found to play a different role in the current account of the three countries; while Brazil has recorded surplus in merchandise and deficit in services, India recorded surplus in services and deficit in merchandise.

Estimate of RCA has shown that with the possible exception of IT software services in India and travel in South Africa, the service sector is an area where IBSA is found to be relatively weak in terms of comparative advantage. The only service sector of Brazil wherein imports showed significant increase are insurance, computer services and other business services. The present study conceives the collective weakness of IBSA as an opportunity for mutually beneficially cooperation in a number of areas. These include IT software services, tourism, traditional medicines, entertainment and animation industries, financial sector cooperation, among others. The study also underscores the need for strengthening people-to-people contact *inter alia* through IBSA Games, establishing an IBSA Network of Think Tanks and promoting great interaction between the media. The service imports of these countries are subject to a number of barriers such as, job quotas and barriers for commercial presence in select sectors. These barriers can be addressed while framing a Comprehensive Economic Cooperation Arrangement among the three countries.

APPENDIX 4.1

WTO Commitments by Sector by IBSA

	Brazil	*India*	*South Africa*
Business services			
Accounting, auditing and book keeping	Participation of non-residents in legal sectors controlled by Brazilian nationals is not allowed. Special registration requirements for accountants who wish to audit such companies as financial institutions and savings and loan associations in case of national treatment.		Citizenship is required for accreditation in auditing.
Architectural services	Foreign service suppliers must join Brazilian service suppliers in a specific type of legal entity (consorcio); the limitations on market access for engineering services is the same as with architectural services.		For building plans of 500 m2 and over the services of a locally registered architect have to be utilised.
Engineering services		Only through incorporation with a foreign equity ceiling of 51 per cent.	
Advisory and consultative engineering services	Foreign service suppliers must join Brazilian service suppliers in a specific type of legal entity (consorcio); the limitations on market access for engineering services is the same as with architectural services.		
Industrial engineering	Foreign service suppliers must join Brazilian service suppliers in a specific type of legal entity (consorcio); the limitations on market access for engineering services is the same as with architectural services.		
Engineering design	Foreign service suppliers must join Brazilian service suppliers in a specific type of legal entity (consorcio); the limitations on market access for engineering services is the same as with architectural services.		
Other engineering services	Foreign service suppliers must join Brazilian service suppliers in a specific type of legal entity (consorcio); the limitations on market access for engineering services is the same as with architectural services.		

Contd. ...

...Contd. ...

	Brazil	*India*	*South Africa*
Urban planning	Foreign service suppliers must join Brazilian service suppliers in a specific type of legal entity (consorcio); the limitations on market access for engineering services is the same as with architectural services.		
Computer and related services			
Software implementation services		Only through incorporation with a foreign equity ceiling of 51 per cent.	
Research and development services			
R&D services on the following natural sciences only: Heat, light, electromagnetism, astronomy, but excluding atomic energy and related matters.		Only through incorporation with a foreign equity ceiling of 51 per cent. However, this category is unbound due to lack of technical feasibility	
Construction services (roads and bridges only)		Only through incorporation with a foreign equity ceiling of 51 per cent.	
Other business services			
Advertising services	Foreign participation is limited to 49 per cent of the capital of companies established in Brazil. In addition, foreign producers must live at least 3 years in Brazil before being authorised to produce films.		
Services related to management consulting	With regard to services relating to management consulting companies must be registered with the Regional Council of Administrators.		
Legal services		An advocate is not allowed to form a partnership/company.	
Financial services			
Direct insurance		Insurance intermediation limited to reinsurance, in which case overseas brokers are allowed to have resident	All insurers need to be incorporated as a public company in South Africa and registered with the

Contd. ...

...Contd. ...

	Brazil	*India*	*South Africa*
		representatives and representative offices who can procure reinsurance business from Indian insurance companies to the extent mentioned above. They can also place reinsurance business from abroad with Indian insurance companies. However, except for the business indicated above the resident representatives and representatives cannot undertake any other activity in India. All expenses of the resident representatives and representative offices have to be met by remittances from abroad and no income can be received in India from Indian residents.	supervisory authority to carry on insurance business in South Africa. The acquisition of shares or any other interest in a registered insurer resulting in the holding of 25 per cent or more of the value of all shares or other interest in that business requires the written approval of the Registrar of Insurance. Apart from this, the executive chairman, public officer and the majority of directors must be resident in South Africa and life insurance actuaries must also be resident in South Africa.
Insurance on freight	Specific type of legal entity is required. Foreign participation is limited to 50 per cent of the capital of a company and to one-third of the voting stock.		
Life insurance	Specific type of legal entity is required. Foreign participation is limited to 50 per cent of the capital of a company and to one-third of the voting stock.		
Medical care	Specific type of legal entity is required. Foreign participation is limited to 50 per cent of the capital of a company and to one-third of the voting stock.		
Property insurance	Specific type of legal entity is required. Foreign participation is limited to 50 per cent of the capital of a company and to one-third of the voting stock.		

Contd. ...

...Contd. ...

	Brazil	*India*	*South Africa*
Liability insurance	Specific type of legal entity is required. Foreign participation is limited to 50 per cent of the capital of a company and to one-third of the voting stock.		
Auxiliary services: agencies and brokers	Open only to natural persons		
Acceptance of funds from the public	The limitations on market access apply to the establishment of new branches and subsidiaries of foreign financial institutions as well as increases in the percentage of the participation of foreign persons and firms in the capital stock of Brazilian financial institutions, which are not permitted. Individual network for ATMs may be set up only by Brazilian banks and minimum requirements for paid in capital and net worth applicable to branches of foreign banks and those banks controlled by foreign capital are twice those established for Brazilian banks.		
Participation in public issues	The limitations on market access apply to the establishment of new branches and subsidiaries of foreign financial institutions as well as increases in the percentage of the participation of foreign persons and firms in the capital stock of Brazilian financial institutions which are not permitted. Individual network for ATMs may be set up only by Brazilian banks and minimum requirements for paid in capital and net worth applicable to branches of foreign banks and those banks controlled by foreign capital are twice those established for Brazilian banks.		
Lending of all types		Acceptance of deposits and other repayable funds from the public and lending of all types including consumer	In banking and other financial services, accepting of deposits and other repayable funds from the

Contd. ...

...Contd. ...

	Brazil	*India*	*South Africa*
		credit, mortgage credit and financing of commercial transactions but excluding factoring are subject to limitations on market access and can operate only through branch operations of a foreign bank licenced and supervised as a bank in its home country. Grant of licence as permissible under existing laws.	public, all dealings in foreign exchange must be carried out through a dealer authorised by the SA Reserve Bank and national treatment is restricted to branches of bank not incorporated in South Africa which maintain a minimum balance of R 1 million on the deposit accounts of natural persons. In lending of all types as well as payments and money transmission services including credit, charge and debit cards, traveler cheques and bank drafts have limitations on market access for foreigners exist, only banks registered to operate in South Africa with the minimum capital base are eligible to seek authorisation as foreign exchange dealer. Companies involved in asset management, collective investment schemes and custodial services and financial instruments for securities and financial instruments need to be incorporated as public companies in South Africa and registered with the supervisory authority to carry on business in South Africa.
Hotels and restaurants	While Brazilian firms operating in the Amazon and North eastern region benefit from certain tax credit incentives, firms with majority of capital held by Brazilian citizen also enjoy other incentives.		
Transport			
Rail freight	Government authorisation required and the number of service suppliers may be limited.		

Contd. ...

...Contd. ...

	Brazil	*India*	*South Africa*
Road freight	Foreign participation is limited to one-fifth of the voting shares of Brazilian companies engaged in this activity.		
Communication services		Voice telephone service, circuit switched data transmission services, facsimile services, private leased circuit services and cellular mobile telephone services will be permitted to be provided only after the operator gets a licence from the Designated authority who shall determine the need if any for issuance of new licences.	Foreign investment in suppliers permitted up to a cumulative maximum of 30 per cent in case of packet switched data transmission services other services like paging services, mobile cellular, and satellite based services. In the case of electronic mail, there are general limitations on the bypass of South African facilities for routing of domestic and international traffic.
Audiovisual services		Market access limitations exist and such services can be offered by foreigners only through representative offices which will be allowed to function as branches of companies incorporated outside India. Limitations on national treatment exist and are subject to the prescribed authority having certified that the motion picture has won an award in any of the international film festivals notified by the Ministry of Information and Broadcasting or participated in any of the official sections of the notified international film festivals or received good reviews in prestigious film journals notified by the Ministry of Information and Broadcasting.	

Source: RIS based on WTO.

APPENDIX 4.2

Overview of Explicit Barriers and Existing Commitments by Brazil

Sector	*Explicit Barriers*	*GATS Commitments*	*GATS MFN Exemptions*
Telecommunications	Mostly liberal. Provision of long distance services requires meeting build-out obligations in local services.	No GATS commitment, currently. MERCOSUR commitment partially liberal, but retaining discretion and surpassed by actual policy.	Reciprocity conditionon telecom services supplied for distribution of radio or television programs directly to consumers.
Distribution Services	No explicit barriers on foreign suppliers.	Commitments mirror policy.	None.
Banking, Insurance, Express Mail and Courier Services	*De facto* liberal, but policy environment is not certain, due to lack of a clear legislative framework on foreign entry. Greenfield entry in banking not allowed.	Reflect executive discretion	None
Maritime Transport	Commercial presence: restrictive, with foreign equity limit. Cross-border trade: international maritime transport quite liberal, but no cabotage rights for foreigners	No GATS commitment.	Bilateral agreements concerning cargo sharing, cargo reservation and reciprocity on access to cargo.
International Road Transport	Commercial presence: restrictions in the form of foreign equity limitations. Cross-border trade: International road transport subject to quantitative limitations. No cabotage rights for foreigners.	Commitment on commercial presence reflects policy.	Agreement on International Land Transport providing national treatment for authorised suppliers of signatories.
International Air Transport	Commercial presence: discriminatory restriction on foreign equity ownership and non-discriminatory restriction on number of airlines. Cross-border trade: quite restrictive as determined through bilateral air service agreements.	Not applicable	Not applicable

Contd. ...

...Contd. ...

Sector	*Explicit Barriers*	*GATS Commitments*	*GATS MFN Exemptions*
Audiovisual Services	Restrictive, with local content rules and foreign ownership restrictions.	No commitments.	Co-production agreements with certain nations.
Construction Services	Some what restrictive, with requirements on the form of foreign entry.	Commitments reflects actual policy.	None.
Professional Services	No major restrictions other than residency requirement.	GATS commitments do not cover all professions. MERCOSUR commitments are wider.	None.
Reinsurance, Postal Services	Closed to domestic and foreign entry.	Commitments reaffirm monopoly in reinsurance, no commitment on postal services.	None.

Source: RIS based on WTO.

Chapter 5

Investments Flows and Technology Cooperation

5.1 Introduction

FDI inflows across the world have seen an unprecedented growth in 2005. They rose by 29 per cent in 2005 and reached US$ 916 billion (UNCTAD, 2006). This upsurge in FDI reflects a greater level of cross-border mergers and acquisitions (M&As). At the same time, performance of developing countries in attracting FDIs was nevertheless outstanding; FDI stocks in developing countries reached to the highest level ever recorded—US$ 334 billion in 2005, with which about 36 per cent of global FDI stocks now belong to developing countries. Among developing economies, Brazil ranks in the list of top 10 largest FDI recipients in 2005, while India and South Africa come next, falling within top 20.

In IBSA, South Africa is one of the leading FDI recipients, with about 21 per cent (US$ 6.4 billion in 2005) of the entire Africa's total inflows, mainly as a result of the acquisition of ABSA (South Africa) by Barclays Bank (United Kingdom). From South Asia, performance of India in attracting FDI has been remarkable. The total FDI inflow into India grew significantly to the highest level ever of US$ 7 billion in 2005. If 2006-07 FY is counted, India with US$ 19 billion FDI inflows comes within the list of top 10 largest FDI recipients from developing countries. Brazil continued to receive substantial FDI till 2004, where a significant proportion of the FDI inflows went into natural resources such as oil and gas. However, FDI inflows decreased in Brazil by 17 per cent in 2005. In general, services in IBSA countries gained the most from the surge of FDI, particularly finance, telecommunications and real estate; whereas it is the manufacturing sector in India which attracted the bulk of FDI.

Notwithstanding significant differences across countries, developing countries (including transition economies) have emerged as significant outward investors as well and IBSA economies are no exception. FDI from developing countries reached US$ 133 billion in 2005, representing about 17 per cent of world outward flows. According to UNCTAD's Outward FDI Performance Index, which compares an economy's share of world outward FDI against its share of world GDP, countries with relatively large outward FDI in absolute terms, such as Brazil, China, and India show considerable potential for future expansion of FDI.

FDI from developing countries accounts for well over 40 per cent of the total inward FDI of a number of LDCs. For example, South Africa is a particularly important source of FDI; it accounts for more than 50 per cent of all FDI inflows into Botswana, Lesotho, and Swaziland. Similar pattern has been witnessed in South Asia, where India is the important source of FDI for Bhutan, Nepal and Sri Lanka. In South America, bulk of the FDI in Paraguay and Uruguay originates at Brazil.

Therefore, the growing outward FDI from developing countries and the flows between developing countries generate considerable South-South investment flows. UNCTAD estimates show that South-South FDI has expanded particularly fast over the past 15 years. According to UNCTAD (2006), total outflows from developing and transition economies (excluding offshore financial centres) increased from about US$ 4 billion in 1985 to US$ 61 billion in 2004; most of these were destined for other developing or transition economies.

However, barriers continue prohibiting investment flows, more acute in developing countries. Countries are now more focused to facilitate cross-border FDI flows. During the last decade, Brazil, India and South Africa have undertaken series of policy reforms in the realm of trade and investment. These policy reforms not only underscored the links between trade and investment but also the primacy of foreign investment as a means of achieving higher rate of economic growth. Such a renewed interest in FDI is based on the generally held view that FDI could act as a source of new technology and management expertise and also helps bridging the saving-investment gap. However, it is often felt that the technologies available especially from the developed countries are very often not suited to the specific factor market and product market conditions that prevail in the developing world. At the same time, there is ample evidence to show that some of the developing countries, notably, Brazil, India and South Africa, during the last few decades have developed substantial capabilities, which in turn leave scope for mutually beneficial cooperation among them. More importantly, if the available empirical evidence is any indication, outward investment is no longer a monopoly of the developed world. A number of firms from the developing world, with substantial technological capability and investible resources, have emerged as multinationals in their own right. This in turn has made efficiency seeking investment restructuring within the developing world more relevant today than ever before. There is a marked increased in South-South investment flows in general, and IBSA countries in particular. We, therefore, need to pay greater attention to the facilitation of FDI in IBSA. There is scope to share the experiences in this area. Cooperation between IBSA countries may enhance opportunities for cross-border investments and contribute to their mutual development.

It is in this context, this chapter undertakes an analysis of the investment inflows into IBSA countries with special focus on investment flows between them. It concludes with some recommendations for promoting cooperation in IBSA.

5.2 Investment Policies in India

Since 1991, India has made significant reforms in her FDI policy and further liberalisation is underway. Today the FDI policy provides for 'automatic' approval in many sectors, by which foreign investors only need to notify the Reserve Bank of India (RBI) of their investments, and need not obtain government licences or approvals. The Foreign Investment Promotion Board (FIPB) clears the proposals that do not confirm to the guidelines of automatic approvals. Government also encourages investment from Non-Resident Indians (NRIs) including Overseas Corporate Bodies (OCBs—a company or other entity owned by NRIs directly or indirectly to the extent of at least 60 per cent). NRIs and OCBs are allowed to invest in housing and real estate development sector. They are also allowed to hold up to 100 per cent equity in civil aviation companies in which otherwise foreign equity up to only 40 per cent is permitted.

Investments and returns are freely repatriable, except where the approval is subject to specific conditions such as lock-in-period on original investment, dividend cap, foreign exchange neutrality, etc. as per the notified sectoral policy. The condition of dividend balancing that was applicable to FDI in 22 specified consumer goods industries stands withdrawn for dividends declared after 14th July, 2000.

The level of FDI inflows into India from August 1991 to March 2007 stood at US$ 54.63 billion.[1] India's talent pool of skilled professionals, the advantages offered by a large English speaking population, increasing disposable incomes, and significant domestic demand have made India an attractive destination of FDI.

The GoI's privatisation policy permits foreign investors to bid for the sale of the state-owned units. Foreign investors are given national treatment at the time of initial investment or after the investment are made. In sectors where licencing is required, procedures do not discriminate against foreign companies.

---

1. Source: *SIA Newsletter*, DIPP, Government of India.

However, in certain consumer goods industries export obligations and local content requirements are imposed on foreign investors.

The policy governing outward FDI (OFDI) has also been liberalised during the 1990s. The Guidelines for Indian Joint Ventures and Wholly Owned Subsidiaries Abroad as amended in October 1992, May 1999, July 2002 and March 2007 provide for the automatic approval of outward FDI proposals upto a certain limit that has been expanded progressively from US$ 2 million in 1992 to over US$ 100 million in March 2007. In order to streamline India's OFDI policy, GoI has allowed Indian corporates/registered partnership firms to invest in entities abroad up to 200 per cent of their net worth in a year, without prior approval of RBI or GoI. The investment can be funded out of balances held in Exchange Earners Foreign Currency Account (EEFC) of the Indian company or 100 per cent ADR/GDR proceeds or by drawing foreign exchanges from an authorised dealer in India up to 100 per cent of the net worth of the Indian company. The earlier monetary ceiling of US$ 100 million (US$ 10 million for partnership firms) was removed by the GoI in the new policy.

Remittances of Dividend and Royalty

There are no restrictions on remittances for debt service or payments for imported inputs. Dividend remittances are permitted without approval from the RBI. There are no delays beyond 60 days on remittances for dividends, lease payments, etc. It only requires income tax clearance to ensure that taxes, if any, have been paid before the transaction is concluded. The RBI's approval is required to remit funds from asset liquidation. Foreign partners may sell their shares to resident Indian investors.

Foreign Institutional Investors (FIIs) may transfer funds from rupee to foreign currency accounts and vice versa at the market exchange rate. They may also repatriate capital, capital gains, dividends, interest income, and any compensation from the sale of rights offerings, net of all taxes without approval.

Indian companies having technology transfer agreements with foreign companies may remit royalties, but recurring royalty payments, such as patent licencing payments, are normally limited to eight per cent of the selling price. Restrictions on payments (currently seven years) and the stipulation of minimum foreign equity holdings have been lifted. Royalties and lump sum payments are taxed at 20 to 30 per cent. Payment of royalty up to two per cent on exports and one per cent on domestic sales is allowed under the automatic route on the use of trademarks and brand names of the foreign collaborator without technology transfer.

Performance Requirements

Local sourcing is generally not required. In some consumer goods industries, the GoI requires the foreign party to ensure that the inflow of foreign exchange and foreign equity covers the foreign exchange requirement for imported goods. In 2002, the GoI removed measures previously requiring local content and foreign exchange balancing in automobile industry.

Plant location: Industrial undertakings are free to select the location of a project; in case of cities with population of more than a million, the proposed location should be at least 25 kilometres away from the standard urban area limits of that city. Electronics, computer, and printing as well as other non-polluting industries are exempt from such location restrictions.

Employment: There is no requirement to employ Indian nationals. Restrictions on employing foreign technicians and managers have been eliminated, though companies complain that hiring and compensating expatriates is time-consuming and expensive. The RBI has raised the remittable per-diem rate from US$ 500 to US$ 1000, with an annual ceiling of US$ 200,000 for services provided by foreign workers payable to a foreign firm. Employment of foreigners in excess of 12 months requires approval from the Ministry of Home Affairs.

Taxes: The GoI provides a 10-year tax holiday for knowledge-based start-ups. Most state governments also offer fiscal concessions. All foreign firms are allowed to participate in government financed or subsidised research and development programmes on a national treatment basis.

Capital Markets and Portfolio Investment

FIIs may invest in all securities traded on India's primary and secondary markets, in unlisted domestic debt securities, and in commercial paper issued by Indian companies. The ceiling of an investment by FIIs is equal to the sector-specific FDI limits. Indian mutual funds may invest in rated securities in other countries. Disinvestments and repatriation of dividends are permitted after payment of capital gains taxes.

SEBI regulates all market intermediaries. The takeover regulations require disclosure on acquisition of shares exceeding five per cent of total capitalisation. In case of acquisition of over 10 per cent, the buyer must make a public offer for a minimum of 20 per cent from the remaining shareholders at a fixed price. Companies may buyback their shares in the market to make inter-corporate investments. RBI and FIPB clearances are required to acquire a controlling stake in Indian companies.

Special Economic Zone

SEZ/EPZ/STP units may import intermediate goods duty-free. The minimum net foreign exchange earning as a percentage of exports by EPZ/STP units is required to be at least 3 per cent. EPZ/STP units may sell up to 50 per cent of their level of exports on the domestic market after payment of taxes. Export Oriented Undertakings (EOUs) are industrial companies established anywhere in India that export their entire production. There are about 2,300 fully operational EOUs in India. They are allowed to import intermediate goods duty-free; have a 10-year corporate income tax holiday; are exempt from excise tax on capital goods, components and raw materials; and are exempt from sales taxes. EOUs may sell up to five per cent of "seconds" on the domestic market after paying appropriate taxes. The government recently extended Special Additional Duties (SAD) exemption to EOUs.

Special Economic Zones (SEZs) are designated duty-free enclaves with developed industrial infrastructure. These zones are regarded as foreign territory for the purpose of duties and taxes, and are excluded from the domain of the custom authorities to enjoy full freedom for the in and outflow of goods. SEZ units enjoy a tax exemption for seven years: 100 per cent exemption in first 5 years, and 50 per cent in the remaining 2 years. They have the facility to retain 100 per cent foreign exchange earnings in Export Earners Foreign Currency Exchange accounts. All SEZ units are free to sell goods in the domestic tariff area (DTA) on payment of applicable duties.

TABLE 5.1

Requirement of Infrastructure Investments in India during 2007-2011

Sector	*Investments (US$ billion)*
Power	90
Road	57
Port	11
Railway	71
Civil Aviation	9
Urban Infrastructure	82

Source: Planning Commission, Government of India.

Infrastructure

India is witnessing rapid development in the infrastructure sector. The infrastructure investment has increased in the past few years, driven by government initiatives and private participation. The GoI has estimated that an investment of over US$ 384 billion during 2007-2012 will be required to fund infrastructure projects alone. Some of the important infrastructure investments are given in Table 5.1. The GoI expects that 22-25 per cent of the investment required is to come from private sector. The Indian infrastructure space has gained much importance in the past few years, and provides immense opportunities for growth and development.

5.3 Policies Governing Investment in Brazil

Along with its liberalisation policies started in early 1990s, Brazil has been encouraging foreign investment to achieve sustained rapid growth as evident from the removal of many restrictions on FDI. Foreign investors are permitted to own up to 30 per cent of media companies and invest in the Brazilian stock market since 1991. The Brazilian Congress passed constitutional amendments in 1995 to open up the formerly closed sectors, such as petroleum, telecommunications, mining, power generation and internal transport to the foreign investors. New or expanded foreign investment in the banking sector has been approved on a case-by-case basis since 1995.[2] New rules in effect from 2000 made considerable liberalisation of foreign investment in equities and putting foreign investors on an equal footing with the national investors. However, restrictions remain on foreign investment on a limited number of sectors, such as nuclear energy, health services, media, rural poverty, fishing, mail and telegraph, aviation and aerospace.

Institutional Framework Governing Investment Policies

Registration of Foreign Capital

All foreign investment must be registered with the Central Bank of Brazil. The bank introduced the electronic registration system for FDI and brought some changes in FDI registration in Brazil and the obtaining of information on these transactions with effect from September 4, 2000. This registration is essential for foreign loans, offshore remittances, capital repatriation, and registration of profit reinvestment. Though usually approval is automatic, some cases may be reviewed by the central bank, and generally the certificate of registration permits remittances of profits and repatriation of capital.[3] Since January 1, 1996, profits are exempt from income tax withholding.

Currency Investments

No preliminary official authorisation is required for investment in currency. The investment to subscribe for capital or to buy a stake in an existing Brazilian company can be remitted to Brazil through any banking establishment authorised to deal in foreign exchange. However, closing of the exchange contract is conditional on the existence of a RDE-IED (Registro Declaratório Eletrônico—Investimento Externo Direto) registration number for the foreign investor and the Brazilian investee. Registration of the investment is made by the Brazilian company receiving the investment within 30 days of closing of the exchange contract for the remittance, together with documents reflecting capitalisation of the funds. The foreign currency investments must be registered in the original currency or, upon express request of the investor, in another currency,

---

2. When the new or expanded foreign investment in this sector was technically forbidden earlier, currently foreign banks account for one-third of the total net worth of the banking system and 27 per cent of total banking assets. (Reference: *US Commercial Service Guide to Brazil*, 2004).

3. For detail on the registration process and procedures, see *Legal Guide for the Foreign Investor in Brazil*, 2003.

maintaining the exchange parity, in addition to the registration in Brazilian currency, as mentioned above. Investment by foreign credit conversion will be subject to preliminary authorisation from the Department of Foreign Capital Control and Registration (Fiscalização e Registro de Capitais Estrangeiros—FIRCE), if the transaction is not registered in the RDE-IED System. After authorisation, a token exchange transaction must be performed, representing the purchase and sale of the foreign currency.[4]

Investment by Import of Goods without Exchange Cover

The investment by import of goods without exchange cover requires the preliminary approval of FIRCE and SISCOMEX. Registration of foreign direct investments resulting from the import of intangible assets without coverage by an exchange contract requires: (i) the value of the registration made through the ROF (Registro de Operações Financeiras—Registration of Financial Transactions) Mode of the RDE System linked to the Import Declaration; and (ii) the currency stated on the corresponding ROF. The import of used goods or under tax incentives is conditional on the absence of similar goods in Brazil. Once the imported goods have been cleared by customs, the Brazilian company has 180 days to incorporate them into its capital and another 30 days to apply for registration of the investment with the Central Bank of Brazil.

Investment on the Capital Market

Any non-resident investors, whether individuals or legal entities, individually or collectively, are allowed to invest on the Brazilian financial and capital markets under the approval of Brazilian Monetary Council. Non-resident investors will now use the same registration to invest in the fixed- and variable-income markets, and may migrate freely from one type of investment to the other.

Repatriation

Foreign capital registered with the Central Bank of Brazil may be repatriated to its country of origin at any time without preliminary authorisation. According to Article 690, II of the 1999 Income Tax Regulations, foreign currency amounts registered with the Central Bank of Brazil as non-resident investments may be repatriated without income tax assessment. In this case, the foreign currency amounts, which proportionally exceed the original investment (capital gain) will be subject to 15 per cent withholding income tax.[5]

---

4. Registration of foreign direct investment resulting from conversion, however, depends on receipt by the Brazilian investee of: (i) a statement from the creditor and committed investor, and (ii) a binding statement from the creditor, agreeing to the conversion. The Brazilian company has 30 days to capitalise these funds and apply for registration with the Central Bank of Brazil.

5. In the specific case of repatriation of capital, it should be noted that the Central Bank of Brazil will normally examine the net worth of the company involved, as shown on its balance sheet. If the net worth is negative, the Central Bank of Brazil may decide that there was dilution of the investment, and may thus deny authorisation for repatriation of a part of the investment in proportion to such negative result.

The ownership in a Brazilian company by a foreign investor may be sold, assigned or otherwise transferred abroad, with no tax implications in Brazil, irrespective of the price paid. The foreign purchaser will be entitled to register capital in the same amount as the registration previously held by the selling company, once again regardless of the price paid for the investment abroad. In this case, the registration number in the RDE-IED Mode of the Central Bank of Brazil should be changed to reflect the name of the new foreign investor, which is essential to allow the new investor to remit/reinvest profits and to repatriate capital.

Policy Induced Barriers to Entry and Operation

Restrictions on Remittances Abroad

Remittance of funds abroad is restricted when such funds are not registered in the RDE-IED System, since remittance of profits, repatriation of capital, and registration of reinvestment are all based on the amount of foreign investment registered.

Restrictions on Foreign Investment

According to Article 52 of the Temporary Provisions Act of the Federal Constitution, the participation of foreign capital in financial institutions is subject to the approval of the Brazilian Government, which will determine if such participation is in the country's best interests.

Participation of foreign capital is restricted and in some cases prohibited in certain areas:[6]

- the development of activities involving nuclear energy;
- the ownership and management of newspapers, magazines and other publications, and of television and radio networks;
- health services;
- ownership of rural areas and businesses on frontier zones;
- post office and telegraph services;
- airlines with domestic flight concessions; and
- the aerospace industry.

Barriers in Access and Operation

From discussion with business sectors it was transpired that, according to Brazilian laws, foreign companies may make investment in goods, which is subject

6. Even Brazilian companies, when under foreign control, may request and obtain permission to operate in certain crucial sectors like mining sector.

to non-voluntary import licencing. For companies set up by foreign companies, their legal representative should have long-term stay status. Otherwise, the foreign company should make an investment of US$ 200,000 to obtain a long-term stay status for its legal representative.

It is understood that stringent administration on foreign currency is enforced by Brazil. Generally, foreign companies or persons may not open foreign currency account in Brazilian banks, and foreign currencies entering into Brazil are required, on the same day, to be converted into Brazilian currency. The remittance of foreign companies' profits is to be made under the supervision of the Brazilian central bank

5.4 Policies Governing Investment in South Africa

The democratic Government established in 1994 has been actively involved in promoting different policies under different programmes.[7] Recognising the link between trade and investment, the government has undertaken certain measures, such as, extensive tariff reform programme, abolishing of most import controls, trade and investment promotion activities, and reforms in industrial strategy and the regulatory environment. Through the government's efforts to liberalise trade and industrial development policies along with a highly developed first-world economic infrastructure, the country has been recognised as the "engine of growth in Southern Africa" and established itself as a dynamic and internationally competitive investment location.

South Africa welcomes foreign investment in all the sectors; national treatment applies to all foreign investors, who can repatriate the proceeds and earnings of their investments after payment of taxes. No government approval is required, apart from the approval required under the exchange control regulations, and there are almost no restrictions on the form or extent of foreign investment.[8]

To achieve regional balance in investment, the country's various regions (provinces) have Development Bodies that offer incentives, varying from area to area, including reduced interest rates, reduced rentals for land and buildings, cash grants for relocation of plant and employees, reduced rates for basic facilities, railage and other transport rebates and assistance in the provision of housing. In June 2003, the South African Government hosted the Growth and Development Summit, aimed at bringing together Government and its social

7. These programmes included Black Economic Empowerment (BEE), Industrial Development Programme (IDP), Small and Medium Enterprise Development Programme (SMEDP), Skill Support Programme (SSP), Critical Infrastructure Facility, Industrial Development Zones (IDZs), Foreign Investment Grant, Strategic Investment Programme, Micro Investor Programme, among others to attract foreign participation in the development process. For details of rules and regulations as well as the protection rights, please refer *Legal Guide for the Foreign Investor in Brazil*, 2003.

8. *http://www.tradeinvestsa.co.za/Investment/story_2405.shtml*

partners to take advantage of the conditions for faster growth and development that exist in South Africa.[9]

Trade and Investment South Africa (TISA) is the country's trade and investment promotion agency.[10] It's core functions are to promote investment—particularly FDI, to coordinate investment promotion in collaboration with the provinces, to market projects to both domestic and foreign investors apart from export development in South Africa. TISA provides investment facilitation services for inbound investors. The agency offers the services to international investors, like, information on sectors and industries; consultation on the regulatory environment; facilitation on investment missions; links to joint venture partners; information on incentive packages; assistance with work permits; and logistical support for relocation, among others. For promoting industrial development and encouraging investment, the old manufacturing support schemes are being replaced by "six pack" of incentives.[11] Under these

9. The major commitments and agreements mostly related to investment reached included the following:
   - All social partners made commitments to work towards creating more and better jobs and decent work for all, through public investment initiatives in partnership with the private sector.
   - Business committed to investing R145 billion over the next five years in the automotive, chemical, mining and oil sectors.
   - All social partners committed to addressing the investment challenge through encouraging investors to invest 5 per cent of their investible income in appropriate financial instruments that are to be developed. See for details, *South Africa Yearbook 2003/04*, "Chapter 7: Economy", p.176.
10. For a detailed information about the functions and operations of TISA, see, *South Africa Yearbook 2003/04*, section on "Trade and Investment South Africa".
11. The Six Pack consists of:
   - Small Medium Enterprise Development Programme (SMEDP), which offers manufacturing, and tourism enterprises with "significant expansions of their operations", tax-free cash grants for two years, based on the cost of the investment in land, buildings, machinery, equipment, and vehicles. A maximum of R 3.05 million per year for enterprises with an investment in qualifying assets of up to R 100 million.
   - Skills Support Programme (SSP) offers a cash grant to cover 50 per cent of the training costs of enterprises under the SMEDP, in order to encourage them to introduce new and advanced skills to their workforce. The maximum assistance an enterprise may receive is 30 per cent of its actual costs.
   - Critical Infrastructure Facility (CIF) supplements the existing public or private sector infrastructure, by funding a top-up grant between 10 per cent and 30 per cent of actual costs.
   - Industrial Development Zones (IDZ) consist of two zones of operation: customs secured area (CSA), and industries and services corridor (ISC). A CSA is a delimited area with entrance and exit points controlled by Customs personnel. Each CSA has a dedicated customs office providing inspection and clearance services, and one-stop administrative centre to facilitate the approval and permit processes. CSA-based enterprises are eligible for: duty-free import of production-related raw materials and inputs; zero rate on VAT for supplies procured from South Africa; and right to sell into South Africa upon payment of normal imported duties on finished goods. ISCs are industrial and office park environments adjacent to CSAs, occupied by service providers to CSA enterprises. The Government will first designate areas suitable for IDZs. Prospective IDZ companies will then have to apply for permits to develop and operate an IDZ.
   - Foreign Investment Grant (FIG) is open to foreign investors (i.e. at least 50 per cent foreign shareholding) located outside SACU and/or SADC, and participating in the SMEDP. It offers up to 15 per cent of the value of new machinery and equipment (a maximum of R 3 million per entity), based on accepted relocation costs.
   - Strategic Investment Programme (SIP) offers a tax allowance of up to 100 per cent (a maximum allowance of R 600 million per project) on the cost of buildings, plant and machinery, for strategic investments of at least R 50 million in manufacturing of food products (excluding tobacco and tobacco-related products), and consultancy in computer hardware and software, data processing and data base activities.

initiatives foreign investors are encouraged in the industrial development process in the country.

South Africa recently implemented stronger competition policy. The new Competition Act also addresses anti-competitive behaviour of state-owned enterprises, especially when they compete unfairly with the private sector.

The financial sector in South Africa is well developed and there are only limited delays in the conversion and transfer of funds. There are hardly any restrictions on foreign firms wishing to invest in share capital. The country has also been progressively removing the controls on financial markets and encouraging foreign participation in the foreign exchange and capital market. Significant progress has been made in the liberalisation of exchange controls since 1994. The financial Rand mechanism was abolished in 1995, removing most controls on non-residents. In June 1997, controls on South African residents were considerably relaxed, and virtually all controls on current account transactions were removed. Resident private individuals who are over 18 and South African taxpayers in good standing have also been permitted to invest up to R 500,000 abroad since 1 July 1997. The limit has since increased to R 750,000 per person.

On February 26, 2003, further measures were announced to relax exchange controls. The changes included the increase of the allowance governing South African corporates' use of South African funds to finance new approved direct investment in foreign countries as well as the unwinding of blocked assets. It was also announced that dividends repatriated from foreign subsidiaries will in future be eligible for an exchange control credit, which will allow them to be re-exported for approved foreign direct investments. Furthermore, the tax payable on foreign dividends was also removed in instances where a South African taxpayer has a meaningful interest in the foreign subsidiary paying the dividend.

In February 2003, tax laws were made simple with a view to further encourage investment. Accordingly, the taxpayers refurbishing a building within designated zones will receive a 20 per cent straight-line depreciation allowance over a 5-year period. Construction of new buildings within such a zone will receive a 20 per cent write-off in the first year and 5 per cent a year for a further 16 years.[12]

Barriers to Entry and Operation

Despite improvements in macroeconomic conditions, policy initiatives and advantages in terms of natural resources and market size, foreign investors have shown limited interest in acquiring, creating, or expanding domestic enterprises

12. The Minister of Finance also announced the scrapping of "a potentially harmful tax practice" in the form of the International Headquarter Company regime as the need for this exemption was obviated by the removal of the foreign dividend tax.

(*Trade Policy Review, 2004*). South Africa still has a number of sectors that are dominated by state-owned enterprises. The former weak competition legislation could be partly blamed for this.

South Africa's policy and regulatory frameworks still serve as disincentives to new investment or impediments to the profitability of firms already operating in South Africa. The immigration legislation and the application of the laws make it difficult to get work permits for the foreign employees. In particular, it was indicated that unnecessary delays, rejections of applications and limits (quotas) on foreign workers in a given field prohibited the potential investors' ability to staff their operations with the necessary skills at a given time.

Poor or unclear regulations in key sectors, such as telecommunications, also act as disincentives to investment. In instances where the regulator is weak and unable to enforce its own regulations, foreign firms are placed in a weaker competitive position compared to the national operator, thereby affecting their profitability. In contrast to domestic investors, foreign investors face local borrowing restrictions imposed by exchange control authorities.

To sum up, the investment regime that exists today in all the three countries in IBSA is highly conducive for promoting investment from abroad. At the same time, each of these countries with a view to promote outward investment have undertaken policy measures that induces the local companies to "go global". Thus, the policy environment today is highly tuned both from the demand and supply side. Against this background let us now proceed to examine the extent to which these countries have been able to attract investment from abroad in general and more specifically to what extent they have been able to emerge as sources of outward investment, which in turn could create facilitating environment for investment among them.

5.5 Investment Cooperation in IBSA

FDI Inflows to IBSA

There has been significant inter-country variation in their success in attracting inward FDI in IBSA. From Table 5.2 it is evident that since beginning of this decade, the record of FDI inflows to IBSA has been unprecedented. In 2005, IBSA received about US$ 28.04 billion FDI inflows, which corresponded to 3.06 per cent of the world inflows of FDI and 8.75 per cent of the flows directed towards developing economies (11.30 per cent if we exclude China), within which Brazil alone has received about US$ 15.06 billion FDI inflows.

FDI flows remained relatively strong despite possible contagion from the crisis in Argentina, Brazil's main trading partner in MERCOSUR (UNCTAD, 2006). During 2001 to 2003, FDI inflows to Brazil felt sharply. FDI flows to Brazil declined from US$ 32.78 billion in 2000 to US$ 10.14 billion in 2003 (Table 5.2).

TABLE 5.2

Trend in Annual FDI Inflows to IBSA

US$ billion

	1981	1991	2000	2001	2002	2003	2004	2005
South Africa	0.065	0.248	0.888	6.789	0.757	0.734	0.799	6.379
India	0.092	0.075	3.585	5.472	5.627	4.585	5.474	6.598
Brazil	2.522	1.102	32.779	22.457	16.590	10.144	18.146	15.066
IBSA Total	2.679	1.425	37.252	34.718	22.974	15.462	24.419	28.044
Share of IBSA in								
World (%)	3.86	0.92	2.64	4.17	3.72	2.77	3.44	3.06
Developing economies (%)	11.11	3.57	14.63	16.49	14.18	8.95	9.38	8.75
Developing economies excl. China (%)	11.24	4.01	17.42	21.22	21.02	12.96	12.24	11.30

Source: RIS based on UNCTAD.

The trend has now been reversed. Brazil has become the second largest recipients of FDI in Latin America. In 2005, Brazil recorded US$ 15.07 billion FDI inflows. Though, the level of FDI inflows declined to about US$ 15.07 billion in 2005, there is hardly any parallels in rest of the world, except perhaps China, to Brazilian FDI performance. FDI inflows to Brazil during the last decade have been induced mostly by the privatisation programme of the Government wherein the foreign firms were allowed to invest in the state owned public sector enterprises. By 2004, Brazil realised US$ 87.5 billion in sales revenues and another US$ 18.1 billion in debt transfer as a result of the national privatisation programme. Of these, 48 per cent was accounted for by foreign firms.

Brazil accounted for an estimated 20 per cent of total manufacturing FDI in Latin America and the Caribbean in 2005. FDI in the Brazilian automobile industry continued to grow in 2005 (by 38 per cent to US$ 1.1 billion) because of a healthy growth in sales, while that in the plastics and rubber industry jumped form US$ 100 million to US$ 600 million because of the soaring global demand for large tyres, which led, for instance, Michelin (France) to undertake important investments in Brazil.

In contrast, South Africa and India witnessed significant inflows of FDI with little fluctuation. In terms of the forms of FDI, a large part is investment in existing assets. Cross-border mergers and acquisitions are increasingly prominent. "Greenfield" investment is relatively uncommon in South Africa (*Trade Policy Review, 2004*). FDI inflows have been relatively diversified in terms of sectoral distribution. On a sectoral basis, banking, telecommunications, and mining and quarrying, have attracted the bulk of FDI, followed by the automotive industry and the food, beverages and tobacco sectors. The largest source of FDI inflows has been the US, although UK was still by far the largest external holder of FDI capital stock by year-end 2000 (this includes the pre-1994 era). Despite South Africa's large mineral reserves, non-mining activities formed a major part of FDI inflows in 2005, with finance and services receiving almost 40 per cent of total FDI, and manufacturing accounting for 26.4 per cent. Inflows to South Africa in 2005 were dominated by the cross-border acquisition of the South African bank, ABSA, by an international banking group led by Barclays Bank of the United Kingdom (UNCTAD, 2006). Foreign companies, particularly banks, have repurchased operations in South Africa (sold at the end of the apartheid regime) as well as in its neighbouring countries (e.g. Namibia). Diamond and nickel mines that had lain dormant in South Africa (because of high extractive costs and low demand), also attracted new FDI as the prices of these commodities skyrocketed in 2005 (UNCTAD, 2006).

India, on the other hand, showed a steady increase in terms of FDI inflows though the total inflow has been much low when compared to that of Brazil. Here it needs to be noted that Indian figures do not follow IMF's BoP manual that is followed internationally resulting in substantial under estimation of FDI inflows to India. The Indian government has taken steps to revise the definition of inward as well as outward FDI flows from the country. In June 2003, Government of India announced that the adoption of international norms led to near doubling of FDI inflow figure from US$ 3.91 billion to US$ 6.13 billion in 2001-02. In 2006-07, India has received a record US$ 19 billion FDI, and which is likely to touch US$ 30 billion by end of 2007-08 FY. The major sectors that attracted investment into India are infrastructure including telecom and power, and services, mostly IT software and services.

The relative role that FDI plays in IBSA countries could be better captured by examining FDI stock as a percentage of GDP (see, Table 5.3). It is evident that while the FDI stock account for 29.05 per cent of GDP in South Africa and 25.17 per cent in Brazil, the corresponding share in India is only of the order of 5.65 per cent, the lowest in entire IBSA.

TABLE 5.3

Inward FDI Stock in 2005 (As a percentage of GDP)

Region/Country	*FDI Stock*	
	US$ billion	*As % of GDP*
South Africa	69.37	29.05
India	45.27	5.65
Brazil	201.18	25.17

Source: RIS based on UNCTAD.

FDI Outflows from IBSA

As we have already noted, one of the basic premises of the present study and factors that act as inducement mechanism for IBSA cooperation is the substantial capabilities across different spheres that these countries have built up during the last few decades. These capabilities in turn have made possible the emergence of a number of companies from these countries as "Third World Multinationals". Thus, India, Brazil, and South Africa are not only major recipients of FDI from abroad but have also emerged as major sources of outward investment. Table 5.4 presents information on FDI outflows from IBSA. It is evident from the Table 5.4 that Brazil with US$ 2.52 billion in 2005 has emerged as the highest outward investor, followed by India and South Africa. However, FDI outflows from Brazil decelerated in 2005. According to UNCTAD (2006), higher growth and commodity prices contributed not only to higher inward FDI, but also to increased outward FDI, as improved earnings enabled Brazilian firms to acquire foreign assets, mainly in telecommunications and heavy industries.

Cross-border M&As were a prime driver of FDI growth in 2005. Their numbers rose worldwide, but the rise was particularly prominent in developing and transition economies in general and countries in IBSA in particular. More than half of all cross-border M&As took place in the services sector. Their growth in the primary sector was mainly concentrated in developed countries, while in developing countries there were more cross-border purchases but fewer sales. Not that primary-sector FDI fell in developing countries; it simply occurred through Greenfield investment. In general, the relatively small value of M&As in the primary sector in developing countries reflects a restrictive regulatory environment.

The growing outward investment by these countries naturally should act as a means of exploiting synergies of their capabilities on the one hand and promoting trade and production for third country market on the other. A close look at the sectors in which these countries invest abroad tends to suggest that

TABLE 5.4

Annual FDI Outflows from IBSA

US$ million

	South Africa	*India*	*Brazil*	*IBSA Total*
1981	643.90	2.00	207.20	853.10
1991	207.90	-11.00	1015.00	1211.90
2000	270.80	509.00	2281.59	3061.39
2001	-3180.10	1397.00	-2257.59	-4040.69
2002	-398.90	1679.00	2482.11	3762.21
2003	565.10	1325.00	249.30	2139.40
2004	1352.10	2024.00	9806.99	13183.09
2005	67.90	1364.00	2516.70	3948.60

Source: RIS based on UNCTAD.

they are having substantial capabilities in high technology areas leaving scope for mutually beneficial cooperation. In case of Brazil for instance, more than 90 per cent of the outward FDI in 2002 was in high technology areas like electrical equipment and transport equipment (see Table 5.5). The financial and technological capabilities of Brazil are further evident from the fact that out of the 25 top TNCs from Latin America, five were from Brazil (UNCTAD, 2006). The largest TNCs of Brazil operate in areas like aircraft manufacturing, where even many developed countries failed to make a mark.

Outward FDI from South Africa, particularly to other African countries, has increased in recent years. The Government is encouraging South African firms through the relaxation of foreign exchange controls on capital destined for the

TABLE 5.5

Industry-wise FDI Outflow from Brazil

US$ million

Industries	*1990*	*1996*	*2002*
Food	14.50	42.29	1.60
Textiles	8.29	9.19	0.00
Lumber & Pulp	0.00	0.00	0.00
Chemical	160.23	1.84	3.19
Metal	24.86	429.31	0.00
Machinery	30.39	43.21	10.37
Electrical	26.24	10.11	133.98
Transport	42.13	28.50	150.73
Others	13.12	10.11	1.60
Manufacturing Total	319.08	574.56	301.46
Farming & Forestry	4.14	1.84	0.00
Fishery	0.00	0.00	0.00
Mining	31.08	136.06	0.00
Construction	4.14	26.66	0.00
Trade	18.65	145.25	23.13
Finance & Insurance	223.08	4.60	66.99
Service	11.05	24.82	3.19
Transportation	4.83	0.00	0.00
Real Estate	0.69	0.00	0.00
Non-Manufacturing Total	296.98	339.22	93.31
Total	616.06	913.78	394.77

Source: RIS based on UNCTAD.

region, to invest particularly in African countries, in an effort to foster industrialisation. Total outward direct investment from South Africa more than doubled between 2003 and 2004, from US$ 565.10 million to US$ 1352.10 million, but decelerated to US$ 67.90 million in 2005.

FDI Outflows from India

The striking development is the rise of OFDI from India. India's OFDI (on approval basis) have been steadily increasing since 1996 both in terms of number of approvals and value. Indian investments abroad has gone up to 1395 approvals (US$ 2855 million) in 2005-2006 as compared to 290 approvals (US$ 557 million) in 1996-97, an increase of 380 per cent in terms of number of approvals and 513 per cent in terms of value of investments approved (see, Table 5.6). Indian OFDI has increased from US$ 2.86 billion in 2005-06 to US$ 7.95 billion in 2006-07 (*Financial Express, 2007*). Till October 2006, 870 approvals were granted to Indian companies for overseas investments worth US$ 6034.87 million as compared to 822 approvals worth US$ 1190.74 million in the corresponding period of last year.

According to the Ministry of Finance, Government of India, during April 1999 to October 2006, the largest amount of approvals for overseas investment was in the manufacturing sector at US$ 11,093 million, followed by financial and

TABLE 5.6

Year-wise FDI Outflow from India

US$ million

Financial Year	*No. of Approvals*	*Equity*	*Loan*	*Guarantee*	*Total*	*Annual Cap*	*Actual Outflows*
1996-97	290	363.73	37.76	155.12	556.61	500	204.99
1997-98	228	482.01	8.34	135.52	625.87	750	120.77
1998-99	275	144.98	18.48	86.21	249.67	750	142.83
1999-00	395	1298.93	50.44	407.64	1757.01	750	318.64
2000-01	714	1176.83	89.84	113.43	1380.1	1000	1211.85
2001-02	908	2712.46	157.21	155.86	3025.53	1000	981.67
2002-03	1034	1298.69	104.49	141.53	1544.71	1000	1799.08
2003-04	1214	822.4	229.9	413.84	1450.56	*	1494.77
2004-05	1281	2010.03	384.39	409.91	2804.33	*	1743.97
2005-06	1395	1887.78	629.74	337.32	2854.84	*	4461.21
2006-07**	870	3685.98	809.29	1539.6	6034.87	*	3319.65

Notes: *–Annual ceiling removed with effect from 1st April 2003. **–April to October 2006.

Source: RIS based on Ministry of Finance, Government of India.

TABLE 5.7

Sector-wise FDI Outflow (Approved) from India

US$ million

Year	Manufacturing	Financial Services	Non-financial Services	Trading	Others	Total
1999-00	548.84	4.26	1143.52	58.31	2.30	1757.23
2000-01	370.74	16.61	876.53	89.17	29.14	1382.19
2001-02	2210.90	48.62	565.49	139.18	61.34	3025.53
2002-03	1056.74	1.82	280.17	69.88	61.69	1470.30
2003-04	765.64	35.11	438.79	76.94	134.08	1450.56
2004-05	2026.43	9.21	548.24	69.12	151.33	2804.33
2005-06	1711.08	167.71	707.44	134.34	134.29	2854.86
2006-07*	2402.76	5.75	2249.96	390.81	985.59	6034.87
1999-2000 to 2006-07*	11093.13	289.09	6810.14	1027.75	1559.76	20779.87

Notes: *–April to October 2006.

Source: RIS based on Ministry of Finance, Government of India.

non-financial services sector (including software development) at US$ 7099.23 million, trading sector at US$ 390.81 million and other activities at US$ 985.59 million respectively, (see Table 5.7).

Investment in India from South Africa and Brazil

FDI from South Africa and Brazil in India has been quite low. Table 5.8 presents an over all picture in terms of FDI inflows from South Africa and Brazil during the 1991 to 2006. While the total cumulative FDI from South Africa and Brazil put together has been of the order of only US$ 67.79 million for the period 1991 to 2006, with bulk of it has been from South Africa (US$ 66.82 million). FDI from Brazil in India has

TABLE 5.8

FDI from South Africa and Brazil to India

Country	1991-2002*	2003	2004	2005	2006	Cumulative Total (1991 to 2006)	
	Rs. million					Rs. million	US$ million
South Africa	103.11	117.4	209.39	972.97	1,653.02	3,055.90	66.82
Brazil	23.76	0	1.12	1.43	7.32	33.63	0.97
Total	126.87	117.4	210.51	974.4	1,660.34	3,089.53	67.79

Notes: * August 1991 to December 2002.

Source: RIS based on Ministry of Commerce and Industry, Government of India.

been very low, which is in order of only US$ 0.97 million. Therefore, total FDI from South Africa and Brazil in India has been minuscule, not only in comparison with the outward investment by these countries, but also in comparison with the inflows into India during the period 1991 to 2006.

There are several studies which have identified a number of factors that influenced the inflow of FDI into an economy. These include structural factors like market size (income levels and populations) extend of urbanisation, quality of infrastructure, geography and cultural proximity and above all policy factors like tax rates investment incentives, performance requirements etc. Table 5.8 clearly indicates that inflow of investment from Brazil has been much lower than that of South Africa. Given the fact that Indian policies towards FDI has been highly liberal during the last decade and India has been perceived as a country with large market, the relatively low investment from Brazil needs to be viewed in terms of geographical and cultural distance. To address this issue, there is the need for focused initiatives to bring together the business communities in the IBSA countries along with measures to intensify people to people contact.

South African Investment in India

Given the fact that Argentina, Brazil and South Africa are major investors abroad it may be pertinent to examine their investment in India. South African firms have of late been investing in India. During 1991 to 2006, about US$ 67 million investment came from South Africa to India. Table 5.9 presents information on major South African investment in India. It is evident that major initiatives relate to food processing (breweries) and those relating to energy (conversion of coal into liquid fuel). South African Breweries is reported to have acquired a majority interest in Mysore Breweries in a US$ 17.5 million deal, after having first invested in Narang Breweries in 2000. Other areas in which South African companies have invested include insurance, diamond exploration and infrastructure. A major South African chain store (Shoprite) has established an outlet in Mumbai. In February 2006, Airports Company of South Africa (ACSA) won the contract for upgrading of Mumbai Airport. The energy giant SASOL is keen to explore the possibility of collaborating in a coal-to-synthetic automotive fuel project in India. Given the enormous capabilities that South Africa has in the field of minerals and metals including gems and jewellery it is suffice to state here that there is much more investment possibilities in India by South Africa which could be of mutually beneficial.

Indian Investments in South Africa and Brazil

As we have seen earlier investment policy in India during the last decade has also laid emphasis on promoting Indian investment abroad. As a result, a large number of firms from India are now investing in a number of countries outside. During the period from April 1996 to October 2006, Russia was the

TABLE 5.9

Profile of Selected South African Investments in India

Name of the Investor	*Field of Investment*	*Remarks*
South African Breweries	Food Processing	Company acquired 76 per cent interest in Mysore Breweries Ltd in Karnataka in a US$ 17.6 million deal. It earlier acquired Narang Breweries near Lucknow in October 2000.
Interpark and Intertoll	Infrastructure highways	These two companies and Group V of South Africa have been executing contracts for highways upgradation on Jaipur-Delhi, Mumbai-Pune and some roads in Uttar Pradesh.
ESKOM	Infrastructure Power	The company has been seeking cooperation with Power Corporation of India and NTPC in the field of power generation and in creating power grids.
LTA Process Engineering	Technology Collaboration	Supplying technology for coal washing for use in power stations in collaboration with Tata Techno Dyne in Kolkata.
SASOL	Energy	SASOL Technology is negotiating with Indian Department of Coal for setting up plants to convert coal into liquid fuel and eventually transfer technology in this regard.
South Africa Department of Trade and Industry	Trade	South Africa Department of Trade and Industry has been exploring export of South African BMWs to India.
Old Mutual	Finance	The company entered the Indian market with its 26 per cent stake into a joint venture with Kotak Mahindra in 2001.
Sanlam Personal Finance	Finance	Sanlam Personal Finance is interested in India's Insurance market.
Shoprite	Retail	Established retail store in Mumbai.
Airports Company of South Africa	Infrastructure Airport	Involved in modernisation of Mumbai international airport.

Source: RIS.

largest recipient of approvals for Indian direct investment at US$ 2830.58 million, followed by USA at US$ 2768.29 million, Mauritius at US$ 2150.72 million, and UK at US$ 2149.62 million. However, Brazil was the largest recipient of approvals of Indian direct investment at US$ 420.12 million in 2005-06 FY, followed by Mauritius at US$ 332.66 million, Netherlands at US$ 284.62 million and USA at US$ 270.25 million.

Compared to other regions, India's investment in South Africa and Brazil has been very low. Table 5.10 provides country-wise India's OFDI in South Africa and Brazil. During April 1996 to October 2006, about 2.25 per cent of India's OFDI (on approval basis) went to the IBSA, amounting US$ 519.48 million, of which Brazil alone attracted over 90 per cent (US$ 467.16 million). South Africa attracted US$ 52.32 million.

The preferred area of investment by Indian companies is found to be in the field of information technology, more specifically IT and software services,

TABLE 5.10

Indian Investments in South Africa and Brazil

US$ million

Countries	*1996–2002**	*2002-03*	*2003-04*	*2004-05*	*2005-06*	*2006-07*	*Total (1996 to 2006)$*
Brazil	12.98	5.17	4.95	17.21	420.12	6.73	467.16
South Africa	21.56	0.07	0.79	2.88	10.42	16.6	52.32
IBSA Total	34.54	5.24	5.74	20.09	430.54	23.33	519.48
Total OFDI of India	7543.06	1472.12	1450.93	2804.01	2859.14	6003.87	22142.89
Share of IBSA in India's Total OFDI (%)	0.46	0.36	0.40	0.72	15.06	0.39	2.35

Notes: *–April 1996 to March 2002. **–April 2006 to October 2006. $ April 1996 to October 2006.

Source: RIS based on Ministry of Finance, Government of India.

including training and human resource development. In addition, a number of Indian pharmaceutical companies have also been investing abroad. Major Indian IT companies like Tata Consultancy Services (TCS) have began their operation in both Brazil and South Africa. Besides TCS, other Indian companies active in the field of IT are Aptech, Satyam Computers, and Ramco.

While Indian investment in Brazil is negligible till date, available evidences suggest that Indian firms are increasingly being present in South Africa. Indian investments take the firm of fully owned Indian subsidiaries and joint ventures. Major Indian subsidiaries include the UB Group of India, Indian conglomerate Tata Group and major pharma companies like Ranbaxy and others (see, Box 5.1). In addition, there are a few joint ventures between Indian companies and their South African counterparts (see, Table 5.11). Investors include the UB Group of India (beer manufacture, hotels) Tatas (vehicles, IT, new investment in a ferrochrome plant), Mahindras (utility vehicles) and a number of pharmaceutical companies, including Ranbaxy, CIPLA, among others. In 2004, Coromandal of India acquired 2.5 per cent stake in Foskor, a major phosphoric acid producing company of South Africa. The Tata Group has 26 per cent participation in the Second National Operator in the telecom sector approved by the government in 2005. Their Ferrochrome plant has also received the go-ahead. They are also interested in moving into power generation and mining in due course. A JV is reported to have been set up between Adlabs Films, India and Pan-African Strategic Investments to produce films, bringing an estimated 50 million Rand of Indian investment. In January 2006, Apollo Tyres acquired Dunlop SA in a Rand 400 million deal. Also in January 2006, an Indian power generating and coal trading company Sandro Power Supply announced its plans to list on the Johannesburg Stock Exchange and to build a terminal to ship coal and iron ore to

India and China. In July 2006, Godrej Consumer Products Ltd signed an agreement to acquire the South African hair colour business of Rapidol, UK, as well as its subsidiary Rapidol International. Indian Hotels, a subsidiary of the Tata Group, has been planning to invest in the hotel industry. Ashok Leyland plans to invest in a motor assembly plant in KwaZulu Natal. Other major Indian companies operating in South Africa include Jindal Steel, Kirloskar, Zensar and Eicher International.

Many South African companies have signed up marketing contracts with Indian companies in the pharmaceutical sector. South African company SPECPHARM has a JV with Lupin for distribution of TB drugs. Another South

TABLE 5.11

Selected Indian Investments in South Africa

Indian Companies	*Year*	*Sector*	*Investment (US$ million)*
UB Group	1996	Food Processing (Breweries)	15.00
Electronic Research	2000	Trade in Electronics	NA
Tata Consultancy Services	2000	Software Development	NA
Tata International	1998	Manufacturing vehicles	2.90
Zenith Rollers	2000	NA	0.07
Usha Beltron	1999	NA	1.26
Lupin Laboratories	1997	Trading in Drugs & Pharma	NA
Mirza Tanners	2000	Tannery	0.22
Maharashtra Hybrid Seeds	1999	Trading in Pesticides and Seeds	0.05
PTS International Trading	1999	Trading of Readymade Garments	0.0174
Southern Travels	1998	Hotel and Restaurants	0.174
Pertech Computers	1995	Software Development	1.50
BPL Telecom	1995	Telecom	5.14
Hindustan Glass & Industries	2000	NA	0.45
Godrej	2006	Consumer Products	NA
CIPLA	2001	Drugs & Pharma	NA
Mahindra	2003	Motor Vehicles	87.50
Tata Steel	2006	Steel	NA
Coromandal India	2004	Chemical	NA
Tata International	2005	Telecom	NA
Adlabs	2005	Film	NA
Apollo Tyres	2006	Tyres	15.00

Source: RIS based on India Investment Centre, Ministry of Commerce & Industry, Government of India, and Indian High Commission in South Africa.

Box 5.1

Major Indian Investments in South Africa

UB Group of India, the largest Indian investor in South Africa, initially invested US$ 20 million in a black-owned brewery (National Sorghum Breweries) and has invested US$ 6 million in a tourism project (Mabula Game Lodge). They have since expanded their operations and investments in South Africa. Shriram Industrial Enterprises Ltd. has invested US $ 7 million in a car air-conditioner manufacturing unit near Durban. Their latest venture is again a tourism project called Imbali Game lodge in Krugar National Park.

Tata's operations in South Africa include three companies. The first one—TATA Africa Holdings is responsible for bringing investments in South Africa in viable areas and supervises Tata companies in Zambia, Zimbabwe, Tanzania, Namibia, Uganda, Mozambique and Ghana. They are exploring other investment projects in South Africa particularly in mining. Tatas have recently launched a project in Richards Bay for manufacture of ferro chrome. The second one, Tata Automobiles, import, assemble, distribute and sell Tata trucks and buses. For marketing of TATA trucks the group entered into a joint venture agreement with ERF Ltd., a subsidiary of DORBYL of South. Tata stands 2nd among six firms short-listed for the Taxi capitalisation. The third one is an IT joint venture between the Tata Consultancy and J&J Group of Companies of South Africa established in 2001.

Ranbaxy, Cipla, Millennium Pharma, Cadilla, Hetro Drugs, Ashok Leyland, Jindal Steel, Kirloskar, Zensar, Eicher International, Interglobe Air Transport, Sahara Computers, Allied Chemicals, Shalimar Enterprises, Godrej Sara Lee, Paharpur Industries, ICICI Bank, and Zee TV are other companies having operations in South Africa. Public sector enterprises based in South Africa include NSIC and GoI Tourist Office.

Source: RIS based on information provided by the Indian Embassy in South Africa.

African Pharma company, Pharmadynamics, has signed a JV agreement with Wockhardt Pharmaceuticals for marketing their products in South Africa. Cape Town-based Sekunjalo has signed a contract with UNICHEM, India for marketing and distribution deal of generic drugs. Therefore, it may be concluded that while the number of investments from India to South Africa has increased continuously since 1995, India is yet to fully exploit the opportunities present in the emerging South African economies.

Indian investment in Brazil has been expanding at a very rapid pace. During 1996–2006, Indian investment in Brazil was about US$ 467.16 million, mostly driven by Indian pharmaceutical companies. As shown in Table 5.12, there was about 32 Indian JVs in Brazil, most of which are placed in pharmaceutical sector (16). Almost all the major Indian companies like Ranbaxy, Strides Acrolab, Dr. Reddy's Laboratories, Cadila Healthcare, Wockhardt, Orchid Chemicals & Pharmaceuticals, Torrent Pharma, Glenmark Pharma, Unichem, IPCA, etc., have established subsidiaries for manufacturing or marketing of drugs and pharmaceutical products in Brazil (see, Table 5.12 and Box 5.2).

Apart from pharmaceutical sector, Indian companies have entered into software, oil and gas, engineering sectors in Brazil. For example, TCS in 2005 and Satyam in 2007 started operation in IT sector in Brazil, and ONGC Videsh Limited (OVL) picked up 15 per cent stake (US$ 410 million) in Royal Dutch Shell for

TABLE 5.12

Indian Joint Venture Partnership in Brazil (as on December 2006)

Industry	*Companies*	*No of JVs*
Software and IT	TCS, Satyam, Aptech, Dexterity Eversystems, I-Flex Solutions, Prologix Support	6
Engineering	Bajaj Kasinski, Elgitread, CRI Pumps, Promac Engineering, Tata Motors, Thermax, TVS	7
Petrochemical & Chemical	Excel Crop. Care/Fersol, Flex Industries/PCE Premium, Reliance Industries	3
Pharmaceutical	Aurobindo Pharma, Bilcare, Cellofarm, Claris, Cipla, Dr. Reddy's Lab., Glenmark Pharma, Hetero, Unichem Pharma, Intas Pharma, IPCA, Orchid, Ranbaxy, Torrent, Wockhardt, Zydus Cadilla	16
	Total	32

Source: RIS based on information provided by the Consulate General of India, Sao Paulo.

exploration of oil and natural gas at a Brazilian oil field in April 2006. Indian automobile company, Mahindra is set to manufacture vehicles in Brazil through a JV partnership with a Brazilian company Bramont.

Technology Flows

It was already argued that countries in IBSA have developed technological capabilities in different spheres. The pattern of FDI has shown that investment between India, South Africa and Brazil is yet to reach a level to exploit synergies between their capabilities. Data on the number of foreign collaborations approved by India from Brazil and South Africa for the period 1995-2001 show that only four foreign collaborations have been approved by India from Brazil. Given the fact that during this period more than 8000 foreign collaborations have been approved by India, the limited technology spillovers from Brazil to India is too evident. This is despite the fact that Brazil is known for its capabilities in some of the high tech areas like manufacture of aircraft and parts, automobiles and parts, electronics goods etc.

In case of South Africa, on the other hand, the number of foreign collaborations has increased from 2 in 1995 to 7 in 2001. It is also worth noting that foreign collaborations in general were in areas where South Africa is known for their technological competence like breweries and diamond mining. At the same time, the present scale of technology transactions and investment flows is too small and that there is significant room for getting benefited by promoting transfer of technology across these countries.

Box 5.2

Indian Pharmaceutical Companies in Brazil

Ranbaxy Laboratories is among the top five generic companies in Brazil and it is the largest foreign generics pharmaceutical MNC in Brazil. The company has two subsidiaries in Brazil, *viz.*, Ranbaxy Farmaceutica Ltda (70 per cent equity holding) and Ranbaxy Do Brazil Ltda (10 per cent holding). The company's sales in Brazil were increased by 37 per cent to US$ 31 million in 2004. Ranbaxy is setting up a new manufacturing plant in Sao Gonzalo near Rio de Janeiro to meet the growing demand.

Torrent Pharma has set up Torrent do Brasil Ltda in 2002-03 with an investment of Rs. 17.79 crore in the equity capital. Subsequently, the company increased its investment to Rs. 31.11 crore during 2003-04. The Brazilian subsidiary commenced operations and within its first year of operations, it has introduced 14 products in the market, so far. The subsidiary is planning to expand its field force, doctor coverage, territorial coverage and distribution coverage in the coming years.

With the restructuring of its Latin America operations, Strides Acrolab strengthened its geographical leadership. A semi-solids facility was commissioned in the Vittoria Pharmaceutical Complex to cater to domestic demand.

Dr. Reddy's Laboratories has set up a subsidiary Dr. Reddy's Farmaceutica Do Brasil Ltda with an investment of Rs. 9.71 crore in the equity capital.

Cadila Healthcare received the approval from ANVISA (the drug regulatory body of Brazil) for its Moraiya formulations factory during 2004-05. The company is now entering the Brazilian market in a big way in the current year. The bio-equivalence facility of the Zydus Research Centre was approved by ANVISA and the company is filing the bio-equivalence products.

Wockhardt Ltd, through its subsidiary called Wockhardt Europe Ltd. (WEL), has set up a subsidiary in Brazil—Wockhardt Farmaceutica do Brasil Ltda for marketing its biotech products. WFL established 10 per cent business of Wockhardt Farmaceutica at a consideration of US$ 21,055. Besides marketing Wockhardt's generic pharmaceuticals, this company will enter into marketing arrangements for biotech products with specialised firms. Brazil is one of the world's top 10 generic markets, growing at 30 per cent per annum.

Glenmark Pharmaeutical is in the process of entering Brazil market. It has acquired Klinger Labs, a ANVISA approved Brazilin company for a consideration of US$ 5.25 million. Glenmark invested Rs. 1.75 crore in equity capital of Glenmark Farmaceutica Ltda, Brazil.

Orchid Chemicals & Pharmaceuticals has set up a subsidiary in Brazil to cater to the product registration and marketing requirements as Brazil is a large and fast growing market for cephalosporins. Orchid has stepped up its investments to Rs. 54.07 lakh in the equity capital during 2004-05.

Ipca has invested Rs. 3.44 crore in equity capital of its wholly owned Brazilian subsidiary Laboratories IPCA Do Brasil Ltda. The company commenced the marketing operations during 2003-04 and its five products are already registered with regulatory authorities.

Another Indian pharmaceutical company, Unichem has strengthened its international operations by opening up subsidiaries in several countries including Brazil.

Source: RIS based on Pharmabiz.com

5.6 Sectors of Investment and Technology Cooperation

The growing outward FDI from India to South Africa and Brazil and the flows between developing countries generate considerable scopes for investment and technology cooperation. Countries in IBSA are focused to facilitate cross-border FDI flows. Brazil, India and South Africa have undertaken series of policy reforms in the realm of trade and investment. These policy reforms not only underscore the links between trade and investment but also the primacy of foreign investment as a means of achieving higher rate of economic growth and transfer of technology. Such a renewed interest in FDI is based on the generally held view that FDI could act as a source of new technology and management expertise and also helps bridging the saving investment gap. There is ample evidence to show that Brazil, India and South Africa, during the last few decades, have developed substantial capabilities, which in turn leave scope for mutually beneficial cooperation among them and also for other countries in the three continents. We, therefore, need to pay greater attention to the facilitation of FDI in IBSA. There is scope to share the experiences in this area. Cooperation between IBSA may enhance opportunities for cross-border investments and contribute to their mutual development.

Aircraft Manufacturing

The demand for aircraft is bound to increase in the developing countries during the years to come. But the Brazilian company EMBRAER is perhaps the only company outside the developed countries to have capabilities for designing and manufacturing of jet aircrafts (up to 100 seats). EMBRAER delivered 101 air planes in 2003 talks about its capabilities. As India is in the process of developing the design and manufacturing capabilities for small aircrafts at HAL, Bangalore, much could be learned and gained by India working together with Brazil in this field.

Auto Components

Brazil is estimated to have a domestic production of nearly US$ 15 billion worth of automotive parts in the year 2004 and is rated as one among the top 10 automotive manufacturers in the world. During the last decade, India also has been developing a vibrant auto component industry and has been in the process of furthering its capabilities in automobiles manufacture. Yet, there has been hardly any interface between Indian automobile industry and Brazil. Tata Motors has entered into a JV with Brazil-based Marcopolo in May 2006 to set-up an automobile company in India that will manufacture and assemble fully built buses and coaches.

Drugs and Pharmaceuticals

Brazil has a large pharmaceutical sector with the sales as high as US$ 5.6 billion in 2003. At the same time during 1999-2003 Brazil imported US$ 1.5 billion annually in pharmaceutical products. India is known for her capabilities in the production of wide range of pharma products at low cost. Till date, about 16 and 12 Indian pharmaceutical companies are operating in Brazil and South Africa respectively. The relatively large production base along with growing domestic market offers highly rewarding areas of cooperation.

Electronics and Computer Hardware

Another industry wherein India and Brazil adopted similar development strategy has been electronics, especially computer hardware. According to the Brazilian electrical and electronic industry association, the local production has reached a level of US$ 22.4 billion in 2003 whereas the total electronics production in India during 2002-03 has only been of the order of US$ 7.6 billion. Both countries were fairly successful in establishing a broad based electronic production base by following the imports substitution strategies. However, the liberalized policies of the 1990s have witnessed marked decline in the rate of growth of electronic production in both countries. Leading producers of hardware in India have moved towards software. In case of Brazil, computer industry came to be dominated by foreign firms like IBM, HP-COMPAQ. However, some of the Brazilian firms like Itautec, Tropcom and Byte On still holds market shares in the range of 5 to 7 per cent (Arora and Gambardella 2004). The crucial issue is, can IT cooperation between India, Brazil and South Africa could help strengthening the hardware production base in IBSA? The cooperation in hardware needs to focus on, among others, development of low cost hardware such that the fruits of such cooperation are not limited to the three countries, but also to the developing world.

Energy (Ethanol)

One of the notable achievements of Brazil, which is of considerable interest to oil importing countries like India, relates to their capability to manufacture ethanol from sugarcane. As is evident from Table 5.13 about 62 per cent of energy requirements of Brazil is met by renewable sources of which ethanol from sugarcane accounts for as much as 10 per cent.[13]

TABLE 5.13

Primary Sources of Energy in Brazil (% of Total)

Source	*1979*	*1983*	*1988*	*1994*
Renewable	54.0	61.7	62.3	61.7
Hydropower	25.1	30.4	33.8	37.8
Wood	22.3	20.7	17.3	12.7
Sugarcane	5.9	9.8	10.2	9.8
Others	0.6	0.8	1.1	1.4
Non-Renewable	46.0	38.3	37.7	38.3
Oil & Products	41.3	32.4	29.7	30.6
Natural Gas	0.7	1.3	2.1	2.4
Coal	3.9	4.7	5.7	5.3
Nuclear	0.0	0.0	0.1	0.1
Total	100.0	100.0	100.0	100.0

Source: http://www.brazil.org.uk/page.php?cid=159&ofset=1

Given the fact that India is the largest producer of sugarcane in the world and has a booming energy oil import bill, the returns from India-Brazil cooperation in this field cannot be over emphasised. There are immense opportunities of Ethanol production in India with Brazilian technology, and sale of ethanol produced in Brazil to India. At the same time, India's capabilities in the field of solar photovoltaic could be of considerable interest for Brazil given the vastness of country and its

13. In April 2002, India and Brazil signed a memorandum of understanding for technology sharing in blending of petrol and diesel with ethanol.

settlement pattern. The opportunities cited above and others that are present though remain unutilised today, may be seen as opportunities to be exploited in the near future. This in turn, however, calls for imaginative policies and action plans to bring together business communities in these countries.

Food Processing

Brazil is known for its capabilities in the food processing industry. Brazil has been able to develop a wide variety of value-added products from root crops like cassava and other horticultural crops. Both India and South Africa may share these capabilities. Cassava is cultivated on a large-scale in some of the South Indian states. Yet, we have not been able to develop and market, value-added products from Cassava. Cassava is also cultivated on a large-scale in some of the African Countries. It has been observed that their success in terms of productivity per hectare is low as compared to India and Brazil and they could also benefit from developing value-added products. Hence, cooperation between IBSA in horticulture and root crops could be beneficial to all the three.

Gems and Jewellery

It is understood that bulk of trade between India and South Africa is in gold, gems and jewellery. However, this trade is today routed through Europe and which in turn leads to a situation wherein neither South Africa nor India has a significant role in the value chain. Therefore, there appears to be immense potential for investment, which enables these countries to capture a significant position in gold, jems and jewellery value chain.

The abundant supply of coloured stones in Brazil and the rich craftsmanship of India in polishing stones provides yet another investment opportunity for the third country market.

Promoting Joint R&D Alliances

During the last few decades, India, Brazil and South Africa have developed significant technological capabilities in different fields. IBSA cooperation should be instrumental in taking these capabilities to new heights for the benefits of countries in the South in general and IBSA in particular. In pursuing this objective, an *IBSA Fund for promoting Joint R&D* could be set up to support joint R&D projects with active involvement of private sector and academia in IBSA. This may facilitate creation of strategic alliances between business enterprises of the three countries. It could also facilitate joint research on common problems of IBSA countries such as development of medicines for tropical diseases, AIDS drugs, Hepatitis vaccines, agricultural research. It could also facilitate joint initiatives for processed food safety, quality standard, quality harmonisation, market research and joint marketing among others. Other areas of cooperation in technology may include capacity building and harmonisation of bio-safety guidelines, IPR regulations, and other regulatory frameworks in tune with the international protocols.

To facilitate flow of technology between IBSA a *Technology Transfer Network* could be set up which may pool information on the availability of technologies with the enterprises/R&D organisations in the region.

Cooperation in SMEs

SMEs not only contribute a substantial proportion of industrial output, employment and exports, but they are breeding grounds for entrepreneurship. All the three countries have very rich experience and exchange of these experiences in promotion of SMEs and micro enterprises is likely to have profound development implications. It is also worth exploring what India could learn from the Black Economic Empowerment programme being implemented by South Africa.

The cooperation might take the form of bringing together the small-scale industry promotion agencies and SME Associations of IBSA to establish liaison with each other and learning from each other's experience and technology sharing.

5.7 Promoting Investment: Role of Investment Treaties

Among the policy factors, apart from tax incentives and investment subsidies, bilateral treaties aiming and promoting investment could be instrumental in attracting investment. Countries therefore increasingly resort to bilateral investment treaties as a means of attracting investment. Given the fact that the policy regime guiding FDI has been progressively getting liberalised and countries are competing among each other, the terms of investment treaties across different countries are becoming similar. As UNCTAD (2003) noted, the scope and content of BITs have become more standard over the years. Today, the main provisions deal with the scope and definition of foreign investment; admission and establishment; national treatment in the post-establishment phase; MFN treatment; fair and equitable treatment; guarantees and compensation in the event of expropriation; guarantees of free transfers of funds and repatriations of capital and profits; and dispute settlement provisions, both State-State and investor-State. But given the sheer number of BITs, the formulations of individual provisions remain varied, with differences in the language of the BITs signed some decades ago and those signed more recently.

Investment Agreements by India

Realising the importance of investment treaties, India has entered into Bilateral Investment Promotion and Protection Agreement (BIPA) with a number of countries. Government of India have, so far, signed BIPAs with 63 countries out of which 50 BIPAs have already come into force and the remaining agreements are in the process of being enforced. In addition, agreements have also been finalised and/or being negotiated with a number of other countries. According to the Model Text adopted by the Government of India, BIPAs apply to all investments made by investors of either Contracting Party (CP), "accepted as such in accordance with its laws and regulations, whether made before or after the coming into force" of the BIPA. Therefore, the coverage and scope of investments is determined by the national laws of the contracting parties. The important features of BIPA are: National Treatment for foreign investment; MFN treatment for foreign investment and investors; free repatriation/transfer of returns on investment; recourse to domestic disputes resolution and international arbitration for investor-State and State-State disputes; nationalisation/expropriation only in public interest on a non-discriminatory basis and against compensation etc. Some key features of BIPAs signed by India are as follows:

Definition of Investment: Since the objective is protection of investment, a broad definition covering every kind of asset established or acquired, including changes in the form of such investment, in accordance with the national laws of the contracting party in whose territory, the investment is made is adopted.

Scope of the Agreements: The agreements apply to all investments made by investors of either contracting party in the territory of the other contracting party, accepted as such in accordance with its laws and regulation.

Most-Favoured-Nation (MFN) Treatment: Investment from the contracting party shall not be given less favourable treatment than that accorded to investors of any third state.

National Treatment: Foreign investments are given the same treatment as given to domestic investments. National treatment is, however, not given to the foreign investors. As per India's present foreign investment policy, foreign investors have to follow a different policy compared to domestic investors. Thus, the treatment accorded is different from treatment extended to Indian investors. However, taxation matters are an exception to MFN and National Treatment. Another exception is existing or future customs unions or similar agreements.

Investment Promotion and Protection: Each CP shall encourage and create favourable conditions for investors of the other CP and will admit such investments in accordance with its laws and policy. Investments and returns of investors of each CP will be accorded fair and equitable treatment in the territory of the other CP.

Expropriation and Compensation: Expropriation/nationalisation of the investments from the contracting country will not be made except for a public purpose. Such an eventuality will be on a non-discriminatory basis and against fair and equitable compensation. Judicial review is available to the affected parties, if desired.

Repatriation Facilities: Free repatriation of its capital, profits, dividends and interest, repayment of loans, royalties and service fees, proceeds of disinvestments or sale of shares, earnings of citizens/nationals etc., is permitted. Also, safeguard is provided for allowing repatriation in the currency of the original investment at the current exchange rate prevailing on the date of transfer.

Dispute Settlement Mechanism: Elaborate provisions exist for resolution of disputes between the investor and a contracting party as well as between the contracting parties. In the former case flexibility is provided for settlement of disputes either under the domestic laws or under international arbitration.

Entry and Sojourn of Personnel: Free movement of personnel is provided in connection with the investment related activities, subject to the domestic laws relating to entries of foreign personnel.

Applicable Laws: The substantive laws applicable on investments will be the domestic law of the host country of investment unless otherwise provided in the agreement. Overriding provisions also exist for the host country to take appropriate action on security and environment grounds.

Duration and Termination of the Agreement: The agreements are initially valid for a period of 10 years and thereafter shall continue indefinitely unless either of the contracting states gives written notice of its intention to terminate the Agreement in which event the Agreement stands terminated one year after the receipt of such notice. In the event of termination of the Agreement, investments made prior to the termination will continue to enjoy the provisions of the Agreement for a further period of 15 years.

The Indian system also has in-built provisions for various elements of the investment protection agreements. It is an accepted principle that all foreign investments at post establishment stage are treated on par and no discrimination is made in the foreign investment made in convertible foreign currencies. Similarly, India's Exchange Control Regulations already provide facilities for repatriation of investment proceeds, return on investment, etc. Thus even without capital account convertibility, there is capital account convertibility in so far as the foreign investments are concerned. In the matter of dispute settlement mechanism, under an act of Parliament, international arbitration provision has also been introduced and thus enables the foreign investors with the option of redressing investment disputes with the state either under the domestic legal régime or going for international arbitration. Similarly, for entry and sojourn of personnel, our immigration laws and the Exchange Control Regulations, permit foreigners to take up employment in India, although with appropriate permissions.

TABLE 5.14

South Africa's Bilateral Investment Treaties (BITs)

Europe	Austria, Belgium/Luxembourg, Czech Republic, Denmark, Finland, France, Germany, Greece, Italy, Netherlands, Russian Federation, Spain, Sweden, Switzerland, United Kingdom
Africa	Algeria, Egypt, Ghana, Libya, Mauritius, Mozambique, Nigeria, Rwanda, Senegal, Tunisia
Asia/Middle East	China, Iran, Korea, Turkey
Latin America	Argentina, Chile, Cuba

Source: SA Department of Foreign Affairs.

Till March 2007, there were about 50 countries with which India has signed and enforced the BIPA. India has also signed BIPAs with 13 countries (as on March 2007) but not yet enforced, and the negotiation with 41 countries is underway (Government of India, 2007). Here it may be noted that neither South Africa nor Brazil are included in the list of countries with which India signed BIPA. However, negotiation for BIPA with South Africa and Brazil are underway. Given the rising investments from India to South Africa and Brazil, it would be worthwhile to conclude the BIPA with these two countries at the earliest.

Investment Agreements by South Africa[14]

As of 2004, South Africa is a party to 32 bilateral investment treaties (BITs), all of which were signed since the country's transition to a democratic dispensation in 1994. The first BIT was signed with the UK in September 1994, symbolising the start of the country's reintegration into the world economy.

Table 5.14 provides an overview of South Africa's 'formal' investment partners by region. It may be noted that India is not a party to this agreement. In addition to these treaties, South Africa has also signed various forms of investment cooperation agreements with Algeria, Canada, Cote d'Ivoire, Malaysia, Paraguay, Saudi Arabia, and the US. Other negotiated drafts (with Angola, for example) remain unsigned. A previous investment cooperation agreement (*Agreement of Co-operation on the Promotion of Investments*') with Taiwan was annulled following South Africa's establishment of formal relations with the People's Republic of China in 1998. Most of South Africa's BITs are with European countries and European Union members in particular, the remainder having been concluded principally with African, certain Asian and Latin American countries. Only two of the African BITs are with co-members in the Southern African Development Community (SADC): Mauritius and Mozambique.

14. For a detailed discussion see Trade Law Center for South Africa (2004).

South Africa's BITs are fairly broad in scope, and cover a wide range of investments. These include movable and immovable property, shares, bonds, and interest in companies, claims to money, assets or performance having economic value, intellectual property, and licences or other rights to exploit a resource. However, the definitions provided in South Africa's BITs are not as specific as in other investment treaties. Key features of South Africa's BITs include following.

Each party to the agreement is to afford investments from the other contracting party the necessary permits in connection with such investments, shall not discriminate against such investments and treat such investments "no less favourably" than domestic investments (National treatment principle).[15]

The BITs contain specific clauses relating to restitution, indemnification, compensation or other settlement, stipulating that this be no less favourable to investors from the other contracting party as it is relating to its own investors. Expropriation of foreign investors' property may only take place under exceptional circumstances where, this is for public purposes, takes place in a non-discriminatory manner, is conducted in a transparent and legal process and against fair, prompt and market-related compensation.

Each contracting party shall allow investors free transfer of payments relating to their investments in a prompt manner at the most recent exchange rate applied to inward investments.

BITs afford dispute resolution an elevated status, as is illustrated by the relatively large number of clauses relating to this matter.

Brazilian Bilateral Agreements to Promote and Protect Investments

Brazil is a signatory of a large number of bilateral agreements (24 in all) designed to prevent double taxation, and has signed almost two dozen bilateral investment agreements with OECD countries and developing countries, two of them with other Latin-American countries: Chile (March 1994) and Venezuela (July 1995). None of the bilateral agreements signed, however, has been ratified by the Brazilian Congress (Veiga, 2004).[16] However, Brazil has entered into agreement with a number of countries for the avoidance of double taxation (see Table 5.15).

While India is a member of such tax treaty, an agreement is yet to be entered into between Brazil and South Africa. Hence, to attract more investment

15. However, the contracting parties are not obliged to afford each other special privileges that may result from any customs union, free trade area or the like that either country may be party to. A notable derogation from the non-discrimination and national treatment principle is contained in seven of South Africa's BITs, namely China, the Czech Republic, Ghana, Iran, Mauritius, Nigeria and the Russian Federation (See for details Vickers, 2003).

16. See in this context Veiga (2004).

from these countries to India and also to promote Indian investment in these countries steps may be taken to enter into trilateral investment agreement in tune with India's BIPA with other countries. Given the fact that India's BIPA takes into account almost all the concerns of investors and also provides a highly propitious environment for investment promotions, the BIPA could be a model for the trilateral agreement between India, Brazil and South Africa.

5.8 Concluding Observations

To sum up, the investment regime that exists today in all the three countries is highly conducive for promoting investment from abroad. At the same time, building on to the technological capabilities built up during the last few decades, each of these countries with a view to promote outward investment have undertaken policy measures that induce the local companies to "go global". Thus the policy environment today is highly tuned both from the demand and supply side, which in turn has made all the three countries major investors abroad. Yet, the investment and technology transactions between India and other two countries are yet to reach its potentials. While a beginning seems to have been made in terms of investment between India and South Africa, that with Brazil is in its preliminary stage. Given the immense potential that exists, present study sets a target of US$ 1 billion FDI inflows to India and puts forward certain specific sectors for investment and technology cooperation. These sectors include aircraft manufacturing, electronics and computer hardware, energy, gems and jewellery, drugs and pharmaceuticals and auto components. To promote investment and technology cooperation the study calls for greater interactions between the investment promotion agencies, an IBSA Investment Agreement, setting up of a technology transfer network along with promotion of jointed R&D alliances especially between private sector firms in these countries.

TABLE 5.15

Bilateral Treaties for the Avoidance of Double Taxation by Brazil

Country	*Year*	*Focus*
United States	1929	Air and Sea Transport
Japan	1967	Income and Capital
United Kingdom	1967	Air and Sea Transport
France	1971	Income and Capital
Portugal	1971	Income and Capital
Belgium	1972	Air and Sea Transport
Finland	1972	Income and Capital
Denmark	1974	Income and Capital
Spain	1974	Income and Capital
Austria	1975	Income and Capital
Germany	1975	Income and Capital
Sweden	1975	Income and Capital
Italy	1978	Income and Capital
Luxembourg	1978	Income and Capital
Argentina	1980	Income and Capital
Norway	1980	Income and Capital
Ecuador	1983	Income and Capital
Philippines	1983	Income and Capital
Canada	1984	Income and Capital
Czech Republic	1986	Income and Capital
Hungary	1986	Income and Capital
Slovakia	1986	Income and Capital
India	1988	Income and Capital
Korea, Republic of	1989	Income and Capital
Netherlands	1990	Income and Capital
China	1991	Income and Capital
Finland	1996	Income and Capital
United States	1997	Air and Sea Transport
Paraguay	2000	Income
Portugal	2000	Income
Chile	2001	Income and Capital
Portugal	2001	Income and Capital
Belgium	2002	Income and Capital
Israel	2002	Income and Capital

Source: UNCTAD database on BITs and DTTs.

Facilitating FDI Flows within IBSA

There have been significant two-way flows between India and South Africa but potential of investment between India and Brazil is hardly exploited. A number of measures can be taken within the IBSA framework to facilitate mutual investment flows between them, as follows.

An IBSA Investment Agreement (IIA)

A trilateral IBSA Investment Agreement (IIA) signed within the framework of IBSA could be a useful component of the IBSA Comprehensive Economic Cooperation Agreement, as proposed in this Report. The IIA could provide a framework for post-investment national treatment, non-discrimination, investment protection and dispute settlement to promote mutual investment flows. It can also be complemented by an IBSA Double Taxation Avoidance Agreement to further promote mutual investment agreements.

Cooperation among the Investment Promotion Agencies

All the three countries are having their respective investment promotion agencies. These agencies may cooperate between themselves and set up their representative offices in other member countries. Such representative offices could be instrumental in the dissemination of information about the policies, rules and procedures of the respective countries, linking the potential investors with local entrepreneurs, facilitating approvals, among other initiatives.

APPENDIX 5.1

Largest TNCs from Brazil and their Major Field of Operation

Name of the Company	*Field of Operation*	*Sales ($ Million)*	*No. of Employees*
	A. Industrial		
Petroleo Brasileiro- PETROBRAS	Petroleum	22612	49049
Group Gerdau	Metal	4590[b]	18955
Companhia Vale Do Rio Doce-CVRD	Mining and Quarrying	2942	10973
Weg	Electrical and Electronic equipment	900[b]	
Marcopolo	Motor Vehicles	310	5000
Tigre Tubos E Conexoes	Chemicals	281	2200
Sao Paulo Alpargatas	Textiles	252	11000
Latasa[a]	Metals	220	1000
IBF-Industria Brasileira de Filmes	Precision equipment	61	750
Forjas Taurus	Machinery and equipment	48	1000
Renner Hermann	Chemicals	20	346
Sisalana-Industria E Comercio	Textiles	11	101
Convex Industria Da Amazonia	Electrical and electronic equipment	11	39
Tupy	Machinery and equipment	1	3
Companhia de Bebidas Das Americas-AMBEV	Beverages		18570
Nemofeffer	Paper		5
	B. Tertiary		
Empresa Brasilera de Aeronautica-EMBRAER	Transport and storage	2676	1227
Viacao Aerea Rio-Grandense-VARIG	Transport and storage	1981	12000
Teka Tecelagem KuehnrichOther business services	168	6451	
Soletur Sol Agencia de Viagens E Turismo	Lesiure	53	
Politec	Other Business services	49	5000
Linksat Sistemas de Comunicacao	Trade	2	9
Seisa Cleman Empreendimentos Imobilliarios	Construction	2	2
Andrade Guiterez	Construction		50
Embratel Participacoes	Telecommunications		12010
Itausa-investimentos Itau	Diversified II		54648
Matrix Informatica	Other Business Services		
Atus Participacces	Other Business Services		2
Banco Bradesco	Other Business Services		74393
Ibest	Other Business Services		
	C. Finance and Insurance	Assets	Employees
Banco do Brasil	Finance	57795	77299
Banco Bradesco	Finance	47659[c]	73943[c]
Banco Itau	Finance	35407	47524[c]
Banco Safra	Finance	12920[c]	3379[c]
Banco Rural	Finance	1496[c]	1667[c]
UNIBANCO-Uniao de Bancos Brasileiros	Finance	431[c]	29704[c]
Banco BMG	Finance	386[c]	500[c]

Notes: [a]-Latasa was sold to Rexam in November 2003; [b]-2003. [c]-December 2001.

Source: UNCTAD (2004d).

APPENDIX 5.2

Bilateral Investment Treaties Concluded during 1995-2003: India

Partner	Year	Partner	Year
Argentina	1999	Mauritius	1998
Armenia	2003	Mongolia	2001
Australia	1999	Morocco	1999
Austria	1999	Netherlands	1995
Belgium/Luxembourg	1997	Oman	1997
Bulgaria	1998	Philippines	2000
Croatia	2001	Poland	1996
Cyprus	2002	Qatar	1999
Czech Republic	1996	Romania	1997
Denmark	1995	Spain	1997
Djibouti	2003	Sri Lanka	1997
Egypt	1997	Sudan	2003
Finland	2002	Sweden	2000
France	1997	Switzerland	1997
Germany	1995	Tajikistan	1995
Hungary	2003	Thailand	2000
Indonesia	1999	Turkey	1998
Israel	1996	Turkmenistan	1995
Italy	1995	Ukraine	2001
Kazakhstan	1996	Uzbekistan	1999
Korea, Republic of	1996	Vietnam	1997
Kuwait	2001	Yemen	2002
Kyrgyzstan	1997	Yugoslavia (former)	2003
Lao PDR	2000	Zimbabwe	1999
Malaysia	1995		

Source: UNCTAD, BIT/DTT database; *www.unctad.org/fdistatistics*

APPENDIX 5.3

Double Taxation Treaties Concluded during 1995-2003: India

Partner	*Year*
Belarus	1997
Canada	1996
Czech Republic	1998
Finland	1997
Germany	1995
Ireland	2000
Israel	1996
Jordan	1999
Morocco	1998
New Zealand	1999
Oman	1997
Portugal	1998
Qatar	1999
Sweden	1997
Trinidad and Tobago	1999
Turkey	1995
Turkmenistan	1997

Source: UNCTAD, BIT/DTT database; *www.unctad.org/fdistatistics*

CHAPTER 6

Firming up the Connectivity

Civil Aviation and Maritime Links

6.1 Introduction

We have seen that one of the factors that stands in the way of trade expansion between IBSA relates to weak connectivity and high transportation cost. Hence, any discussion on promoting the trade and investment relations between IBSA countries remains incomplete without addressing the issues relating to connectivity. In this chapter, we review the transportation linkages between India and South Africa, and India and Brazil. Since, shipping and airways are the only modes that connect these three countries and also carry the merchandise trade and people, an attempt is also made here to understand present profile of maritime and air transportation linkages in the region. Cross-country movement of goods through this network, particularly between India and South Africa, and India and Brazil, is dealt in the next section. Finally, based on above analysis, conclusions and policy implications are drawn in the last section.

6.2 Transport Linkages

High intra-regional trade has long been recognised as being necessary for all economies aspiring to form regional trading arrangement. We have seen in previous chapters that even though absolute volume of intra-IBSA trade at present is found to be low, compared to the same registered with predominant regional trading blocs, trade within these three countries has been remarkably growing over 50 per cent every year since 1991, where India's trade with South Africa and Brazil shows a consistently rising trend in recent years. This brings enough reasons to investigate whether the region is equipped with adequate transportation facilities to enhance intra-IBSA trade at a crucial point in time when intra-IBSA trade is growing at a faster rate. In view of the above, we will be discussing the present status of transportation linkages, pertaining to India's connectivity with the two countries in IBSA. It is widely accepted that intra-IBSA trade is mostly carried out through sea and a very negligible part by air (De, 2006b). Hence, while making any policy formulation for enhanced trade in the region, importance of maritime transport sector in integrating these three economies needs special attention.

Ports and Shipping

Even though India, Brazil, and South Africa are located in three separate continents, they are embedded with ample open outlets for merchandise trading. All the three countries are endowed with vast coastline (5560 kms for India, 2798 kms for South Africa, and 7491 kms for Brazil) and are dotted with many working ports—28 of India, 7 of South Africa and 46 of Brazil. At present, ports of these three countries together handle 1.32 billion tonnes of cargo including 13.40 million TEUs of container, sharing 3.62 per cent of world container traffic (Table 6.1). Richards Bay in South Africa is the largest port in IBSA in terms of annual port throughput. With 98.35 million tonnes of cargo in 2003-04, this South African port alone shares 72 per cent of total South African annual port throughput. Bulk and break bulk cargos, coming from Indian Ocean region (India) to South Africa are normally unloaded at the port of Richards Bay. This port's

TABLE 6.1

Ports of IBSA in 2004

Countries	*Length of Coastline* KM	*No of Ports*[1]	*Total Cargo* MT	*Container Cargo*[3] MTEU	*Top Ten Ports in IBSA*[4]
India	5560	28	520.72	4.94	Richards Bay (98.35), SA Tubarao (82.12), Brazil Itaqui (72.90), Brazil Santos (60.50), Brazil Sao Sebastio (59.27), Brazil
South Africa[2] (SA)	2798	7	190.50	2.87	Vizag (50.15), India Chennai (43.81), India Kandla (41.55), India Haldia (36.26), India
Brazil	7491	46	610.48	5.60	Durban (31.74), SA
Total	15849	81	1321.70	13.40	

Notes: 1. No of major cargo handling ports.
2. Data for South Africa is reported for the year 2003-04.
3. Data for the year 2005-06.
4. Port traffic for India is for 2004-05, and the same for Brazil and South Africa is for 2003-04.
Data in parenthesis are the throughput of the respective ports.
MT and MTEU stand for million tonnes and million twenty foot equivalent units respectively.

Sources: 1. Ministry of Shipping, Government of India for Indian ports.
2. National Ports Authority of South Africa for South African ports.
3. United Nations Economic Commission for the Latin America and Caribbean (ECLAC) for Brazilian ports.

inherent strength is its deep-water infrastructure, with a maximum permissible draught of 17.5 metres. With annual throughput of 82.12 million tonnes, the Brazilian port, namely, Tubarao, comes next to Richards Bay. India's largest port, Vizag, occupies the sixth position in the league. Some common features of top three largest ports of the three countries in IBSA are: (a) all seaports, located on the east coast of their respective countries, (b) all predominantly bulk ports, thereby representing these countries' heavy reliance on bulk trade, (c) all endowed with deep draught in the range between 14-18 meters, and (d) all regulated by the Government.

Richards Bay (South Africa), Tubarao (Brazil), and Vizag (India) are three largest ports of three countries in the region, which are predominantly bulk ports. In case of containerised cargo, the aforesaid order does not follow in IBSA. With 2.37 million TEUs in 2004-05, India's Jawaharlal Nehru port occupies the top position in IBSA, whereas with 1.90 and 1.65 million TEUs, Santos (Brazil) and Durban (South Africa) come next to Jawaharlal Nehru port, respectively.

A possible explanation for the low intra-regional sea freight, resulting in low intra-regional maritime interdependence, might be the absence of intensified merchandise trade. This is some way captured in Table 6.2. Table 6.2 shows that

TABLE 6.2

*Port-wise Intra-IBSA Sea Freight: India vs. IBSA**

'000 Tonnes

Ports	*Year: 2000-01*			*Year: 2001-02*		
	India's Sea Freight (Exports + Imports) with					
	South Africa	*Brazil*	*IBSA*	*South Africa*	*Brazil*	*IBSA*
Paradip	0	0	0	22	0	22
Vizag	32	4	36	66	44	110
Chennai	0	7	7	0	48	48
Tuticorin	191	0	191	69	0	69
Cochin	74	0	74	0	0	0
New Mangalore	9	0	9	8	0	8
Mormugao	431	0	431	1233	0	1233
Jawaharlal Nehru	0	138	138	0	0	0
Mumbai	151	11	162	49	0	49
Kandla	453	84	537	659	169	828
Total	1341	244	1585	2106	261	2367
Total (million tonnes)	1.341	0.244	1.585	2.106	0.261	2.367

Note: *-Excluding containerised traffic.

Source: Ministry of Shipping, Government of India.

intra-regional sea freight to the extent of India's trade with rest two members of IBSA is very low (1.59 MT in 2000-01 and 2.37 MT in 2001-02), which is accounting for only 0.52 per cent of India's total sea freight. Table 6.2 also indicates that India-South Africa freight component alone shares more than 90 per cent of total India-IBSA sea freight, which has gone up from 1.35 MT in 2000-2001 to 2.12 MT in 2001-02. India's sea freight with Brazil is very negligible at about 0.24 million tonnes.

India's port-wise trade, which is reported in Table 6.2, is also extended to commodity-wise and is reported as Appendix 6.1. It may be observed from the Appendix 6.1 that imported coking coal from South Africa is handled at Mormugao port, and imported phosphoric acid from South Africa is unloaded at Kandla and Tuticorin ports. India imports good amount of edible oil from Brazil, which is normally handled at Kandla and Jawaharlal Nehru ports. Indian foodgrains to South Africa is exported mostly through Mumbai and Kandla ports, whereas petroleum, coke and ores are exported to Brazil through Vizag and Chennai ports. Jawaharlal Nehru, Mumbai, Mundra and Tuticorin ports handle most of the containerised traffic going to (and coming from) South Africa and Brazil. Hence, except Kolkata and Haldia ports, rest of the Indian ports have direct/ indirect trade and shipping linkages with South African and Brazilian ports.

This low volume bulk sea freight does not attract regular services of general cargo carriers. What is important is that there is high potential of bulk shipping as countries in IBSA are aspiring to attain high intra-regional trade.

Containerised Shipping

Unlike bulk and break bulk shipping, we have rather considerable presence of liner shipping companies in IBSA because container business volume is comparatively bigger than that of bulk and break bulk segments. To assess the liner shipping deepening process, we have estimated the containerised traffic, generated from India's trade with South Africa and Brazil, in Table 6.3.

Table 6.3 shows that India's containerised trade with IBSA generated approximately 105,458 TEUs in 2005-06, out of which 87 per cent (91,780 TEUs) generated from India's trade with South Africa and 13 per cent (13,678 TEUs) with Brazil. Even if India's containerised trade with IBSA is too small, compared to her total global containerised trade, there is high potential for higher containerised trade in IBSA when intra-regional trade has been growing at a faster rate. This potential is apparent if we look into the quantum jump of containerised trade in the region. India's containerised trade with IBSA estimated to be 44,620 TEUs in 2000-01, became 105,458 in 2005-06 within a span of five years. This jump in containerised trade, mostly generated from between India and South Africa, has attracted many noted shipping companies in the region.

TABLE 6.3

Estimated India's Containerised Trade with IBSA

TEUs

Category	*2000-01*	*2001-02*	*2002-03*	*2003-04*	*2004-05*	*2005-06*
Exports to South Africa	9449	29135	51631	50320	62430	76092
Imports from South Africa	22833	23015	14690	14046	14821	15688
Total Trade with South Africa	32282	52150	66321	64366	77251	91780
Exports to Brazil	2595	3185	3473	2904	3760	4128
Imports from Brazil	9743	9092	9245	8765	9073	9550
Total Trade with Brazil	12338	12277	12718	11669	12833	13678
Exports to IBSA	12044	32320	55104	53224	66190	80220
Imports from IBSA	32576	32107	23935	22811	23894	25238
Total Trade with IBSA	44620	64427	79039	76035	90084	105458

Source: Calculated from Export-Import Database, Ministry of Commerce and Industry, Government of India.

Table 6.4 reports that operational profile of shipping lines, which are operating in IBSA. Brazilian and Indian ports are not connected by any direct call service, whereas the same exists between India and South Africa, and Brazil and South Africa. Due to low volume of containerised traffic, we have no direct shipping lines operating between India and Brazil. There are at present 12 and 18 lines operating in India-South Africa, and South Africa–Brazil sectors respectively. Most of these lines offer "fixed-day-sailing" and operate once in a week in the containerised segment. At present, due to absence of direct calls between Indian and Brazilian ports, most of the Indian cargos, going to Brazil (or coming from Brazil), are transhipped at either Durban (South Africa) or Dubai JA (UAE) or at Salalah (Oman). There are some common shipping lines, which operate

TABLE 6.4

Liner Services in IBSA in 2006[1]

	India–South Africa	*South Africa–Brazil*
No of Liner Companies	12	18
Ports Connected		
India	Mundra, Jawaharlal Nehru, Tuticorin, Mumbai	
South Africa	Port of Elizabeth, Durban, Cape Town	Port of Elizabeth, Durban, Cape Town
Brazil		Paranaqua, Santos, Itaqui, Rio Grande, Rio de Janeiro, Sao Francisco do Sul
Average Voyage Time	16-18 days	9-12 days
Frequency	1 call per week Fixed Day Sailing	1 call per week Fixed Day Sailing

Note: 1. As on December 2006.

Source: CI Online, Containerisation International, Informa UK Ltd., London.

liner vessels in both India–South Africa and South Africa–Brazil sectors, such as Maersk Sealand and P&O Nedlloyd. While most of Maersk vessels, originating from Brazil and coming towards South/Southeast Asia, cross Atlantic, P&O Nedlloyd's vessels normally cross Pacific and then Hong Kong, Singapore and finally South Asia. There is also one established shipping conference in India and South Africa sector, named "Indian Ocean Vessel Sharing Agreement", participated by P&O Nedlloyd and Gold Star Line, which is formed to handle container traffic between South/East Africa to Indian Subcontinent/Middle East. The liner shipping network in IBSA is shown in Figure 6.1.

FIGURE 6.1

*Liner Shipping Network in IBSA**

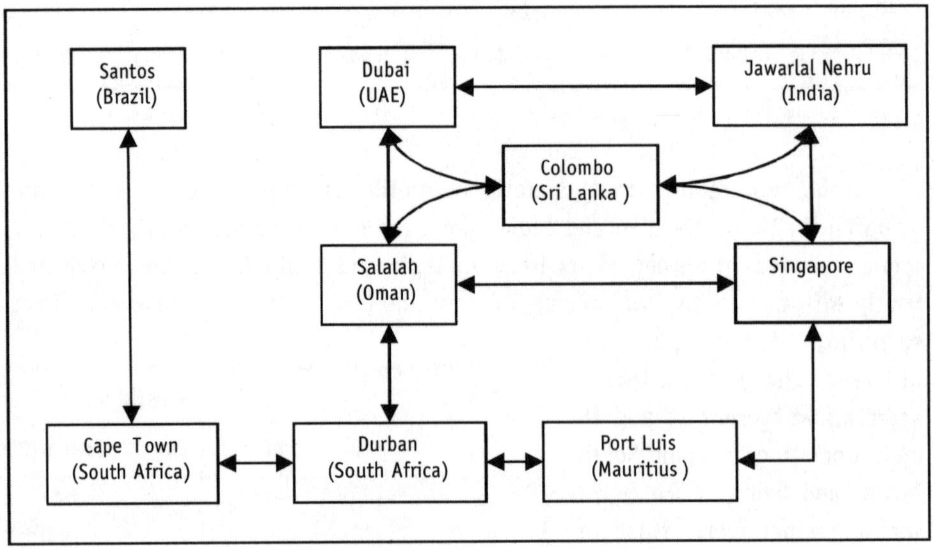

* Diagramatic representation of present liner networks.

From the foregoing analysis, it may be concluded that lower intra-regional trade has resulted in lower intra-regional sea freight. Moreover, there has been some sort of inter-linkage in the non-containerised trade between the ports of India and South Africa, and India and Brazil, while the same is more intensified in the containerised trade. Hence, one of our prime tasks would be to remove the inconsistency in bulk shipping by encouraging more merchandise trade in IBSA. Over and above, forming a regional shipping network, "IBSA Liner Network", would pave the way in achieving an intra-regional maritime integration process. The foregoing analysis also calls for an urgent effort to form a regional shipping conference in IBSA. We will have to keep in mind that all our efforts should lead not only to reduce the cost of transportation among the three countries, but also to enhance the containerised trade in the region.

Transportation Costs

Recent literature has emphasised the importance of transport costs and infrastructure in explaining trade, access to markets, and increases in per capita income. A possible explanation for the low intra-regional trade might be a supposed presence of high transaction costs. There are a number of studies, which show that higher the volume of intra-regional trade, better the economies of scale in transportation and lower the transaction costs. In case of IBSA, we have encountered not only with low volume of intra-regional trade but are also involved in multiple transhipments.

The intra-regional transportation cost, particularly between India and Brazil is abysmally high due to cost of transhipment and long journey. There are high frequencies of transhipment resulting in high transportation costs between the countries in IBSA. Poor performance of ports also adds to the cost of transportation.

Table 6.5 reports the inter-continental transportation costs in IBSA. As usual, India's imports from Brazil (and also Brazil's imports from India) involve higher transportation costs compared to the same generated out of their bilateral trade with South Africa. Since, India and Brazil are located at two extreme points in IBSA and due to absence of direct shipping linkage between the two countries, average 26 per cent of total value of Brazil's imports from India and about 34 per cent of India's total imports from Brazil in 2006 incurred as international transportation costs. However, the merchandise trade between India and South Africa and that between Brazil and South Africa are associated with about 9 per cent international transportation costs. Higher transportation cost increases the costs of import through which it negatively affect the growth of intra-regional trade. Hence, efforts should to be initiated to minimise the international transportation costs, failing which growth of intra-regional trade will hamper.

TABLE 6.5

*IBSA Transportation Costs (TC) in 2004**

Importer	*Exporter*	*TC (%)*
India	South Africa	9.09
India#	Brazil	34.36
South Africa	India	9.09
South Africa	Brazil	9.09
Brazil	India	25.81
Brazil	South Africa	9.09

Notes: *: Calculated based on [(cif/fob)-1]*100; represented as percentage in terms of total imports.

#: Adjusted with cif factor due to data discrepancy in reported trade statistics.

Source: RIS based on DOTS, 2007, IMF.

Nonetheless, there exists good potential to promote intra-regional trade by integrating liner shipping companies and also by improving transport services. It is found that there does not exist any direct services, particularly between Brazil and India. As on date, only 2 liner services that call in India-South Africa region also call in South Africa-Brazil region. In addition, due to the increase in transhipment services, trade between India and Brazil is slowly becoming uncompetitive.

Airways

Air transport sector is one of the fastest growing industries in IBSA. In 2005, IBSA generated 2.26 per cent of world air freight, carried 3.81 per cent of world air passengers, and operated approximately 1 million world aircrafts (see Table 6.6). In terms of aforesaid three indicators, Brazil stands at the top among the three. It alone carried 47.43 per cent of air freight and 48.89 per cent of passengers, and operates 51.98 per cent of aircrafts in IBSA in 2005. The growth in air transportation sector in IBSA is influenced by the rise of domestic air transport sector. With opening of economies coupled with growing services sector (such as tourism and information technology) international air transport in IBSA has also been growing fast. All the three prime airlines in IBSA, namely, South African Airways (SAA), Brazilian Airways (Varig Brazil) and Air India (Indian) have stepped forward to strengthen their respective fleet sizes and international networks. In general, all the three airlines in IBSA are desperately looking to strengthen their fleets, alliance partners, and opening new operations.

TABLE 6.6

Air Transport Sector in IBSA in 2005

	Country	*2005*
Air transport, freight (million tonnes per km)	Brazil	1530.68
	India	773.22
	South Africa	923.38
	World	142570.78
	IBSA share (%)[1]	2.26
Air transport, passengers carried	Brazil	37661733.00
	India	27527738.00
	South Africa	11844657.00
	World	2020603951.00
	IBSA share (%)[1]	3.81
Air transport, registered carrier departures worldwide	Brazil	514700.00
	India	327388.00
	South Africa	148146.00
	World	24877724.00
	IBSA share (%)[1]	3.98

Note: 1. Share in world.

Source: RIS based on *World Development Indicators CD ROM 2007*, World Bank.

Although the air transport sector has been playing a greater role in integrating the three economies, there is a missing link in direct air connectivity between India and Brazil, due to which, South Africa has been found as one of the preferred transit point for passengers moving between India and Brazil using SAA. This is an area, which needs special attention. In so far as fleet strength is concerned, South African Airways, which is fully privatised, comes in leading position. With 60 own fleets in the international sector, SAA serves 91 international destinations individually and more than 600 along with its alliance partners in the current year (see Table 6.7), even though it has less alliance partners than Varig and Air India. It amply indicates that SAA has been performing well for quite sometime now, and their experiences can be extended to IBSA for further consolidation of the air transport industry in the region.

TABLE 6.7

Airlines Performance Indicators in IBSA in 2004

Particulars	*SAA*	*Air India*	*Varig*
No. of International Own Fleets[1]	60	34	47
International Destinations Served[1]	91	32	63
Alliance Partner	12	16	16
Member of Star Alliance	No	No	Yes

Note: 1. Without any code sharing.

Sources: RIS based on individual web sites of the Airlines.

TABLE 6.8

South African Airways in IBSA (As on December 2005)

Sector	Frequency	Fleet Type	Capacity	Travel Time
Mumbai–Johannesburg–Mumbai	4 flights per week Non-stop	A340-200	236 passengers 42 business class 194 economy class	8 hours
Johannesburg–Sao Paolo–Johannesburg	Daily Non-stop	A340-300	269 passengers 38 business class 231 economy class	10 hours

Sources: RIS based on individual web sites of the Airlines.

At present, except South African Airways, no other airlines from India and Brazil fly in IBSA. South African Airways has direct non-stop flights to Mumbai in India and Sao Paolo in Brazil. Timing of the flight is also very much convenient to Indian passenger going to (or coming from) Brazil via Johannesburg (JNB); a passenger has to wait just 3 hours at JNB to catch next flight to Sao Paolo. Moreover, SAA has deployed a latest Airbus fleet, A340-200, in India-South Africa sector, and A340-300 in the South Africa-Brazil sector. Table 6.8 captures some of the features of SAA.

In most of cases, passengers, travelling from Mumbai to South Africa, choose SAA or Emirates for travelling to South Africa. Since there are multiple options, it is found that in some cases passengers, mostly tourists, also choose Emirates and/or some other African airlines such as Kenyan Airways, Ethiopian Airlines, Tanzanian Airways, etc. for travelling to South Africa. However, in case of travelling to Brazil, Indian passengers have no option rather to choose SAA, which is most convenient in terms of travelling time and cost.

SAA is also found as most convenient airline, in terms of both travelling time and air fare, for those who are going to South Africa or to Brazil (Table 6.9). In terms of air fare, SAA is competitive in the sector Mumbai–Brazil–Mumbai but not in Mumbai–JNB–Mumbai. For instance, a General Sales Agent (GSA) of SAA in New Delhi charges, on an average, US$ 780 for economy class and US$

TABLE 6.9

Air Fare of Selected Airlines in IBSA (As on December 2005)

Sector	Airlines	Air Fare[1] (US$)	
		Economy	Business
Mumbai–JNB–Mumbai	SAA	780	1845
	Emirates[2]	735	1710
Mumbai-JNB-Sao Paolo–Mumbai	SAA	1690	6090
	KLM[3]	1835	4960
	BA[4]	2230	6780

Notes: 1. Excluding taxes, gross fare.
2. Transit at Dubai.
3. Transit at Amsterdam.
4. Transit at London.

Source: RIS based on information gathered from GSAs of SAA/KLM/Emirates in New Delhi.

1845 for business class return fare for travelling in Mumbai–JNB–Mumbai sector, whereas Emirates offers lower fare in both categories. In case of Mumbai-Sao Paolo-Mumbai sector, SAA's fare in economy class is quite lower than those offered by KLM and British Airways. Therefore, to enhance more air passengers in IBSA, one may need to look into not only the cost of travelling but also the travelling facilities as due to competition alternate traffic routings have increased in recent period.

Even though there is price competition among the airlines, operating to and from Africa and Middle East, SAA has witnessed 18 per cent jump in passenger traffic in 2002-03, compared to the last year. This finally helps us to estimate that SAA is operating at average 75 per cent occupancy, which is quite higher than other airlines doing business in this sector (see Table 6.10). Seeing the jump in passenger traffic, SAA has increased the frequency from 4 days/week to 5 days/week from March 2005. SAA is also planning to start a flight from New Delhi to JNB. According to GSAs of SAA in New Delhi, on an average, 20 per cent of total passengers carried in a year in India-South Africa sector (specifically Mumbai to JNB) by SAA travel to Brazil using JNB as transit point. This amply indicates low volume of air travel between India and Brazil and vice versa.

TABLE 6.10

Passengers and Freights Carried to and from India by SAA

Year	*Passenger No*	*Freight Tonnes*
2000-01	53,683	1,533
2001-02	54,542	1,147
2002-03	64,810	901

Source: RIS based on *Air Transport Statistics 2003*, Director General of Civil Aviation, Ministry of Civil Aviation, Government of India.

The air transport sector in IBSA is large enough to raise each individual countries presence in the international civil aviation sector. Greater cooperation will help them to attain this objective. Sharing each other's experiences will certainly enhance IBSA's competitiveness in the international air transport market at a time when this region alone shares about 2 per cent of world air freight and about 4 per cent of internal air passengers. To enhance travelling within IBSA, we may learn from MERCOSUR Civil Aviation Plan, which allows passengers, coming from MERCOSUR, to travel the region without much hassle.

In regard to air transport sector, governments in IBSA should also aim at providing adequate capacity in accordance with demand by first restructuring their national carriers and maximising their equal participation in the IBSA air transport segment. Adequate capacity will certainly ensure development of trade and tourism in IBSA. Liberal regional rights should also be given for promoting international operations to less developed regions in IBSA as well as to ill-connected two extreme countries (e.g. India and Brazil) in IBSA to promote trade and tourism.

Governments in IBSA should establish an objective and well-defined mechanism for sharing of international traffic rights amongst airlines in a transparent manner so that people in the region can avail more international flights going to (or coming) from Asia, Africa or Latin America. Efforts should also be made by each other's national carriers, following Varig, to join global alliances (such as Star Alliance) in their own commercial interest and in the interest of travelling passengers through code-sharing, exchange of frequent-flier programmes, etc. Governments in IBSA may also consider tourist charters from domestic airports to foreign destinations in IBSA subject to safeguards for scheduled operations.

In regard to promotion of travel and tourism, we have to acknowledge that tourism and trade sectors are closely linked to civil aviation sector. Therefore, it is important that airport infrastructure and air services are planned keeping in view the requirement and promotion of these sectors. Multi-modal approach should be used for planning to ensure better connectivity. A thrust for international tourism in IBSA will be given by providing freedom to International Tourist Charters to all airports linking places of tourist interest.

Efforts should also be made to issue visa on arrival at the airport in case passenger coming from IBSA. Following SAA's experiences, Air India can introduce EDI (Electronic Data Interchange) interlinking trade agencies, customs, and immigration for faster efficient trade transactions. Private sector participation in cargo handling for increasing competition and improved services should be welcomed.

6.3 Concluding Remarks and Recommendations

The foregoing analysis clearly indicates that there are ample opportunities for growth in maritime and air transport sectors in IBSA. In general, we have seen that maritime and air linkages between India and South Africa, and South Africa and Brazil is stronger than that of India and Brazil. However, there are potentials for higher growth in air and maritime transport sectors between India and Brazil provided we strengthen the transportation linkages between the countries. Governments in IBSA should try to remove the structural asymmetries in the air and maritime transportation sectors which are found to be quite significant.

The Political Agenda

The goal of increased trade in IBSA has to overcome a number of obstacles: attractive package for transportation exchange has to be identified, a way has to be found to reduce transport costs for such products and the commercial links between the countries have to be strengthened.

The need for the deepening of commercial linkages between the three continents should also be emphasised. Member countries in IBSA must agree on the need to combine the efforts of the public and private sectors and relevant specialised organisations to facilitate *inter alia* coordination between shipping companies, provide improved information on trade flows, identify hubs and improve port infrastructure.

The role to play for ports, shipping services, airways and improved transport links will be an essential element of further progress.

The low volume of trade makes the business relatively unattractive to the main-line shipping companies. Competition for business is therefore weak. However without competition, efficiency cannot improve and costs are unlikely to decline. Similarly, the small scale of many of the ports makes the purchase of gantry cranes apparently uneconomic and tends to prevent high productivity in container handling.

The alleged lack of coordination between the different carriers offering feeder and inter-island services and between these carriers and the main-line services may tend to increase costs and impair service frequencies. One suggestion that has been made is to discuss the feasibility of a common feeder structure as used in the Mediterranean, whereby the main-line carriers agree to use regional feeders and inter-island carriers operating as a pool.

The Increasing Role of Transhipment

The new element in the equation is the emergence of a geographically dispersed range of ports offering transhipment services. This offers the possibility of providing even the smaller destinations access to increased regional trade. The principal transhipment ports on the basis of geography for the IBSA trade should be at Durban or Cape Town.

The transhipment ports need to be linked by connector shipping services, for example from Jawaharlal Nehru. Additional feeder services are needed from the transhipment ports to final destinations. Transport costs may be lower with a pattern of main-line services, connector services and feeder services, concentrating on fewer routes and ports, rather than the present confusion of roles.

The existence of frequent and inexpensive liner shipping services does have a positive impact on trade and integration. Higher frequencies are statistically linked to lower transport costs. Hence, with regard to trade in IBSA, more and better services would also promote intra-regional trade. However, it appears that today there are actually not many services and options available. We find only two liner shipping services call at ports of India, Brazil and South Africa. However, the same is irregular in bulk shipping. Trade between India and Brazil increasingly involves at least one transhipment and often main lines connect to the region's economies at the same transhipment port for IBSA, thus also facilitating connection among these countries. It can be expected that transhipment in the IBSA will continue to grow, with the positive side effects of generating income for those ports and countries which supply such transhipment port services, and simultaneously helping the region's shippers to get access to additional transport options within and outside the region.

Demand Might Follow Supply

Existing trade flows are small, freight rates are high and services frequencies and journey times are in general unsatisfactory in IBSA. Despite these obstacles, there are trade flows between the countries in IBSA. What is needed is a programme to encourage this traffic, through additional contacts between the exporters and importers of the three countries and by the alleviation of present transport-related obstacles. Cheaper transport between ports is the priority.

Contacts between trade associations and others concerned with trade among the IBSA countries should be encouraged. The officially sponsored bodies for the promotion of exports, which exist in nearly all the countries concerned, have an important role in promoting such contacts.

Improving Transport Services

What can be done to improve transport services in IBSA? First, we can encourage micro-level cooperation among leading transport operators of the three countries, primarily in maritime, air and railways sectors as because countries in IBSA have immense opportunity to learn from each other's experiences. Say for example, India's vast expertise in automation of railways can be extended to South Africa and Brazil. Similarly, India and South African can also learn from the Brazilian experiences in introduction of private capital in improving railway efficiency. It would be good idea to form a commercial venture among three leading logistics operators from these three countries. Say for example, formation of any commercial venture among Container Corporation of India (CONCOR from India), Transnet Ltd. (from South Africa), and Companhia Vale do Rio Doce (CVRD from Brazil) could be of great boost to closer transport integration among the three countries. While CONCOR and Transnet are public sector companies, CVRD is Brazil's largest logistics company in the private sector.

Similarly, Air India can learn from the success of South African Airways and Varig Airways. Here also apart from code sharing, joining together to promote trade and tourism and to exchange technical experiences will certainly pave the way in sustaining closer integration in near future.

There are also immense opportunities for all the three countries to induce cost-effective and quality shipping provided they establish a regional shipping service for IBSA. Experience in the area with shipping lines such as WISCO in the Caribbean and with Namucar in Central America may be explored. We should always be careful that such a service should lead to generating profits. A variant of this idea envisages the creation of a joint public-private Non-Vessel Operator (NVO). However, it would be seen more promising for governments to improve the conditions under which the existing NVOs operate, than to enter the business themselves. Unlike infrastructure investments, international transport services are not usually suitable to be provided by the public sector. This does not mean, however, that the public sector has no options to promote regional integration. India, with its renowned maritime training institutes, can offer modern maritime training to seafarers of South Africa and Brazil. Similarly, South Africa's wide experiences of port management can also be extended to Indian port authority. Shipping lines in all the three countries can forge a network to exchange experiences in implementing ISPS code. However, some following activities would be beneficial to trade in this region in general.

- Work to reduce transport costs through international benchmarking and the provision of better information to shippers. A regional data base might help to set benchmarks and encourage improvements.
- General work to alleviate other transport restrictions in the fields of telematics, facilitation and port and labour reform. Indian and Brazilian ports, in particular, could learn from successful reforms from South African ports.
- A regional legislations in IBSA should be supportive of the NVOs and multimodal transport providers, with the identification of obstacles to their more effective functioning. UNCTAD is currently carrying a consultation exercise in this area.
- The public and academic sector could cooperate with service providers in the identification of ways to improve the linkage between main-line and feeder services at the different transhipment points, through common feeder services or other mechanisms.

Whilst high transport costs are not the only reason for present low intra-regional trade levels in IBSA, they are a contributory factor. Transport is playing an increasing role in the countries' competitiveness in each others markets. Realisation of the potential for increased trade in IBSA will require action both by the private sector and by the concerned public sector institutions.

To attain this object, governments in IBSA should enhance cooperation leading to higher intra-regional trade. One urgent task is to bring under some sort of common market enhancement policy in IBSA. If such a modest degree of policy harmonisation or centralised oversight cannot be secured, it is hard to imagine that there will be progress toward deeper forms of policy coordination, such as regional policies for compensating structural asymmetries, regional competitiveness programmes or enhanced macroeconomic coordination.

APPENDIX 6.1

India's Cargo-wise and Port-wise Sea Traffic with IBSA: 2000-2002

('000 tonnes)

Indian Ports	*Cargo*	*2000-01 Import SA*	*2000-01 Import BRZ*	*2000-01 Export SA*	*2000-01 Export BRZ*	*2001-02 Import SA*	*2001-02 Import BRZ*	*2001-02 Export SA*	*2001-02 Export BRZ*
Paradip	Misc.							22	
Vizag	FRM (Dry)	32				18			
	FRM (Liquid)					30			
	Foodgrains							18	
	Granite Blocks				4				
	Petroleum coke								44
Chennai	Other cereals		3						
	Iron & Steel (Mftd.)		1						
	Chemicals		2		1				
	Other ores								38
	Iron scrap						10		
Tuticorin	Phosphoric acid	21		3		20			
	Industrial coal	85							
	Timbers and logs	49				49			
	Misc	33							
Cochin	Coal	74							
New Mangalore	Timbers and logs	9						8	
Mormugao	Coal (Thermal)	299							
	Coking coal	132				1233			
Jawaharlal Nehru	Edible oil		138						
Mumbai	FRM (Dry)	99				15			
	Iron & Steel					29			
	Foodgrains			52				5	
	Edible oil		11						
Kandla	Edible oil		75				169		
	Chemicals		9			69			
	Phosphoric acid	157				183			
	Coal (Thermal)	278							
	Coal (others)					182			
	Timbers and logs					30			
	Foodgrains (Rice)			13				166	
	Foodgrains (Wheat)							10	
	Containers	4				11		8	
	Misc.	1							
	Total	1273	239	68	5	1869	179	237	82

Source: Ministry of Shipping, Government of India.

Chapter 7

Strategic Cooperation in Shaping the International Trade and Financial Architecture

7.1 Introduction

The coming together of three leading economies from the South is taking place at a historical point in time wherein the developing countries in general after experimenting in globalisation for more than a decade find themselves at cross roads. While the developing countries have faithfully embraced globalisation as a development strategy, there is a general disenchantment among them primarily on account of the unequal distribution of returns to globalisation. This in turn has made the leaders of developing countries to search for new trade geographies. In this concluding chapter, we consider the formation of IBSA not only as a means of strengthening cooperation among the three countries concerned but also as a powerful institutional arrangement to address the wide ranging development problems that countries in the South face today by providing an impetus to South-South cooperation. In fact, the New Delhi Declaration made by the leaders of IBSA clearly acknowledge their key role in not only evolving a new world order but also to participate actively in alleviation of poverty and hunger. At the multilateral level, the New Delhi Declaration called for cooperation among IBSA to realise the reforms of United Nations to make it more democratic and responsive to the priorities of its members state, particularly those of the developing countries. The commitment of the three countries to address the problems associated with poverty and hunger in the developing world is evident from the setting up of IBSA facility for alleviation of poverty and hunger. In what follows, we shall highlight certain specific action points that could be considered by IBSA towards addressing the asymmetries in the world trading system and achieving the millennium development goals.

7.2 Relevance of IBSA Cooperation in Multilateral Forums

The strategic importance of IBSA cooperation in shaping the outcome of multilateral negotiations cannot be overemphasised. As emerging powers they can provide leadership to the developing world in these negotiations and thus help in evolving more development-friendly framework for multilateral trade and financial architecture. If the recent experience of their cooperation in multilateral trade negotiations is any guide, this partnership is going to have a major influence on the shape of multilateral negotiations in future.

7.3 Reform of International Financial Architecture and the United Nations

Considering the common development concerns of IBSA countries, they could also coordinate their positions and provide leadership to developing countries in pushing reforms of international financial architecture including reform of IMF conditionalities to prevent reoccurrence of financial crisis and making it more development friendly and sustainable. Both Brazil and South Africa have suffered from mild crises in the past. The reform of the UN with expansion of the UN Security Council is also a common agenda and Brazil and India have announced support of their candidature for permanent membership of the UN Security Council on a mutual basis.

7.4 Cooperation in Multilateral Trade Negotiations

Over the past years IBSA countries have already cooperated within the framework of the G-20 of developing countries at the Cancun Ministerial Conference of WTO and subsequent negotiations in a very fruitful manner. G-20 led by Brazil, India, South Africa, (and China), proved to be an effective coalition, which submitted a counter proposal to the US-EU proposals on agriculture negotiations at the Fifth Ministerial. It is to the credit of the leadership of the G-20 that it has held together despite the attempt by the developed countries to break their ranks by offering to phase out export subsidies for select products of interest to some leading countries. Later on in the negotiation of the July framework, India and Brazil represented G-20 in the Five Interested Parties (FIPs) that hammered out the agreement. Given the fact that the G-20 was led by Brazil, India and South Africa, it can be said that the trilateral engagement by India with Brazil and South Africa under the IBSA framework has facilitated coalition-building on WTO issues. The Ministerial Meeting of the IBSA Trilateral Commission IBSA held in New Delhi in early 2004 emphasised on the importance of a common approach with regard to WTO among other priorities. It is important that IBSA countries continue playing such leadership role in the multilateral trade negotiations as they have been over the past. Furthermore, it is important for the longer-term sustainability of the coalition of G-20 in WTO to develop a more constructive proactive agenda. In this context following specific actions may be worth considering.

A WTO Watchdog of Developing Countries

IBSA could consider assuming the responsibility of creating a WTO Watchdog of developing countries. While implementation of their WTO commitments and complaints brought on any cases of under-implementation by developing countries are carefully monitored by developed countries, the developing countries, individually, lack the capacity—physical, analytical and financial—to identify and pursue the cases of non-implementation or unilateral policy decisions concerning trade policy on the part of developed countries and seek their redressal under the existing framework. The recent case of the trade distorting export subsidy valued at $4 billion under Foreign Sales Corporations (FSC) by the US government which was successfully brought by the EU to the DSB is a case in point. Needless to mention that no developing country possesses the capability to do the same

Reform of the Decision-making at WTO

The general perception is that the decision-making process in WTO is non-transparent, and non-inclusive. The will of a handful of powerful countries, viz. Quad countries, is imposed on the entire membership in the name of 'Consensus'. In an organisation whose membership comprises countries at varying levels of development, their concerns and interests are expected to be different. Obviously these differences limit the possibilities of arriving at a consensus. Hence, IBSA under the aegis of G-20 should come up with a comprehensive reform of the WTO decision-making process to make the process more inclusive and participatory.

Capital Flows and Reform of International Financial System

IBSA should seek a consensus on the urgent need of reform of the international financial architecture and develop a development friendly agenda for it. This agenda should emphasise on the need for restoring long-term resource flows to low-income countries. The expanding magnitudes of private capital and FDI, while a welcome development in itself, cannot substitute for the falling levels of official development finance in view of the inability of poorest of developing countries to tap these resources due to their low income levels, poor infrastructure, undeveloped capital markets, among other reasons. Industrialised countries should offer assistance to developing countries with a renewed commitment to restore official development assistance in the spirit of global interdependence in the globalising world economy. In the interdependent global economy, any flow of resources to developing countries revert eventually in the form of enhanced imports by them. Implementing the UN target of ODA level at 0.7 per cent of their GDP, agreed to earlier, would lead to an additional flow of US$ 100 billion of resources to poorer countries at the present levels of GNP of industrialised countries. A flow of that amount of additional resources, if employed properly, could lead to additional growth stimulus not only in the developing world but in the world economy at large. In order to enhance the effectiveness of aid for promoting growth and poverty removal, ODA should be untied and be available to development policy making and implementing bodies so that it effectively supplements the domestic resources.

7.5 Promotion of South-South Cooperation

South-South Cooperation (SSC) received considerable attention as a philosophy for development during the 1960, 1970s and 1980s. These were the times when developing countries, having coming out of the yoke of colonisation, were struggling with poverty and underdevelopment. Lack of financial and technological resources and the western apathy forced them to look to collective self-reliance as an engine of growth.

In the 1990s, however, globalisation took the centrestage and SSC was put on a backburner. The process of globalisation was promoted by the Brettonwoods institutions and GATT and its successor, WTO. A large number of developing countries, which faced financial crisis in the 1980s and 1990s against the backdrop of declining resource flows, were forced to approach the Brettonwoods institutions for assistance which generally came with the conditionalities binding them firmly with the Washington Consensus. The latter required the borrowing countries to liberalise their trade and investment regimes to integrate themselves more firmly with the world economy.

Recent trends suggest that developing countries are revitalising on SSC as a new engine of growth in the new millennium, partly as a result of their growing discontent with 'selective' globalisation. Developing countries in different regions are also establishing their own schemes of regional economic integration, e.g. MERCOSUR, COMESA and SACU. In Asia, there is an ASEAN FTA, and SAFTA and BIMSTEC FTA are taking shape. The Bangkok Agreement is being revitalised. Several alternative plans for evolving a broader pan-Asian grouping are also being discussed such as East Asian Economic Community, Asian Economic Community or JACIK. In this context, IBSA being represented by the three leading economic powers from three continents could be instrumental in building new bridges in SSC by prompting the trade, investment, and technology flows between them.

G-20 could also become a forum for promoting SSC such as mutual cooperation in implementation of commitments, technical assistance for compliance of emerging standards, etc., besides evolving approaches for promoting South-South trade. They could discuss ways and means for revitalising the GSTP for promoting their mutual trade besides addressing non-tariff barriers to it. IBSA could take lead in making G-20 pursue these proactive measures.

South-South Cooperation in ICT: The e-South Framework

Given that Information and Communication Technologies (ICT) have emerged as a key engine of growth in the 1990s and an instrument for addressing many development issues, the New Delhi Declaration has called for cooperation in projects involving, e-governance, local content development, capacity building, e-health and others in the framework of a Trilateral Memoramdum on Cooperation on Information Society.

The present study, however calls for IBSA to promote South-South Cooperation by spearheading a **e-South Framework Agreement** aimed at bridging the digital divide through an integrated development of ICT sector in the developing countries. Towards achieving this objective, the Agreement, in tune with the Information Technology Agreement of WTO, should facilitate free trade in ICT goods and services among the developing countries. At the same time, drawing from the e-ASEAN Framework Agreement, the e-South Agreement should be instrumental in building capacity both for production and use. This calls for measures to promote investment in the ICT sector such that new income, employment and export earning opportunities are generated. Given the paramount importance of human capital in developing ICT production and promoting ICT use, special focus may be given to developing IT manpower base wherein there is the need for relaxing the restrictions on the mobility of skilled manpower across the developing world. In general, the Agreement should facilitate an integrated development of the ICT sector wherein both production and use are promoted instead of the ongoing lop-sided approach towards making many a developing countries passive adopter of technology.

References

Arora, Ashish, Alfonso Gambardella (2004). "The Globalisation of the Software Industry: Perspectives and Opportunities for Developed and Developing Countries", *NBER Working Paper Series*, No. 10538. Cambridge: NBER.

Baldwin, R. (1994). "Towards an Integrated Europe". United Kingdom: London Centre for Economic Policy Research.

Balassa, Bela (1967). "Trade Creation and Trade Diversion in the European Common Market", *Economic Journal*, Vol. 77: 1-17.

———. (1975). *European Economic Union*. Amsterdam: North Holland Publishing Company.

Botelho, A.J.J., Jason Dedrick, K.L. Kraemer and Paulo Bastos Tigre (1999). *From Industry Protection to Industry Promotion: IT Policy in Brazil.* Irvine: Centre for Research on Information Technology and Organization, University of California.

Botelho, A.J., G. Stefanuto and Francisco Veloso (2005). "The Brazilian Software Industry", in Arora, A. and A. Gambardella (eds.), *The Rise and Growth of the Software Industry in Some Emerging Economies*. Oxford UK: Oxford University Press.

Central Bank of Brazil (2003). *Annual Report.* Available at *http://www.bcb.gov.br*

Chaudhuri, S., Mattoo, A., Self, R. (2004). "Moving People to Deliver Services: How Can the WTO Help?", *Journal of World Trade*, Vol. 38(3): 363-93.

Charlton, A. H. and Stiglitz. (2005). "A Development-friendly Prioritisation of Doha Round Proposals", *The World Economy*, Vol. 28(3): 293-312.

Cogburn, D.L. and Catherine Nyaki Adeya (2001). "Prospects for the Digital Economy in South Africa, Technology, Policy, People, and Strategies", *Discussion Paper No.* 2001/77. Helsinki: UNU WIDER.

Correa, C.M. (1990). "Software Industry: An Opportunity for Latin America? UNDP/UNIDO Regional Coordinator, Programme on Informatics and Microelectronics, Buenos Aires", *World Development*, Vol. 18(11): 1587-98.

De, P. (2006a). "The Growth of International Trade in Services in Developing Countries: Some Implications", *Journal of International Logistics and Trade*, Vol. 4(2): 75-106.

———. (2006b). "Trade in IBSA Economic Cooperation: The Role of Transportation Linkages", *RIS Discussion Paper* No.104. New Delhi.

Ferreira, F.H.G., Carlos E. Velez and Ricardo Paes de Barros (2004). *Inequality and Economic Development in Brazil.* Washington DC: World Bank.

FICCI and EXIM Bank of India (2004). *Potential for Enhanced India-Mercosur Trade in Creative Industries.* New Delhi: FICCI.

Frankel, Jeffrey A. (1997). *Regional Trading Blocs: In the World Economic System.* Washington DC: Institute for international Economics.

Gabriele, A. (2004). "International Trade in Services and the Evolving Position of Developing Countries", *Journal of Economic Integration*, Vol. 19(4): 780-803.

Government Communication and Information System (n.d.). *South Africa Yearbook 2003/04*. Available at *http://www.gcis.gov.za/docs/publications/yearbook.htm*

Government of Brazil (n.d.). *Investment Opportunities in Brazil, Investebrasil*. Available at *http://www.investebrasil.org*

Government of India (different years). *Foreign Collaboration: A Compilation*. New Delhi: Department of Scientific and Industrial Research.

———. (n.d.). *India's Current Engagement with RTAs*. New Delhi: Ministry of Commerce and Industry. *http://commerce.nic.in/india_rta.htm*

———. (2002). *SIA Newsletter 2002: Annual Issue*. New Delhi: Secretariat for Industrial Assistance, Department of Industrial Policy and Promotion, Ministry of Commerce and Industry.

———. (2004). *India-Brazil-South Africa (IBSA) Dialogue Forum Trilateral Commission Meeting: New Delhi Agenda for Cooperation and Plan of Action*. New Delhi: Ministry of External Affairs. *http://meaindia.nic.in/*

———. (2006b). *WTO Negotiation on Trade in Services: A Backgrounder*. New Delhi: Ministry of Commerce and Industry. Available at *http://commerce.nic.in/wto_sub/services/wto_service.htm*

———. (2007). *India's Outward FDI*. New Delhi: Dept. of Economic Affairs, Ministry of Finance. Available at *http://finmin.nic.in/the_ministry/dept_eco_affairs/index.html*

Government of South Africa (n.d.). *Tradeinvestsa*. Department of Trade and Industry. Available at *http://www.tradeinvestsa.co.za/Investment/story_2405.shtml*

———. (2003). *Using Open Source Software in the South African Government: A Proposed Strategy Compiled by Government Information Technology Officers' Council*. Available at *http://www.oss.gov.za/docs/OSS_Strategy_v3.pdf*

Greenaway, David, T. Hyclak and R. Thornton (eds.) (1989). *Economic Aspects of Regional Trading Arrangements*. London: Harvester Wheatsheaf.

Greenaway, David (1989). "Regional Trading Arrangements and Intra-Industry Trade: Evidence and Policy Issues, in Greenway, David, T. Hyclak and R. Thornton (eds.), *Economic Aspects of Regional Trading Arrangements*. pp.31-42. London: Harvester Wheatsheaf.

Gunter, F.R. (1989). "Customs Union Theory: Retrospect and Prospect", in Greenway, David, T. Hyclak and R. Thornton *op. cit.* pp.1-30.

Heckscher, E. (1919). "The Effect of Foreign Trade on the distribution of Income", *Ekonomisch Fidskrift*, 21.

Henwood, R. (1997). "South Africa's Foreign Policy: Principles and Problems", *Monograph*. *http://www.iss.co.za/Pubs/Monographs/No13/Henwood.html*

Hoddinott, John, Michelle Adato and Tim Besley (2000). "Participation and Poverty Reduction: Issues and New Evidence from South Africa", *World Bank Working Paper* No. 27896. Washington DC: World Bank.

Hoekman,B. and C. Primo Braga (1997). "Protection and Trade in Services: A Survey", *Open Economics Review*, Vol.8: 285-308.

Hoekman,B. and D.E. Konan (1999). "Deep Integration, Non-Discrimination, and Euro-Mediterranean Free Trade". *World Bank Policy Paper*, No. 2130.

Holden, M. (2001). "Trade Policy in a Liberalizing Economy", *Journal of International Development*, Vol. 13(6): 711-723.

International Monetary Fund (Different years). *Balance of Payments Statistics Yearbook*. Washington DC.

———. (2002). *Determinants of FDI in South Africa*. June. Washington DC.

———. (2007). *World Economic Outlook 2007*. April. Washington DC: International Monetary Fund.

International Trade Centre (2000). *The Andean Community, MERCOSUR and Chile, Sub-regional Trade Opportunities*. August. Project No. INT/W2/09. UNCTAD and WTO.

Kumar, N. and K.J. Joseph (2005). "Export of Software and Business Process Outsourcing from Developing Countries: Lessons from Indian Experience", *Asia-Pacific Trade and Investment Review*, Vol. 1(1): 91-110.

Kumar, Nagesh and Sachin Chaturvedi (2007). "BICS in the Doha Round: Building a Development Friendly World Trading System?", Paper presented in international workshop on *Emergence of Large Developing Countries (BICS) and Implications for International Development* organised by RIS and Common Wealth, 28-29 June, New Delhi.

Kumar, Nagesh (2002). "Towards an Asian Economic Community: The Relevance for India". *RIS Discussion Paper* #32. New Delhi.

———. (2004). "Tackling Selective Globalisation", *Financial Express*, March 10.

Linnemann, H. (1996). *An Econometric Study of International Trade Flows.* Amsterdam: North Holland Publishing Company.

Lucian, Cernat (2003). Assessing South-South Regional Integration: Same Issues. Many Metrics. *Policy Issues in International Trade and Commodities Study Series,* No. 21. New York and Geneva: UNCTAD.

Mattoo, A. (2000a). "Developing Countries in the New Round of GATS Negotiations: Towards a Pro-Active Role," *World Economy,* Vol.23(4): 471-89.

Markusen, J.R. (1987). "Trade in Producer Services and in Other Specialized Intermediate Inputs" *American Economic Review* Vol 79: 85-95.

Mehta, Rajesh (2003). *Indian Industrial Tariff: Towards WTO Development Round Negotiations.* Report for the Ministry of Commerce. New Delhi: RIS.

Mehta, Rajesh and S.K. Mohanty (2001). *WTO and Industrial Tariffs: An Empirical Analysis for India.* New Delhi: RIS.

Moguillansky, Graciela and Ricardo Bielschowsky (2001). *Investment and Economic Reform in Latin America.* United Nations Publications.

Mohanty, S.K. (2007). "Rise of BICS and the World Economy: Implication of India's Recent Economic Expansion on Developing Countries", Paper presented in the international conference on *Emergence of Large Developing Countries (BICS) and Implications for International Development,* joining organised by RIS and Common Wealth, June, 28-29, 2007, New Delhi.

———. (2002a). *Possibility of Close Economic Cooperation between India and Singapore.* Report submitted to the Ministry of Commerce, Government of India. New Delhi: RIS.

———. (2002b). *Feasibility of Extending Unilateral Tariff Preferences to Newer Members of the ASEAN: From an Indian Perspective.* Report for the Ministry of External Affairs, Government of India. October. New Delhi: Research and Information System for the Non-Aligned and Other developing Countries.

Mytelka, Lynn K. (ed.) (1994). *South-South Cooperation in a Global Perspective.* Paris: OECD Development Centre.

NASSCOM (2007). *Strategic Review 2007.* New Delhi: National Association of Software and Service Companies.

Ohlin, B.G. (1933). *Interregional and International Trade.* Cambridge, MA: Harvard University Press.

Pavlic, B. *et al.* (eds.) (1983). *The Challenges of South-South Cooperation.* Colorado: West View Press.

Rakshit, M. (2007). "Services-led Growth: The Indian Experience", *Money and Finance,* Vol. 3(1): 91-126.

RBI (2007). *Database on Indian Economy.* Mumbai. Available online at *https://reservebank.org.in/cdbmsi/servlet/login*

Reddy, E.S. (1985). *India and the Struggle Against Apa*rtheid. Available at *http://www.anc.org.za/ancdocs/history/solidarity/india-sa.html*

Ricardo, David (1817). *Principles of Political Economy and Taxation.* London: John Murray.

RIS (1987). *South-South Economic Cooperation: Problem and Prospects.* New Delhi: Radiant Publishers

———. (2003). *World Trade and Investment Report 2003: Cancun and Beyond.* New Delhi: Research and Information System for Developing Countries and Academic Foundation.

———. *South Asia Development and Cooperation Report.* New Delhi: RIS.

———. (2004b). *ASEAN Vision 2020.* Report to be submitted to the Head of States of India-ASEAN Summit. November.

———. (2004c). *BIMSTEC Vision Document.* Submitted to the Heads of the States in the BIMSTEC Meeting. Bangkok.

———. (2007). *SACU-India-MERCOSUR Economic Cooperation: A Framework for Trade and Investment Cooperation.* Interim Draft. Study conducted for thr Ministry of Commerce and Industry, Government of India, New Delhi.

Sanchez, O. (2003). "Globalisation as Development Strategy in Latin America?", *World Development,* Vol. 31(12): 1977-97.

Smith, Adams (1776). *An Enquiry into the Nature and Causes of the Wealth of Nations.* (Edwin Canan ed.). London: Methuen and Co. Ltd.

South Commission (1990). *The Challenge to the South: The Report of the South Commission.* New York: Oxford University Press.

Sung, Keuk-Je. (2004). "The Doha Development Agenda and the General Agreement on Trade in Services Negotiation and Regulatory Reform in Korea", *Journal of International Logistics and Trade,* Vol. 2(2): 29-39.

Tigre, P.B., Botelho, A.J. (1999). "Brazil Meets the Global Challenge: Its Policy in a Post Liberalization Environment", *Paper No.* 4. Irvine: University of California.

Trade Law Center for South Africa (Tralac) (2004). *Investment Project.* South African Case Study prepared by Tralac for IISD. May. *http://www.iisd.org/investment/dci/sai.asp*

Trade Policy Review Body, The (1996). *Review of Brazil: TPRB's Evaluation.* SICE. Foreign Trade Information System. WTO-PRESS/TPRB/47. November 01. *http://www.sice.oas.org/ctyindex/wto/tprbr47.asp*

UNCTAD (1986). "South-South Economic Cooperation: Some Issues in the Field of Trade and Finance". *RIS Occasional Paper* No. 7. New Delhi: Radiant Publishers.

———. (2000). *FDI Determinants and TNC Strategies: The Case of Brazil.* Geneva: United Nations.

———. (2003). *World Investment Report FDI Policies for Development: National and International Perspectives.* New York and Geneva: United Nations.

———. (2004a). *Bilateralism and Regionalism in the Aftermath of Cancun: Re-establishing the Primacy of Multilateralism.* TD(x1)/BP/12. Geneva: UNCTAD.

———. (2004b). *Regionalism and South-South Cooperation: The Case of Mercosur and India.* TD(X1)BP/11. Geneva: UNCTAD.

———. (2004c). *World Investment Report 2004: The Shift towards Services.* Geneva.

———. (2004d). World *Investment Directory: Volume IX, Latin America and the Caribbean 2004, Part I.*

———. (2005). *Handbook of Statistics CD-ROM 2005.* Geneva.

———. (2006). *World Investment Report 2006.* New York.

———. (2007). *Trade in Services and Development Implications.* Geneva: Trade and Development Board, United Nations Conference on Trade and Development.

———. (different years). *World Investment Report.* Geneva: United Nations.

US Department of Commerce (2004). *South Africa Country Commercial Guide FY 2004.* US Commercial Service.

———. (2004). *US Country Commercial Guide: Brazil- 2004.* US Commercial Service. *http://www.focusbrazil.org.br/ccg/*

Veiga, Pedro da Motta (2004). *Foreign Direct Investment in Brazil: Regulation, Flows and Contribution to Development.* Available at *http://www.iisd.org/pdf/2004/investment_country_report_brazil.pdf*

Vickers, B. (2003). *Investment Policy, Performance and Perceptions in South Africa: Final Report of the Investment for Development Project in South Africa.* Johannesburg: Institute for Global Dialogue.

Viner, J. (1950). *The Customs Union Issue.* New York: Carnegie Endowment for International Peace.

Wade, R. (2004). "Is Globalization Reducing Poverty and Inequality?", *World Development*, Vol. 32(4): 567-89.

Whalley, John (1990). "Non-Discriminatory Discrimination: Special and Differential Treatment under the GATT for Developing Countries", *The Economic Journal*, Vol. 100: 1318-28.

Wilson, Dominic and Roopa Purushothaman (2003). "Dreaming with BRICs: The Path to 2050", *Global Economics Paper* No. 99. Glodman Sachs Global Economic website, *https://www.gs.com*

Winters, A., and M. Schiff (2003). *Regional Integration and Development.* Washington DC: The World Bank.

Winters, L.A. (1990). "The Road to Uruguay", *The Economic Journal*, Vol. 100: 1288-303.

World Bank (2000). *Trading Blocs.* Washington DC.

———. (2004a). *Sustaining India's Services Revolution: Access to Foreign Markets, Domestic Reform, and International Negotiations*, New Delhi

———. (2004b). *Brazil's Services Trade and International Trade Negotiations.* Washington DC.

———. (2007). *World Development Indicator 2007.* Washington DC.

World Trade Organization (2001). *Guide to the GATS: An Overview of Issues for Further Liberalisation of Trade in Services.* World Trade Organisation. The Hague: Kluwer Law International.

———. (2003). *Trade Policy Review—Southern African Customs Union*, Annex 4: South Africa. Geneva.

———. (2004). *Trade Policy Review: Brazil.* Report by the Secretariat. Geneva.

———. (2006) *World Trade Report 2006.* Geneva.

———. (2007). *Services Gateway.* Geneva. Available online at *www.wto.org*